****

THE OFFICIAL HISTORY OF

HAVERHILL CRICKET CLUB
(1861-2012)

ROY BRAZIER
© 2013

****

ISBN 978-0-9536518-5-6

All rights reserved. No part of this publication may be produced, stored in a retrieval system, or transmitted in any form, or by any means, electronic, mechanical, photocopying, recording or otherwise, without prior permission in writing from Romary Books.

Roy Brazier has asserted his moral right to be identified as the author of this work

First Edition August 2013

Published by

ROMARY BOOKS
01440 714877

CONTENTS

OVERTURE	1
IN THE BEGINNING	2
ORGANISATION AT LAST	7
INTO THE 20th CENTURY	43
LET'S START AGAIN	74
THROUGH THE THIRTIES	91
A PERIOD OF WAR	107
FRESH BEGINNINGS	114
A DOWNWARD TREND	191
RISE FROM THE ASHES	211
NEW CENTURY, NEW HOPE	219
2013 AND BEYOND	243

ACKNOWLEDGEMENTS

To the Haverhill & District Local History Group, South-West Suffolk Echo, Halstead Times, Bury Free Press, Cambridge Newspapers, Cambridgeshire Collection, British Newspaper Library (Colindale), Haverhill Cricket Club, Colin Cracknell, Ray Shanks, Chris Whiting, Michael Farrant, Dick Poole, Michael Rinaldi, Christopher Gurteen, Tony Turner, Patrick Crouch, Marty House, Megan Woodley.

OVERTURE

Cricket is one of the oldest games still being played in modern times, and as with many such pursuits it is quite impossible to put a certain date on when it actually started. A reference to the Prince of Wales playing 'creag' appears in the Royal Household Accounts of King Edward I towards the end of the thirteenth century. This is sometimes put forward as one of the earliest references to the game of cricket, creag being the name of the most basic game nearest to the cricket played today, but again there is no proof of this. There is no doubt that cricket was played around the middle of the sixteenth century, and the period between 1650 and 1700 saw a considerable advance in the popularity of the game. The first eleven-a-side match took place in Sussex in 1697, while the earliest known laws of the game are dated 1744. The Hambledon Club and their ground at Broad Ha'penny Down in Hampshire is the usual place seen as the home of modern cricket.

In the first code of rules the wicket consisted of two stumps one foot high, placed about two feet apart and joined by a third stump laid across them like a bail. The space between the stumps was called 'the popping hole', into which the batsman had to thrust the end of his bat before the wicket-keeper could 'pop' the ball into it. The bowler delivered the ball fast along the ground, but the batsman was not out if the ball passed between the stumps. The modern wicket replaced this odd arrangement at the turn of the century. There were many loop-holes in these premature rules and a certain gentleman named Thomas White profited from one such omission when he went out to bat in

1774 with a bat so wide that the stumps could not be seen; a quick rule change saw the measurements of the bat limited to four and a half inches.

There are details of the first known inter-county match being played between Kent and London in 1719. A team from Surrey started off for Paris in 1789 to play a game of cricket against a French side, but at Dover they met the Duke of Dorset fleeing home to England from the French Revolution, so the Surrey men also turned back.

It was the game of cricket which extended over the divide of the class system when the ordinary village or townsfolk took up the game. When in 1746 Lord John Sackville played in a well documented match of cricket under the captaincy of his own gardener, it certainly raised a few eyebrows upstairs and downstairs. Thomas Lord opened the first of his grounds in 1787 and the Marylebone Cricket Club (MCC) was formed the same year. However it was not until 1859 that an England touring side went to Canada for a short tour, with no war to intervene this time.
****

IN THE BEGINNING

In the eighteenth century the first reference to the game of cricket in Haverhill is an unfortunate one. *"4 August 1786. Abraham Goodlad was stabbed in an unhappy affray between some persons who had been playing at cricket in Haverhill; he died thirty-two hours later. He was a fine blooming young man aged twenty-seven"*. It is about the mid 1850's that we find one of the earliest mentions of a properly organised cricket match played by Haverhill, which does not mean there was a suitably formed Club in the town, as nothing has been discovered along these lines. In August **1856** the Bury and Norwich Post and Suffolk Herald newspaper reported. *"Clare v Haverhill. This match was played in the Bailey at Clare on Monday last 28th. The Haverhill score was greatly augmented by the fine batting of Messrs Humphrey and Deed from Bumpstead, the first mentioned player scoring thirty-four runs in one innings. Clare first innings 54 and second innings 4. Haverhill first innings 130."* From this earliest report Haverhill were not adverse to borrowing a few players to strengthen their line-up, and also appear to have some good bowlers as witnessed by the Clare second innings of a mere four runs

Nothing more is found until the same newspaper carried another report, this time containing the names of a Haverhill team in 1857, again in a match versus Clare. From this report it seems that they had been opposing each other for some time, although it could have been just the second time of asking. *"Tuesday 15 June 1857. Haverhill v Clare. The annual match between these two sides was played on the Clare ground on the 9th inst, and terminated in favour of Haverhill by forty-six runs."*

HAVERHILL

E.A.S.Walton b Fisher	13	lbw	9
Cornell c Barnes	7	b Mortlock	3
C.Basham c Sams	2	b Fisher	5
Knapp b Mortlock	15	c Hammond	1
D.Gurteen b Mortlock	0	run out	10
Berry b Fisher	0	run out	0
W.Gurteen b Mortlock	0	run out	2
Mason lbw	0	b Fisher	1
Gowers b Fisher	8	c Barnes	1
Hall b Fisher	7	b Fisher	2
Blandon not out	0	b Fisher	4
Extras	9		1
	61		39

In the Clare first innings they scored 48, with Mason (Haverhill) taking six wickets, all clean bowled. In the second innings Clare were all out for 12 runs, Walton and Blandon taking three wickets each for Haverhill. It is interesting that the same two Clare batsmen were run out in both of their sides innings, and with three Haverhill batsmen also being run out - Mr Berry, D Gurteen and W Gurteen - can we conclude that not all the local cricketers were very fast on their feet? From these findings cricket was being played on Mondays and Wednesdays, and even allowing for the fact that Wednesday in Haverhill was probably half-day closing for the shops, half the cricket eleven consisted of businessmen of the town.

Again from the Bury and Norwich Post newspaper dated 30 June 1857 comes the report of another game. *"Haverhill v Clare. The return match between the above teams was played on the Haverhill ground on 23rd inst, when Haverhill again came off conquerors."* The Haverhill team was the same except that J Basham replaced Hall. E A Walton seems to have been the team's wicket-keeper and the top scorers for the winners were Cornell (21) and D Gurteen (12) while Blandon took six wickets. Moving on to the next year we find in the Bury and Norwich Post for Tuesday 20 July **1858** *"Haverhill v Thurlow & Wrattings. An interesting and well contested game was played at Haverhill between the above sides. Won by Haverhill. Newcomers to the Haverhill eleven for this year are the Rev Roberts, Mr Martin and Mr Hicks."* The return match resulted in a win for the combined village side. Haverhill scored 31 and 35 while their opponents notched up 32 and 44 the margin being just ten runs. The Haverhill eleven consisted of W Gurteen, J Elles, A Basham, D Gurteen, Berry, Mason, Halls, Hicks, Martin, Walton and the Rev Roberts.

After this flurry of early reports no certain starting date comes forward for the beginning of cricket in Haverhill. It is more likely that while there was no official cricket club in the town in the very early days, cricket was played in the way of some sporting lads of the town getting together and making their way to nearby places to play the game. These contests were always versus a village close to the town or to another town on the rail network after the railway reached Haverhill in 1863. Trips to the closest villages to the town were often made by horse and cart even on foot which possibly gave the home side a good start to the games. While there is nothing much to be found on Haverhill playing cricket, many local villages were being consistently reported; Stoke-by-Clare v Thurlow and Horseheath v Wratting are two games that spring to mind.

Over the years the cricket in Haverhill has fluctuated and there have been several instances of the club not being active, but the year 1861 has been the most mentioned of the dates for the formation of an official cricket club for the town. With this in mind and with no evidence available as to why 1861 shall be the date decided on a trip to the Newspaper Library in London was undertaken by three members of the Local History Group to see what could be unearthed to prove or disapprove this theory and date. The **1861** regional newspaper covering this area has no mention anywhere in its pages of a Cricket Club being formed, which would be thought to be newsworthy. It seems this year does not live up to its history of being the starting date of an organised Cricket Club in Haverhill.

There was plenty of Haverhill news however which was interesting in itself; the sale of the old church clock which for one hundred years had no face or hands, and a death of a young girl by a garden pea; but these did not help in the cricket quest. But then on a Monday in August of 1861 eleven of the Silkweavers of Haverhill played a cricket match against eleven of the Tradesmen of the town. This took place in a field belonging to Mr Boreham and kindly allowed for the game. After this match they all went to the Greyhound Hotel for an excellent supper provided by host Clark. The Silkweavers won the match by an innings and one run, the Tradesmen scoring 24 and 33 and the Weavers 58, their highest scorer being 'Byes & Wide's' 22. Again we have the names of the two teams, showing who was playing cricket in Haverhill when the opportunity presented itself.

TRADESMEN	SILKWEAVERS
H Blanden	J Backler
C Mason	Elijah Amey
S Suckling	H Whybrow
W Hawes	J Berry
C Basham	R Freeman
T Jarvis	G Whybrow
J Campion	P Wallis
W Fairweather	J Whybrow
J Brown	J Bigmore
J Turpin	George Webb
F Carter	C Brown

The return game followed soon after when J Gurteen came into the Tradesmen XI and the Silkweavers included eight fresh players, none of whom were named. The Traders had their revenge skittling the Silkweavers out twice for 53 and 32 and scoring 88 themselves for a victory by three runs

The following year, **1862**, also furnishes us with one solitary account of a cricket match being played in Haverhill. The newspaper is the 'Halstead Times, Haverhill and Colne Valley Advertiser' dated Saturday 30 August 1862. *"On Monday last a friendly game of cricket was played between the married men and the single men of Haverhill, in a field kindly lent by W W Boreham Esq. The scores were Single Men 1st innings 14 and 2nd innings 44. Married Men 1st innings 44 and 2nd innings 33."* The names of both teams are also given.

MARRIED	SINGLE
-Claydon	- Whybrow
- Reardon	W Sharp

- Whiffing	C Bigmore
S Suckling	J Backler
G Webb	J Webb
W Webb	W Poole
S Sharpe	E Fuller
J Bigmore	W Westrop
J Farrant	- Wells
J Webb	S Webb
W Mead	- Schribs

Lots of old Haverhill names are amongst these two sides, with the Webb family well represented. With Mr Boreham residing at the Mount the meadow used for this game could well have been round about the site of the present cricket ground.

Not much is reported of cricket in Haverhill in the next few years, but in 1864 there were matches going on around and nearby the town. There were games such as Stoke College versus Newton, and a special match between a Juvenile Party selected by Mr Robert Partridge playing a similar party of Mr F C Fitch's young friends at Baythorne Grove. Also in 1865 the newspaper carried a paragraph that the nearest match to the town was at Helions Bumpstead where a match took place, again between the Married and the Single of the village. Its hard to believe there was no cricket involving Haverhill, but in the years before the local 'South-West Suffolk Echo' we have to rely on newspapers which were based in other towns such as Bury St Edmunds, Halstead and Cambridge

1870 came along and we learn in April that cricket is to be provided at Clare for the season at Mr Deeks at Church Farm, and that one of their early visitors was Steeple Bumpstead.. Ridgewell had a taste of the game when Mr C G Wynch's eleven played their match in that village against Gosfield, a side which seemed to flourish in that period. On 30 April 1870 a match opening the season was played at Haverhill between eleven selected members of Messrs Gurteen's firm and eleven members of the Haverhill Choral Union. The day was fine and a good attendance of visitors witnessed the interesting and well fought game, after some very good cricket on both sides. This resulted in victory for the Choral Unionists by 16 runs. Choral Union 43 & 42. Gurteens 20 & 49. Names mentioned for this seemingly one-off encounter= Hall, Suckling, Bigmore, Mason, Webb, Turpin, Gurteen, Sizer,

French and Farrant; again all good Haverhill stock. Then on 25 June 1870 Chauntry Mills provided the twenty-two players for a 'Married v Single' game at Haverhill. The Singles team included, W B Gurteen (bowled out by J Gurteen for 1), Poole, Webb, Sizer and Farrant. W B Gurteen took 7 wickets for his team (Single). Amongst the Married team were Whiffen, Webb, and J Gurteen (who took 5 wickets). The final scores were Single 63 Married 49.

It is were easy to see how a Haverhill Cricket Club was eventually formed in whatever year; it could well have been born out of the scratch games being played between different workmen or districts of the town. Names in these early cricket matches include several who are mentioned later when a bona-fide club was operating in the town. Looking at the scant evidence available and the fact that the Gurteen Factory played several of these in-town and sometimes inter-town games, I have come to the conclusion that the formation of a Town Cricket Club resulted from these selected matches.

****

ORGANISATION AT LAST

An early match in 1883 was at Little Wratting - who also had a football club before Haverhill did - and they entertained the mighty Clare and beat them; a fine win. Then came a noteworthy newspaper report *"The opening match of the NEWLY-FORMED Haverhill Cricket Club took place on Whit-Monday between Mr W B Gurteen's eleven and one selected by the Rev T J Smith, the former being victorious by forty-two runs. At two o'clock the members of the club sat down to an excellent luncheon provided by Mrs Fell of the Rose and Crown. The chair being taken by the Rev T O Roberts and the Vice-Chair was Mr D Gurteen jnr. It is understood that a number of matches have been arranged with local clubs, and a successful season is anticipated."* Sometimes this was said to be the newly reformed cricket club which meant a club existed before this date, but this is the first written evidence available of the Haverhill Cricket Club.

When football began to take a hold, the cricketers in Haverhill were often members of the football team as well. One season could not start before the opposite game had completed their season, and this saw the formation of the Haverhill Cricket and Football Club. This was an arrangement which went on for a good number of years before they went their separate ways.

Now there was a properly constituted Haverhill Cricket Club matches were reported in the newspapers more regularly. One due to become a local derby among the fixtures and greatly contested was versus Sudbury. The first game of the 1883 season in June went the way of Haverhill, and when the return was played in August, Haverhill again came out on top; bragging rights to the town at the start. Another such fixture which became an annual event was against Cambridge Cassandra, and the game at Haverhill saw the home team win by an innings and five runs, F Whiting hitting the highest score of 48 in the total of 124. Balsham were the next to face a strong Haverhill eleven and lost 213 to 73, with P A Mann registering a magnificent 112 runs, arguably the first century by a Haverhill cricketer.

This grand start for the newly born club saw Cavendish beaten, with Mann again up front with a score of 60 not out, while a Thursday match went Haverhill's way against Saffron Walden 80 to 27. This run of success then came to a halt when the second match with the Cassandra Club in Cambridge saw the University students side victors over the town, who tasted defeat for the first time. The Haverhill side for this year was usually F Whiting, H Leonard, W Suckling, Rev J T Smith, F C Wayman, J Gardiner, P A Mann, J Gurteen, T Hall, J Beasley and J Martin.

Scratch matches were still part of the pattern of cricket in Haverhill with the Haverhill Steam Factory taking on the Haverhill Steam Cutters eleven, this match taking place on the Hamlet Croft, this time by permission of Mr D Gurteen Junior. J T Mason's XI took the field versus E Thorpe's XI and not to be outdone Haverhill Boys cycled over to Kedington to play the village Boys XI, Kedington being the winners in that one. Haverhill Butchers played two games against Haverhill Bakers which resulted in one win to each team, and near the end of the season W Poole's XI opposed W Shipp's XI. Meanwhile the Haverhill town club finished off their season with two more wins and a narrow loss at Little Wratting. The most unusual cricket match this year was the one between the Abstainers v Non-Abstainers played at Haverhill; I hope they all had a good time in spite of the conditions laid out, and the two sides contrasting beliefs.

Finance was paramount in the running of the club and every so often the cause of sporting clubs almost closing down. Most, including the Haverhill Cricket Club, struggled along on the proverbial shoestring. An early attempt to raise funds was to hold an evening of 'entertainment' to which members contributed various turns, so keeping the costs down. One such event made the pages of the local newspaper when in November 1883 there was a large attendance at the town hall. The menu set before the audience was *"Overture- Caliph of Bagdad (String Band), Reading (Mr T Bates), Song by Mr Walker, The Glees 'Hark to the Rolling Drum', Song 'Yesteryear' by Miss Nice, and Mr Vincent song 'I Really am so Sleepy'. This was followed by 'an hours magic' very cleverly performed by Mr Mallinson (an amateur conjurer), interspersed with more impromptu songs from Mr Deards. This was a decided success and we learn that a balance of about nine pounds will be available to hand over to the Cricket and Football Club."*

This accomplishment was quickly followed by another such evening at the beginning of the next year in which there were *"Good songs and solo instruments and the glees received well-merited encores, but the readings were mostly long and tedious, and at times the audience manifested unmistakable signs of impatience, but Mr Emson created roars of laughter with his character songs. Mr Gurteen and Miss Hudson presided at the pianoforte with their usual ease."*

But enough of the fun evenings; and how were the games of cricket panning out? In the 1883 season there had been twenty matches arranged and played of which eleven were won by the Haverhill team and nine games lost; altogether an even balance of power. However, no-one could speak in flattering terms of the clubs cricket as they had been sadly defective in batting and fielding, and with one or two minor exceptions it was anything but good. The towns batsmen were too fond of hitting out and while it was very pleasing to feel the ball going to the boundary, it was very annoying to be bowled out the next ball. These observations were made at the Annual Meeting of the Club, which went further: *"Young men must not begin the cricket alphabet the wrong way, they must acquire a good defence and hitting would follow. As to fielding there seemed to be an erroneous idea that anyone could field or there was not much honour in fielding well; consequently the bad show in that branch of the game. But what could be more pleasing than to stop a ball well or make a clear pick-up and return. Now this could not be done without plenty of practice; fielders should remember that runs saved were towards winning a match."* It was more pleasing to talk of the bowling and the wins resulting from Haverhill's superior bowling ability, but not in so many words the cricketers of Haverhill were not amongst the best in the county.

With the club captain Mr J Gurteen not present, most of the aforementioned remarks were made by Mr P A Mann, one of the younger members of the Cricket Club. He was one player who took his cricket seriously. He was way ahead in the batting averages and had throughout the season proved valuable to the club in advice, batting and bowling. One wonders how the rest of the team took the sometimes negative comments by a young upstart

In the December 1883 issue of the short-lived Haverhill & District Magazine, the Annual Meeting of the Cricket Club held on 5 November, saw the treasurer, Mr C H Vincent, produce the balance sheet showing receipts for the year of £44-15-6d, and expenditure £50-6s. However friends and members assisted and the slight loss was hurriedly cleared. Small losses like this were very often turned around by donations from those at the Annual Meetings throughout the years. The Rev T Roberts was the President, Mr W Hammond secretary, and the first cricket captain was Mr W Wayman. As it was usual at that time the meeting closed with 'God Save The Queen' although it could be sung 'God Save Our Team'. This AGM was also that of the Haverhill Town Football Club with both sports operating in tandem for a number of years. The report ended, *"The clubs which are yet in their infancy bid fair to be useful and appreciated institutions."*

In the same magazine for May **1884** it was mentioned *"The opening game of the Cricket Club for this year was played on Easter Monday at the Clubs ground, after which a social tea was provided at the Rose & Crown. The club commences its second season under favourable auspices, and it is to be hoped it may have a prosperous time, and afford the young of the community especially much helpful and pleasurable recreation."*

This Haverhill & District Magazine also carried an article written by Mr P A Mann, the young man who had spoke at the club's Annual Meeting *"As there is every prospect of Haverhill being able to field a strong cricket side, a few remarks on cricket in general may not be out of place, and may prove helpful to the juveniles and some of the adults. In endeavouring to run a club the promoters of the game should first ascertain the desirability for cricket in* the town where the club is to be formed. Always remember that cricket is an expensive game and needs the support as well as the sympathy of the many. Taking it for granted they have a good ground, those wishing to learn and excel in the good old English game to be persistent in their practise, not just once in a while but at least twice each week. All class and individuality should be laid aside, and possess patience, good temper and plenty of pluck and nerve. Mr Mann showed good writing skill as he continued to try to pass on his knowledge of the game and how it should be carried out, such as by the batsmen. "The bat must strike the ball, not the ball on the bat; this is a very common error. The batsman then to take a proper stand at the wicket, placing his right foot just inside the popping crease and his left about a foot-and-a-half in advance of the right, firmly gripping the bat. Beginners sometimes bat at random and get careless and treat the bowling without caution." This is only part of the article which was continued with bowling advice in the following edition.

It is in **1885** that we find one of the anomalies of Haverhill cricket which appear from time to time throughout the years. For some reason this particular year saw the cricket club playing on Saturdays take the name of the Haverhill Rose Club, although when they played matches during the week they were known simply as the Haverhill Cricket Club. Most of the personnel in these teams were the same throughout. Playing against the village team of West Wratting the details were Haverhill Rose Club 44 West Wratting 26, the Haverhill eleven being F Whiting, W Freeman, H Leeks, E Gunnell, S Poole, H Mason, C Wolsley, W Willison, F Mason, G Clarke and L Smith. Others also noted playing for Haverhill Rose were J Gowers, J Radford, W Murton, T Whiting and J Kemp. The next week Haverhill Rose put up a great total of 197 against Earls Colne of which P A Mann rattled up 92 runs. On the other hand the midweek side playing against Saffron Walden saw Mann again amongst the runs scoring 58 not out; unfortunately they lost the match to their opponents who even played the match one man short. Others appearing in the town team at this time included J Gowers, J Radford, J George, W Bailey, R Walton, J Gurteen and H Thake. Some were playing for the Rose and tyher Cricket Clubs including S Poole, P Mann and F Whiting. There was also a solitary appearance for the midweek eleven from Adam Pitchforth who was bowled out first ball in the first innings against Cambridge Cassandra and for the second innings marked down as absent.

In the early and mid eighties the Rose and Crown was the accepted headquarters of the Cricket and Football Club, and the Annual General Meetings were laced with a sit-down meal and ended with songs and toasts. Members around this time included Dr Simpson, C H Vincent, F Bates F Taylor, G Gunnell, W Mason, A Carter, W Hayward, J Arber, E W Griggs and W Ashplant. Looking through this list it becomes apparent that these are mainly the businessmen of the town, maybe because the working men did not have enough time off from their jobs to play the game, and also from quite early days the young men of Haverhill found it hard to burst on to the sporting clubs of the town. Indeed they sometimes had to prove themselves worthy of a place in Haverhill's leisure history.

However it was the Cricket Club captain, Mr W Wayman, who found that owing to his work pattern and other engagements he had to resign from the role of captain, and from this Mr J Gurteen was elected to fill that position with Mr P A Mann as vice-captain The election of Mr Taylor as a vice-president gave another clue as to how long cricket had been played in Haverhill, the new vice-president saying "*I look upon myself as one of the fathers of cricket in the town, and I remember with clearness when we had a match in the afternoon and spent all the money in the evening. We were not particular about the ground we played on and sometimes the Market Hill was the chosen spot.*" The chairman also spoke of the pleasure of watching the young men of the town enjoying themselves on the cricket field, and that everyone must be aware that Haverhill was a self-improving place. He proposed the toast to the club coupled with the health of Mr Gardiner who frequently acted as umpire at matches. The cricket club was to play their games only on Saturday afternoons from then on; it seemed they fixed a match whenever the right number of men were available, and more than likely the mid-week matches were the domain of the businessmen as others were busy at work.

Rivalry was set aside in April of 1887 when the Clare Amateur Dramatic Society gave an excellent evening of entertainment in aid of the funds of the Haverhill Cricket and Football Club in the Town Hall. There was a large attendance which resulted in £7 being handed over to the club. Two small plays were acted out, 'Bitter Cold' and 'Mrs Green's Snug Little Business'. The Shepherds Brass Band conducted by Mr C Milligan were also on the bill and the evening was "*very much appreciated by the audience who frequently applauded the performers."*

It was in **1887** that the first full list of games for the cricketers were printed in the local newspapers. These saw the likes of Cambridge Swifts, Cambridge Idlers, Sudbury, Long Melford, Sawston, Clare, Bury United, Saffron Walden and the Tom-Tits (Cambridge) as opponents. Mention was also made of a Haverhill Cricket Club Reserves (2nd XI) fixing games against Birdbrook, Withersfield, Walden Friends School, Hedingham and Halstead Factory. As seen, all these clubs were on the railway network except nearby Withersfield when no doubt 'Shanks pony' or a wagon ride sufficed. It was also in this year that the Local Almanac and Directory mentioned the Haverhill Cricket and Football Club and their ground was stated as Mr Cross's field in Hamlet Road.

The 1887 season went well on the performance side as out of the fourteen games played ten were won and four lost. The lost matches were said to have been played without a proper captain to guide the side when he was unavailable, and that was the one important thing that needed to be sorted out before the next year. Again there was a loss on the season of £6 but as had been the case in the past a subscription list was opened at the next meeting and the books were made to balance once again.

A year later the cricket club was going through one of its adverse periods and in February **1888** a special meeting was swiftly convened to be told *"The outlook is not so satisfying as might be wished, but it is hoped that the club may not be allowed to fall through, as it has been the means of affording many a pleasant afternoons entertainment."* Another such meeting took place the next month and after some soul searching the committee agreed to carry on the club for the present but to try and encourage and attract more members. To help this happen the subscriptions were reduced from six shillings to five shillings. The opening match was arranged for Easter Monday; this day was the first of the cricket season for a long time to come.

The situation had not improved very much by the next month when the Annual Meeting took place as there were only forty-six fully paid up members, these being listed as the Secretary Mr W Backler, Treasurer Mr C H Vincent, nine Vice-Presidents, sixteen hon members and nineteen youth members. The secretary reported *"I regret very much that I have to announce*

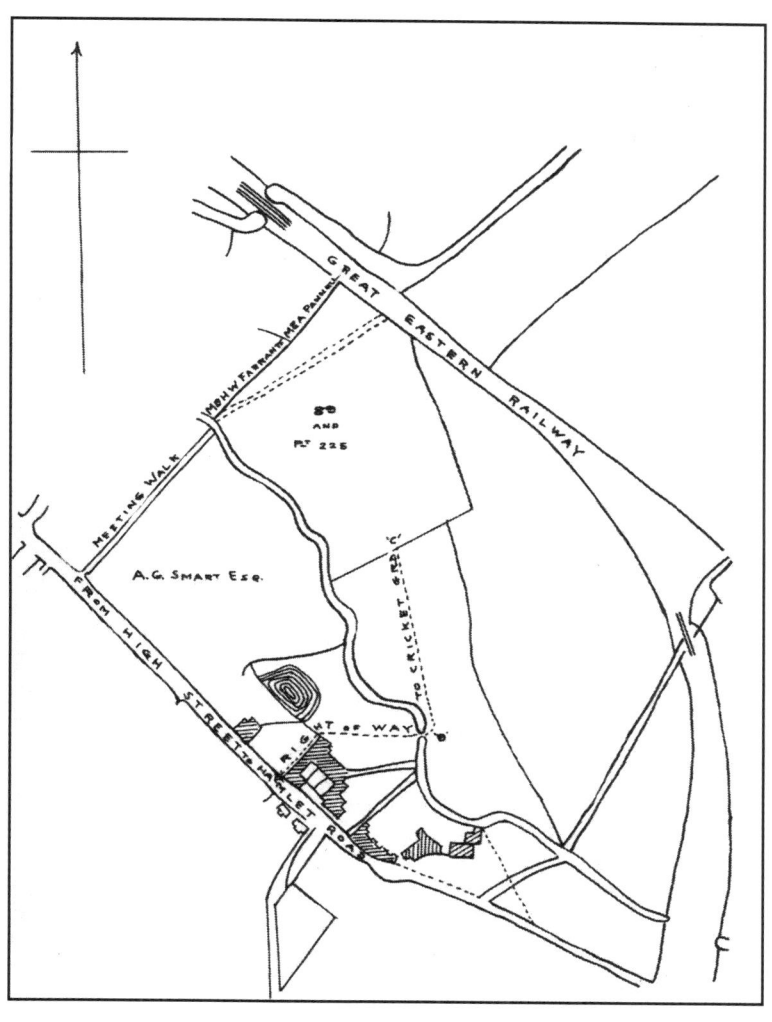

IN EARLY DAYS THE WAY TO THE CRICKET FIELD WAS FROM HAMLET ROAD
THROUGH MANOR FARM AND VIA A FOOTPATH ACROSS THE NOW NORTH
STREET GARAGE SITE OR VIA MEETING WALK

the withdrawal from the club of eight honorary members and six ordinary members, reducing the income by £6-0-6d. I cannot offer any reason or excuse for our friends leaving us but I hope and trust that the loss will be made up by new members joining us before the season starts." The Vice-Presidents listed were Mr W C Quilter MP, Mr H Gardener MP, Mr G Newnes MP, Mr D Gurteen JP, Mr D Gurteen Jnr JP, Mr W B Gurteen, Mr Jabez Gurteen, Mr W Ward, Mr J Bevan and Mr W W Boreham JP. The captain for the next campaign was to be W B Gurteen, and things were looking up after the business ended. Several toasts were offered, the 'Queen', the 'Trade of Haverhill', the 'worthy Secretary', the 'worthy Treasurer' and the 'Umpires'. Some members were also encouraged to stand up and render a song or two.

A visit was made to Hedingham for the opening match of 1888 and won 62-41, quite low scoring. On Whit Monday Haverhill entertained Cambridge Cassandra in a day long match. The ground was visited by a large number of people, but as there appeared very little to excite them they soon drifted away again. The Cambridge side proved victors in spite of the home team having a guest player in Mr J George from Sudbury. Players were often borrowed by most teams as there was no registering of players and all the games were classed as friendly encounters anyway.

In spite of the Haverhill Cricket Club having problems with selecting a side plus other things to hold them back, the game was popular all over town and odd matches cropped up during the week. A Tuesday game saw the Warehousemen from the cotton department of Gurteen's Factory take on the Woollen Department. There was certainly more to interest the spectators in this game which went to the Cotton XI. The schoolboys were not to be left out when the St Mary's Choir Juveniles walked to nearby Withersfield to play the juveniles from that village, the choir boys singing all the way home after a win by four runs. Things looked promising for the future in the hands of the younger elements of Haverhill.

The sport was not without its injuries as in the Haverhill visit to Thurlow at Thurlow Hall. The Rev R Jackson fractured one of the bones in his finger when batting, and Mr F Mason of Haverhill received a severe blow to the mouth while keeping wicket, the ground being hard and dry. There were three vicars in the village side, Rev Fleming and Rev Gover together with the unfortunate Rev Jackson. To entice the younger lads to the cricket field a match was arranged between Haverhill Juveniles and Thurlow Juveniles. In the Thurlow first innings they were all out for just two runs, these coming from their opening batsman; they managed to muster nineteen in a second attempt. There was no doubt that the home youngsters won the game with the eleven of T Winney, F Edwin, R Backler, E W Griggs (wicket-keeper), G Collar, H Wiseman, A Whiffing, F Unwin, F French, J Byham and J Basham. Then the Haverhill boys took on Clare Juniors on the Croft Field, which was at the end of Chauntry Road and owned by Mr Gurteen, now part of the Recreation Ground.

Most of the Haverhill matches were low scoring and nobody could really forecast the way games were going to work out as the town eleven were sometimes very good and at others equally bad. In fact the match versus the Halstead and Gosfield Club found the town side wanting when five players failed to score and three more got just one run each. The spectators were probably ready to shout out to the feeble Haverhill batsmen but thought better of it as the Rev Fleming and the Rev Jackson were in the town side. There were newcomers to the town eleven at times and H Leeks made fifty not out in his first appearance and a R H Holloway was reported as being very useful when he made his debut

Regularly in the fixture list were games against West Wratting Park, which was a Boys School at the time and always led by their sports master Mr William H Cobbold who had been an international footballer for England in his time and no mean batsman in the summer game. Other games were occasional Wednesday afternoon matches by the Shopkeepers XI, the shops in the town then having a half-day closing. Sometimes the Haverhill Club would put out a Secretary's XI to play them and provide some exercise. After these mid-week games both sides would retire to the Croft for tea, and drinking to success no doubt.

In August 1888 Haverhill received a visit from bitter rivals Sudbury. The result this time was in favour of the home side for whom Mr J Gurteen and Mr Mann were top scorers. The bowling of Mr H Leeks was exceedingly destructive as he took eight wickets, and the final score was 78 to 54. Interestingly in the Sudbury team were A Backler, W C Griggs and H Dare; Sudbury must have arrived short of an eleven as some teams often did, and borrowed these Haverhill gentlemen.

Towards the end of the season two fatal accidents related to cricket happened In the first a young man named Charles Wolsley went to West Wratting from Haverhill to be an umpire for the Withersfield v West Wratting match. All went well until ten o'clock in the evening when he was seen to be missing. A search was made and it was the next morning when he was found in a pond near the public house where the team had been drinking. He left behind a young wife and a little daughter. Wolsley had played cricket for the Haverhill Club in former years. The other incident was in December and came about because the footpath which went across part of the Haverhill cricket field had been moved much nearer the river. An old lady of sixty-four named Mary Mead drowned. It seemed she had slipped in as she was said to have been near-sighted, and the water had been exceptionally deep as well. The location of this footpath was to cause other incidents over the coming years.

Instead of the usual 'entertainment' evening which was the most accepted way of generating finance the Cricket Club arranged a 'Cinderella Dance' in February **1889**. Upwards of 130 people indulged in some spirited dancing to the strands of a band provided by Mr Mann of Colchester. The club's debt which had appeared once again - £10 - was soon wiped out.

The footpath question was raised at a meeting of the Haverhill Local Board, and a letter from Messrs Backler and Robson, the secretaries of the Cricket Club and the Gala committee was read out, asking for the Board to divert the existing footpath from the Chapel Bridge to the Railway Crossing, to its original position near the hedge. After much discussion, the Board thought it was for the owner of the property which the footpath crossed, to approach the Great Eastern Railway to sort this out between themselves, a definite case of 'passing the buck'. Meanwhile six loads of shingle were laid on the path to the cricket ground.

As for the actual playing of cricket the season opened as it usually did with the Captains XI v the Vice-Captains XI, and then the first match was against Clare. If last year the scoring was low throughout the season Haverhill surprised everyone in the second match when they hit 171 for 5 wickets before they retired under new Marylebone Club rules. Their opponents were

Hedingham who went in and quickly out for just seventeen runs, eight of their batsmen failing to score. For Haverhill H Leeks got 64, and P A Mann 25. With their tails up, Haverhill entertained Halstead and Gosfield (a combined side) and slipped back into old ways by losing 50-29 as the home side registered four 'ducks' and four others managed a single run each. The Whit Monday fixture against Cassandra saw wet weather set in for the whole day and the Cambridge based side coming to Haverhill by an early train only to have the game postponed. Both elevens took an early lunch at the Rose & Crown before the opponents set off for home.. Another match had to be postponed when a week-end of stormy weather left the cricket field and the whole of the meadows looking like a large lake when the river flooded parts of the town.

So the season progressed with fine victories interspersed with equally poor displays. Trying to fit in games on weekdays was not a very good idea, and two Thursday matches against sides from Cambridge University had to be cancelled when Haverhill could not find enough to make up an eleven, letting down two sides from Cambridge University. But then one Tuesday afternoon Haverhill again piled up 171 runs, this time versus Linton (T Mitson 45, J Twitchett 38, J Gurteen 34) The first two batsmen mentioned were borrowed from Clare. There was always a chance to organise an interesting game for holiday week-ends and Haverhill took on 'The Unknowns' which turned out to be another name for the Cassandra side from Cambridge. The Shepherds Brass band came along for this match and played a selection of popular tunes.

One game at Gosfield had to be hurriedly abandoned as a heavy storm swept over the proceedings, while the return Sudbury match was declared a tie when each side scored 71. The Haverhill Junior side also played three matches during the 1889 season. Also that year the Haverhill Rovers Cricket team was formed, which later became the football club. Many local sportsmen took part in several different sports which included athletics at the prestigious Haverhill Gala.

The Cricket and Football Club held their Annual Meeting slightly earlier than usual. Before any business it was decided to end the season with a 'Steeplechase' starting from the cricket field at 2-30 in the afternoon. All members of the club were ordered to take part as some people had questioned the fitness of the members of each sport, and this was a chance to prove that they deserved a place in the teams. The next day a match was arranged between the Haverhill Stars and the Odd XI. At the Annual Tea at the Rose & Crown the club said it was important to keep the football and cricket club up to a good standard and encourage healthy exercise amongst the young men. It was queried at the time as to how many young men were given a chance in the Cricket Club's 1st XI to which no answer was given.

For a change the treasurer was applauded when he announced that the balance was £2-1-7d to the good, but then added in a more sober tone that £25 was still owed by the club from the previous year. Also the fencing needed much repairing and although Mr Mason let them have the field at a reduced rent, no admission could be charged as footpaths run through the ground. In a lengthy speech Dr Tandy, who had been elected secretary as Mr Backler stepped down, remarked that membership had fallen which he thought was due to non-members being allowed to play in matches Mr Backler had been hard pressed not to resign but he declined through private reasons.

The river near the cricket ground then nearly claimed another victim when Mr and Mrs Sizer were walking in the cricket field with their small child when the child wandered away and fell into the river. Fortunately it was not very deep and on hearing the child's cries, the father, with another gentleman passing by, managed to rescue the child from its sudden immersion. This incident no doubt made the footpath question more urgent and a petition was handed in to the Haverhill Local Board. *"We the undersigned of Haverhill desire to call your attention to the footpath over the meadow in the Hamlet, now in the occupation of the Cricket and Football Club, and crossing the Great Eastern Railway line. Before the railway was formed and when this path was less in request, it ran along the fence on the Northern side of the meadow, as will be seen by the tithe map. It has since been diverted to the inconvenience of those using the meadow, and the crossing over the line is attended with great danger, indisputable evidence of which can be furnished if necessary. The meadow is now habitually frequented by the townspeople and owing to this fact, and also to the great increase in population, the footpath and crossing are very much more used than was the case formerly, and the risk to life and limb lies thereby also increased. The Railway Company are about to make various alterations and improvements to their line near this spot, and it has been thought that if proper representations were made to them by the Local Authority, the Company would be willing to do away with their crossing so that the footpath may be restored to its original side, and be continued through a tunnel under the line. We therefore ask that you will be pleased to forward this object in such manner as may be deemed best for the safety and advantage of the public."*

The question of the footpath and the railway crossing carried on into 1890 as the petition was passed by the Haverhill Local Board to the Great Eastern Railway, and included a suggestion that the footpath be removed from across the cricket meadow to alongside the hedge as far as the Chapel Bridge. In March came a reply, they were quite willing to contribute half the cost of removing the footpath and crossing over the railway next to the cricket ground, the path to go nearer the hedge and away from the river. To do this a subway was to be made under the railway track; this costing in the region of £240. This reply was passed to the cricket club who asked Mr C H Vincent to act on their behalf. As the cricket club could not see their way to providing any cash for this project, the decision went to the Local Board yet again. The Board dragged their feet once more.

Meanwhile a grand ball was held in March for the funds of both the Haverhill Cricket and Football Clubs. An attendance of close on 150 attended and music was provided by a 'very good' swing band from Bury St Edmunds. With most of the organising done by a Ladies Committee £20 was raised and the cricket season started with the Haverhill club able to pay off old debts and begin with a clean sheet once more. However when an evening of entertainment came along there was not such a good response and members of the two sports clubs were conspicuous by their absence. For this evening the Haverhill String Band rendered good service under their conductor Mr D Gurteen Jnr, and Mrs Beer was applauded for her songs, while Mrs Blanch Crowe was noted for her fine playing of the harp

The usual teams from around the district were on the fixture list again, but Haverhill did not strike the winning habit until well into June, in spite of the fact that S Poole was in impressive form with his bowling, 4 wickets for 13 runs in the first game versus Long Melford. It was reported that the town's opponents in early season had the Haverhill fielders 'leather hunting to a high degree', and it was as before when a match was won in style, only to be just the opposite the following week and lost again. To boost the batting Haverhill resorted to bringing in 'guests' borrowing two from Cambridge Cassandra and then three University men, including a certain Kumar Shri Ranjitsinhji who later forged a magnificent career in top class cricket. But in this match for Haverhill he was run out for just four runs.

It was against their long term rivals Sudbury that Haverhill performed unfavourably in front of a large crowd at the cricket field and conceded victory to their visitors by nine wickets. This caused the local newspaper to comment. *"I hear the members of the Sudbury cricket team were somewhat discourteously treated by the home representatives, only one of the latter entertaining them at the luncheon which was provided by them at the Rose & Crown. This does not speak very highly for the courtesy of our local cricketers especially as in view of their defeat by the visitors - and what a licking it was - their conduct is open to some misrepresentation. At any rate the Sudbury gentlemen must have experienced something of the feeling which a man feels when he is invited to a dinner and on going finds that his hosts are conspicuous by their absence."*

As the Australian cricketers were touring England in the summer of 1890 some special excursion trains were run to see them in action versus Cambridge University on a Thursday, Friday and Saturday in June. One wonders how many local cricketers took this opportunity to see the stars of the period in action, and pick up a few tips on the way.

Then came another reminder that the river was too near the paths. This time it was an unfortunate decision by a local youth of seventeen to try and end his own life. He had been discovered kneeling in the river with his head under the water by Mrs Nunn who was walking close to the cricket meadow, and a Mr Rash pulled him clear, assisted by P C Smith. The young man was taken back to his lodgings in the town which he had given up the day before, his landlady giving him blankets and some stimulants; letters in his pocket indicated he had lost his job at John Atterton's the day before.

At last, a reply came from the Great Eastern Railway Company but they would not be accepting the cost of a new subway as the amount of traffic using it did not justify the expense (There were seventeen trains each day, plus some on Sundays, while the Colne Valley Railway ran twelve daily and three on Sundays.) They also pointed out that if the Local Board would buy the subway from them afterwards they would be inclined to say yes to the project. The Local Board said no to buying the subway when and if it was built. A check was made on Sunday 1 June 1890 and showed that just over 400 foot passengers passed over the crossing that day; a week-day average was around one hundred. It seemed that only a nasty accident would shake those responsible into any action at all.

Local rivalry was on show when a Haverhill Cricket Club eleven played against the Haverhill Rovers Cricket team which paraded sixteen players, the Rovers won by 64 to 40. This was beginning to show that there were several very good young cricketers currently in the town, and the fielding of the Rovers team was capital but that of the older players was not all it should have been. This prompted a letter to the 'Echo'. *"When I wrote last week of seeing a team of boys pitted against the Haverhill Cricket Club, I had no idea that I should so soon have my desire gratified. As maybe supposed I did not miss seeing the match and the victory was no more popular with anyone more than the juniors themselves. The Town eleven however bore their ignominious defeat with good grace, and admitted that they had been fairly beaten. The fielding of the youngsters was superior and young Backler admired for his bowling."*

This criticism of the Haverhill club had an effect when the town's eleven went out the very next week and defeated a previously unbeaten Saffron Walden side, but the margin was only five runs in a close finish. P A Mann was in form with the bat, showing style and vigour, however he forgot the rule of hitting the ball twice and was declared out. Sometimes it was the batting, at other times the bowling which let Haverhill down. In one loss it was noted that the fielding was not up to the mark except for the efforts of Kemp at long-stop. However Haverhill did have two bowlers who could up their game when needed; Mann and S Poole ended one match with 5 wickets for 7 for Mann and 5 for 9 runs for Poole. In the next game Poole proceeded to record the following statistics, 11 over's, 18 runs and 7 wickets.

In September the annual match against West Wratting Park took place, the Park winning 149-54; there were some fine cricketers at this finishing school over the years. During the game F Whiting who was batting in fine form for Haverhill, received a severe blow on the forehead, knocking him down and rendering him insensible for a short time. As a result he had to retire from the field having notched up 18 runs.

In a review of the season it was found that after a bad start to the year the Haverhill Club had won eight and lost nine of their matches, one other being declared a draw. This was the first time for more than a few years that Haverhill had not won more matches than were lost, and a voice at the Annual General Meeting ventured the following, *"Opinions will be offered and given by those in the club and others who go along to watch each game, on how Haverhill should be playing the game. The first thing to look at was the lack of sufficient funds which come along every year, in other words the club is not being supported as well as it ought to be in such a town. There is a big field of titled gentlemen not too far from Haverhill who could be approached for subscriptions."* Another failure was the use of a good ground. Everyone knew the wretched nature of the cricket meadow, and there was not a batsman in the other clubs who didn't dread playing on it. The bumpy ground made it not uncommon for the ball to rise over head high. Also, in a hot summer cracks formed on the ground; to stop these they were just filled up with loose earth. The ground was more or less a public one and youngsters often played about on it with no regard for the surface. Another important point was the officers and committee. They were no doubt doing what they thought best for the club, and that was a extremely delicate matter, but the Cricket Club needed to have players who played just for the love of the game. Approaching gentlemen for subscriptions seemed to have worked for the young Rovers Cricket Club at first when the local Member of Parliament, Mr W Cuthbert Quilter, donated half-a-guinea, accompanied by a letter saying he should like to see the club a strong one.

A cricket tea was partaken at the Club's headquarters in October when twenty gentlemen sat down to one of Mrs Fell's legendary spreads. A business meeting took place afterwards mainly to keep track of the money side of the clubs operations. The treasurer presented a balance sheet showing £1-11-8d in hand, with seventy-nine members which included twenty-three playing members. For the following season the Rev Fleming was to be captain, with Vice-Captain Mr R Walton and Secretary Mr T J Mason.. There was also a suggestion that the Rovers Cricket Club be amalgamated with the town club so as to take advantage of some rising town stars, but this was almost immediately voted down.

There was a surprise in store for the Haverhill Club when they started the 1891 season. They responded to a challenge from a small club operating at Baythorne End and met them for a match on a Wednesday. Even allowing for the fact that the town eleven was not as strong as it could have been, the villagers won by 112 to 63. Both teams then sat down to a dinner at the Swan public house. The next was against Steeple Bumpstead who were one of the strongest village sides in the area. This time Haverhill were successful scoring 115 in their innings while the opposition managed only 21 in the first innings and 77 when they batted again. Haverhill's team was F Smart, F Whiting, D Gowers, T Mason, R Gibson, P Mann, H Fleming, R Walton, S Poole, W Backler and J Backler:

On a holiday weekend, Clare Cricket Club came to Haverhill. The Brass Band played during the interval and several couples got up and danced to the music. The British summer brought brilliant sunshine for some week-ends and the attendance at the cricket matches was higher than for some previous years. It was also evident that more ladies were being seen in the crowds. The cricket was also reasonably better, and scores for teams of over one hundred runs were frequent, but not always for the Haverhill team. S Poole continued to excel in bowling and versus Gosfield, he was described as a most destructive bowler taking 6 for 28, and he followed this with figures of 8 wickets for 18 runs in the Sudbury match. P Mann was not far behind when he chalked up 6 wickets for 8 runs versus Great Bradley. Extra players making a first appearance in the Haverhill team included G Harrison, J Bedford, F D Sladen, E Parson, P Taylor and T Mitson.

The river and footpath still occupied a quantity of space in the local newspaper when another small child named Hawes, who lived in nearby Hamlet Road, was saved from a watery grave by Mr H F Thake, a builder in the town. It appeared that the child was playing in the cricket field near the river when he fell in, and would have drowned but for the opportune rescue. This seemed to be an unfortunate spot as one or two persons had now fallen in at this part of the river. Other trouble at the cricket field saw Inspector Smith taking some young boys to the local court for 'wilful damage to the Cricket Club's property'; the boys were fined 6d each and also had to pay costs of 1d each.

One of the most exciting matches of this season was at Haverhill when Mr

T Mason's XI met the Steeple Bumpstead Working Mens Club one Wednesday. Mason's XI scored 23 and 22 while the Club managed 26 and 35. There were twenty cases of players out for a duck in the match; not many good batsmen in this encounter! Games between scratch elevens often provided great entertainment and even the athletic club Haverhill Harriers turned out for a cricket match against Mr Mostyn Sedgewick's XI from Birdbrook, while the Haverhill Matweavers entertained Castle Camps in a field lent by Mr W B Gurteen. The Haverhill Harriers were a fairly new club and had already held some athletic meetings on the cricket field.

By the close of the season eighteen matches had been arranged but two had been called off because of the weather. Haverhill were beaten by Clare (twice), West Wratting Park (twice) and once by Sudbury, but had won six matches; the batting and bowling seemed to have improved slightly. Alas, the fielding was said to be on a par with infants starting school. P A Mann topped the batting averages with some vigorous batting at times, and was thought by the own team to be the best all-rounder the club had produced for some time; his forty-one was the highest individual score in the year. Newcomer Gibson, who hailed from Yorkshire was the top bowler but did not appear very often so Poole and Mann were looked on as the town's best bowlers.

At the annual tea and business meeting the treasurer showed another loss on the year of £2, but as subscriptions were already coming in for the next season this was soon covered. A new captain was elected in Mr W Price with his vice-captain Mr B Gibson. The question of forming a Junior Branch was again spoken of and left for the Annual General Meeting, where it was suggested that younger players be encouraged to join the town Club. This was to help strengthen it and also bring in some new blood. A committee was formed to see if this was possible but nothing seemed to happen as the AGMs were always talking of this but no proceedings were ever taken.

Early in **1892,** Haverhill had received a letter from Mr Taylor of Cambridge inviting the Haverhill Cricket Club to compete with other clubs in the Cambridge district for a ten-guinea cup, and asked a deputation to attend a meeting in Cambridge to draw up some rules. Although Haverhill agreed to enter a team, no one representing the club went to the meeting and as a result, this new competition fell by the wayside. The idea of League Cricket was some time in the future when clubs settled down and looked for more intense matches.

The Haverhill captain this season was Mr F G Smart and Mr F W Gurteen took on the post of treasurer, while there was one overall committee of twelve for both sports of the Club (six for cricket and six for football), and as always the cricket could not begin until the winter sport had concluded their matches. Meanwhile a Dance was arranged in aid of the football section on 6 April at the Town Hall; Mr Smart was put in charge of engaging a suitable dance band.

One of the first matches this year was a Past v Present at Haverhill, the older eleven scoring 106; Radford was barred from bowling as he was declared too good for the old-timers. The Present side replied with 116. The Past XI included P Mann, H Thake, F Bates, G Halls, H Peck, G Poole, J Arber, F Mason, W Wash, Rev Smith, and W Shipp; the Present XI, as well as the regulars consisted of W Price, E Gunnell, H Pearson, B Gibson, W Ashplant, D, W, & T Smith: There were thirteen players on each side and of these 18 were clean bowled. Wednesday afternoon being a general holiday a cricket match was arranged between eleven of the Co-op employees and eleven Publicans. There were a great many spectators, and the latter team, who were evidently not used to such activity, although some of them showed they had not altogether lost their form, caused much amusement. Nevertheless, the youthful Co-operators were too much for them, and going in first, they scored 173 runs. The men of the 'Bar' only scored 23 for 6 wickets when a very heavy downpour of rain put an end to the play: Amongst the scratch elevens this year were the Matmakers who went to Hundon one Saturday in July with the following men = Bigmore, Spicer, Poole, Phillips, Beavis, Mildenhall, Brown, Whittle, Harrington, Webb and Smith. They made 15 in the first innings and then 21, but the village side with 20 and 30 beat this.

The Haverhill 2nd XI began with a visit to Thurlow but terminated rather unpleasantly when the visitors were dissatisfied with the very early drawing of the wickets especially when they were in a very good position to win the game On Whit-Monday the Haverhill 1st XI met an eleven from the Cassandra Club in Cambridge. The day being extremely fine, a large number of people paid a visit to the cricket field during the afternoon. (pity they could not charge for admittance) The Shepherds Band was also present and played a selection of music. The result was Haverhill (63) Cassandra (99).

Midweek games were being played more often and the Haverhill home match versus the Anchor Club (Cambridge) on Tuesday resulted in an easy win for the home club who put up the big score of 237 (R.Gibson 60, H.Leonard 34, T Mitson 33). The Anchor scored 41 with only one player in double figures. Haverhill played Rev Fleming but he only scored 6 and not a big score as he had made against Haverhill in a previous match with Thurlow. On Tuesday at Haverhill versus Sudbury, Haverhill nearly reached one hundred being all out for 98. Sudbury then passed this total and ended with 177 runs. In another game against Sudbury Haverhill went just one better and posted a score of 99 all out. It was in this fixture that Haverhill bowler J Radford managed eighteen overs of 'lightening deliveries' and taking 7 Sudbury wickets for a meagre 9 runs.

Just one week after totalling one of its highest scores the Haverhill Club found itself on the other foot when they made their annual visit to West Wratting Park. The home team went in first and quickly the score mounted up to 268 with their master W Cobbold hitting a masterful 97 before Radford managed to bowl him, and with two others scoring 51 and 47 the omens looked bad for Haverhill. However there was not much time left before the close of play and they had reached 72 for 3 wickets and the match was declared a draw.

Typical of the Haverhill side, they had rarely appeared to a greater advantage than the following week when they went out and beat a powerful team representing the Leys School of Cambridge by 57 runs. Haverhill knocked up 96 runs before the Haverhill bowlers got to work on the Cambridge side who could do little against Radford and Young and backed by some excellent fielding (for a change) they disposed the School for just 39. This season ended on a high note when the Haverhill Local Board agreed to enlarge and repair the footpath into the cricket field, employing their own men.

In January **1893**, the Annual Cricket Tea was held at the Rose & Crown although the attendance was not as significant as other years for such a healthy occupation. Those there were anxious that enough finance was forthcoming to enable the club to carry on successfully. After the meal, the officers and committee were voted on with the Rev Roberts taking the chair. This year saw a Ladies Committee formed, mainly to run the Dances and other pursuits that the feminine side of the club could organise much better than the gentlemen. Also under discussion was the state of the Cricket Field bridge at the end of Meeting House Lane. The Local Board had found that a new bridge would cost twenty pounds, which was too much for them as they said they were willing to spend up to fifteen pounds but no more. This was then passed to the Highways Committee to sort out; shifting the responsibility!

As the Football Club were playing their home games on the cricket field this season the summer pastime had to wait until they had completed the fixtures before they could take over. However, by Whit Monday, the field was ready for cricket and the Cambridge Cassandra club made their regular visit to Haverhill, this time to open the new season. There was a good wicket prepared and a large attendance in the fine weather saw the visitors rattle up 165 runs to start with. The Haverhill bowling was on the weak side and the fielding was loose, and when the town went in to bat H Grey's fast bowling for Cassandra wrecked havoc in the Haverhill batting ranks and the innings closed at 53. There were five 'ducks' in the Haverhill innings including the Rev Fleming whose wickets were sent flying several yards from where they were set up. This quite early finish saw the home side have another go and when stumps were drawn, they had scored another 60 runs. However, this was not a good commencement. Although there seemed to be many spectators at the Whit-Monday game, the following appeared in the Echo paper, "*I am afraid most of our Haverhill friends found the cricket match in the Meadows hardly attractive enough to keep them in the town on Bank Holiday. Some went to Lavenham to the Foresters Gala, while a contingent left for Colchester to return in the wee small hours of Tuesday morning. In addition, a large number spent the afternoon witnessing the sports at Clare. The weather was delightful and many people enjoyed it in the countryside.*" I wonder where the writer got his information; perhaps he was a resident of Sudbury who was always on the look out for running Haverhill down.

However, it all came good a few weeks later when in brilliant sunny weather Clare were the visitors and were sent home defeated by Haverhill by an innings and eighteen runs. This was in spite of Clare calling upon the help of three Cambridge players, and could do little against the bowling of J Radford (5-14) and S Poole (5-21) and only managed 42. Haverhill scored 87 of which D Whiffing made 36 including six three's! Clare fared worse, when they went in again and Poole and Radford scuttled them out for a mere 27; all the batsmen being bowled out. The young Rovers Cricket Club were also given a game and although the Town club played a weakened team the Rovers boys were beaten by sixteen runs. Everyone knew the cricket season was upon them when the advert appeared in the local newspaper from William Newman. He offered for the new 'Cricket and Tennis Season' wire netting, lawn mowers, garden seats and a selection of ready mixed paints. All local clubs were supplied at special rates.

Up to the match between Haverhill and Sudbury, the weather stayed fine but after Sudbury had their innings and put up a decent 105, rain fell as the teams were having lunch at the Rose & Crown and Haverhill batted on a rather damp wicket. Gowers was in fastidious form and hit a five and a six in successive deliveries in his innings. Then a somewhat unpleasant incident occurred when Mann and Radford appeared to be well set and there was a prospect of the home team winning. Mann was given out by the Sudbury umpire, caught by the wicket-keeper who had appealed. The batsman disclaimed having touched the ball with his bat, and at the close of play, the Haverhill captain said to the Sudbury captain that they would not play the return game if the same gentleman were umpire. Mann also apologised for the disturbance at the time.

Glemsford had just formed a cricket team and Haverhill sent an eleven to play their first match. Haverhill proved much too strong and scored 201 when they batted and then bowled the Glemsford side out for 28 and 69. All the Haverhill batsmen got double figures except one, and Radford was responsible for a vigorously hit 65. The 1st Kings Dragoon Guards, who were quartered in the town over a few days, took the time out to play a match versus Haverhill. They marched into the town from Bishops Stortford on the Saturday morning and the townsfolk turned out to watch them depart on early Monday morning bound for Bury St Edmunds. On another open date, a match took place between a Chauntry Mills XI led by Mr J Gurteen and Dr Hargrave's XI, the factory winning.

Frequenters of the cricket meadow and others who had the occasion to cross the river at Meeting House Lane appreciated the great improvement that had been brought about by the town's Highway Committee. One twice its width, standing on brick pillars had replaced the old narrow bridge, and the work was completed by making-up the riverbank on the cricket meadow side by adding some old railway sleepers. This work was felt by both cricket and football clubs which were beginning to attract larger crowds, of which the bridge was the principal means of going to and fro on Saturday afternoons. The next thing wanted by the sporting clubs of the town was for the adjoining fields to be created into a public recreation ground. Matches were also starting to be played on weekdays, mainly between scratch teams and others representing different businesses in Haverhill - Co-op v Grocers XI and the Matmakers v Mr Gowers workers.

An interesting letter appeared in the Echo newspaper towards the end of the summer. _"From a paragraph about footballers in an earlier edition it seems that the football section of the two clubs (cricket & football) as one club, were dissatisfied with the treatment at the hands of the committee and were determined to establish a separate organisation. A committee was formed to see if a suitable ground could be obtained, but no further meeting has been called, as I understand no such ground has been obtained, so a forming of a new club is somewhat damaged. What the precise grounds for dissatisfaction were I know not, but it seems that the root of the matter is the contention that the club exists primarily for the benefit of the cricketers. The footballers assert that they do not get their fair share of consideration, notwithstanding that the subscribers subscribe for the common benefit of both sections. They especially complain of the lack of interest in the football section on the part of many committee members, and in the manner in which their business is looked after, pointing to the fact that last year the season was nearly over when the captain, secretary etc, were officially appointed. Another sore point with the footballers is that several members are said to be determined that football matches this season must be played at the bottom end of the field, and to this the football section object. One can understand that playing football on a cricket pitch does not tend to improve the latter, but at the same time, considering that the club exists for the benefit of all, and that the field is too small to permit half being reserved for cricket and half for football, it is difficult to see that the cricketers have any more right to dictate to the footballers than the other way around. One thing is certain that *properly managed football is the more paying game and commands the greatest interest. It seems that the way to go is to put both sections on an equal footing. As far as the ground is concerned, until it is enlarged it is unfair that one section of the club should have the advantage over the other. A LOVER OF SPORT."* This seems to be the beginning of the end of both sports being operated by just one committee and the split was soon to happen. Meanwhile the Matmakers firstly opposed the Rovers and then the cricketers from Castle Camps on the Camping Close (this ground is now covered by the Alsi Supermarket) by kind permission of Mr W B Gurteen.

The most serious thing that affected both the cricket and football clubs was the financial difficulty they were under, and they could both sink and not surface again. For the past three or four years it had been a struggle to get on a sound footing, and if nothing was done in regard to the 'in-fighting' the town would be without either. Money, re-organisation and loyalty were required to sort this out, even more so when it emerged that the football team had more games arranged than before and membership was on the increase. It was hoped that some of the younger members would be given a chance in the coming season, with notions of a Reserve XI being created.

Entering **1894** at the annual supper of the town's Cricket and Football Club at the Rose and Crown members were greeted with a balance sheet showing a liability of £41-9-9d. The President addressed the meeting saying *"Congratulations to the club on its position and I express my pleasure that despite religious and political differences found, the club continues to be a means for social discourse."* Two or three of the club's gentlemen had already promised to make donations to support the club. A motion was also passed that the yearly subscriptions would be for both sports, to try and bring the two factions closer together; the under twenties fee was to be two shillings and sixpence. It was of note that A J K Smith the son of the Rev J T Smith had won a challenge cup at St Mary's College Sports in London, this being the third time in as many years. He played cricket for Haverhill from time to time when he was at home in the town.

On the question of a new recreation ground it was suggested that both the cricket and football clubs play a big part in this - the Haverhill Harriers Athletic Club now being defunct - and that the wealthy gentlemen of the town dip into their pockets as well, together with the School Board and the Education Department getting involved. This recreation ground would be ideal for the children of the town as they only had the streets or somebody's fields to play in. In a recent court hearing three young men and two boys were summoned for playing football and cricket in certain fields. *"These youths are to be pitied as they have no other place for their activities,"* remarked the Magistrates. Even the thousand children at school had no real area to use for any sort of organised games in the summer, and the small playground at the Board Schools was inadequate.

At this time the Cricket Club drew the attention of the Echo newspaper to the fact that for some period past a number of young men and boys had been in the habit of nightly visiting the Cricket Ground for the purpose of playing cards and other similar activities, although they had been requested not to do so. This had now become a nuisance of considerable magnitude and the committee were determined that if the practice persisted, the offenders were to be prosecuted. It was also added that recently damage had been done to the scoring huts, boards being wrenched from the sides, and the zinc covering being torn off. It was trusted that this hint would not be without its useful effect. Another spot of bother was a break-in to the hut on the cricket field when a pair of boots and a flannel jacket were stolen. A cricket bag was also broken open but the contents were untouched.

As usual the season began with a visit from the Cassandra Club from Cambridge on Whit-Monday, and for this opener Haverhill had the services of G Brown from Stowmarket and W Young from London. The visitors proved very much stronger this year. They included four county players, including H Gray who was exceptional; the very next week he played for the University against the Gentlemen of England at Lords, who had W G Grace in their side. Gray was very destructive against Haverhill taking 6 wickets for 13 runs as the home team were all out for 38, and the Cambridge side won easily. Haverhill went to Cambridge the next week to play the Leys School who proceeded to pile up 223 for 7 wickets, the Haverhill fielding being very indifferent. Haverhill lost this second match. The Haverhill team was T J Mason, T Mitson, D Whiffing, H Leonard, D Gowers, F Smart, P Taylor, P A Mann, F W Gurteen, W J Backler, H Cornell and J Radford.

The Haverhill seconds started with a visit to Halstead Grammar School.

The school were easily defeated by the Haverhill side who knocked up 108 with Ashplant top scorer on 31. Meanwhile the first eleven entertained Cambridge University Press on a cold and showery afternoon; play was suspended three times because of several heavy showers. S Poole was the best bowler with 8 wickets for 29 runs as the home side won between the rain stoppages. The following match saw J Radford taking the bowling plaudits with 7 wickets for just 9 runs versus Clare. The spectators were treated to some vigorous hitting by the Haverhill batsmen, D Gowers playing a slashing innings for his 63, which included two fours, six threes, thirteen twos and eleven singles. Last man in J Backler also hit out for his 35 runs.

A fixture which had been played at various times over the years was resumed this year when the Town v Factory sides met on the Cricket Ground. Against all odds the Town eleven came off best by winning. For the losers F G Smart was the pick while F W Gurteen was the best bowler for the Factory. The return match found the revenge of the Factory side. A visit to Denston saw Mr Morgan-Kirby's XI well beaten by Haverhill who had a demon bowler in J Radford; he took 6 wickets for 10 runs in the first innings and six wickets for one run in the second, including a hat-trick in a spell of phenomenal success with the ball. For this feat he was presented with a new bat by Dr Hargrave; should it have been a new ball? After seven games D Gowers was top of the batting with a total of 161 runs.

For a match at Bury St Edmunds the Haverhill side travelled by road instead of the usual rail journey, travelling in two charabancs. The return game versus Bury United took place on the Hamlet Croft as part of the Horticultural Show in August and was witnessed by a bumper crowd who saw a home victory. The fielding on both sides was not up to standard as there was a very bumpy outfield. Haverhill's score of 199 was mainly due to D Whiffing who frequently sent the ball into the nearby refreshment tents as he amassed 61 runs. The able manner of Mr Marsh the groundsman was acknowledged with a benefit match when a collection was made on his behalf. After this match he received £1-7s. Mr P A Mann opened a subscription list with a view to present a new bat to 'Duke' Whiffing for his performance at the Hamlet Croft, many people saying they had not seen such a exhibition of vigorous cricket for many a long day.. Several matches were closed with a visit to the Rose and Crown for a lunch or tea from the excellent Mrs Fell's kitchen.

A wonderful catch was taken by G A Gamble playing for Haverhill at Shudy Camps Park, interesting as he had never been in the Haverhill side before and did not come from the town, but guest players were often brought in. The next week the Grocers and Drapers XI went to Withersfield to play the village team, and up popped Mr Gamble once again in the Withersfield eleven. It was certainly an apt name for a sportsman. This match was very low scoring the home team being all out for 9 runs, then 46 in the second innings with Fred Bradnam on 10 runs. The Haverhill XI put up 13 and 23; there were twenty-one batsmen out for 'ducks' in this game.

Of the seventeen matches played by Haverhill, eight were won and nine lost. D Gowers' average of 18 saw him top the batting. T J Mason was the top bowler despite the performances of Poole and Radford, as Mason had not played in so many games. Newcomer Nicholson was high in the batting and looked a good acquisition. The annual tea and meeting once again saw the club in the 'red' by £17-18s, but it was agreed that the youngsters and the footballers would pay a reduced sub' when joining the Cricket and Football Club. It was also decided to institute legal proceedings against any persons not members of the Club, playing games on the Cricket Meadow, without the permission of the Cricket and Football Club. A notice was also displayed in the 'Echo' newspaper to this effect. With a view to inducing shop assistants and others who had only Wednesdays off, they could be members on payment of 2s 6d, this to include Wednesday evening practice. A Cricket League was once again discussed but once again after contacting the local sides this was still a closed book.

In February **1895** the Ladies Committee put on a club ball at the Town Hall which was fully decorated with flags, banners, plants and Chinese lanterns, together with footballs and cricket bats. Dancing to the modern day tunes from Mr C E Skipsey's Quadrille Band the event raised £321-2-8d profit which was promptly handed to the club to pay off the debts once again. The young Rovers Cricket Club was also finding it hard and asked the Town Club for help but they decided to take *"no notice of the Rovers debt of £1-7-6d."* Elected once again were the President=Mr W B Gurteen, and Joint Secretaries = F W and D M Gurteen. Before the games were due to begin, the Club decided to try and obtain a lease on the ground, and also to put up a fence on Mr Mason's side of the ground, but then decided that a lease on the ground was first in line before any fences, but some chairs and a bench were bought with crossed fingers for a bright summer.

The new season started this time with a Captains XI v Vice-Captains XI which took place in delightful sunny weather. The second XI opened against Halstead Grammar School at Haverhill, the homesters winning by an innings and 110 runs in a rather one-sided game. The second XI consisted of R Backler (captain), J Mann, W Argent, W Ashplant, W Poole, A Freeman, W Mason, F Whiting, E Rust, C Mason and E Farrant, a good smattering of worthy Haverhill names. The annual match versus Cambridge Cassandra attracted a substantial crowd to the Cricket Meadow where they were also entertained by the Shepherds Brass Band in the interludes. Haverhill paraded S Wright of Leicestershire who was visiting the area but the strong Cambridge side were worthy winners.

The beautiful summer weather continued for several weeks and some fine cricket was seen although the town team were not always victorious. In the game versus Clare the trundling of Gurteen and Backler was the winning factor for Haverhill, the first named performing a hat-trick when taking 4 wickets for 6 runs. Later Jack Backler showed some vigorous hitting with the bat. A visit to Thurlow saw the game played on a somewhat dangerous pitch and resulted in Chapman forced to retire after receiving a nasty blow on the head. It was during the outing to Cavendish that the fine weather broke and a heavy downpour prevented the game from starting. There was also some big hitting when Bury United came to Haverhill, Whiffing, Gibson and Radford opening their shoulders for the home team, Gibson often *"swiping the leather over the hedge."*

Wednesdays this year often saw a match being played such as the Echo Staff opposing Mr T Jarvis Staff - the newspaper men winning - and Haverhill Commercials versus Hempstead, with the village team containing players from Helions Bumpstead and Finchingfield. The Town side also put out a Wednesday team against long standing rivals Sudbury and was reported *"Sudbury compiled one hundred runs and a special mention to Nicholson who took a exceptional catch to dismiss the Rev King who was their top scorer. A quarter of an hour before lunch Haverhill started batting and after making a single Nicholson was given out 'caught at the wicket' a decision which created great dissatisfaction, the batsman not touching the ball within

(1) 1893; Back-D Smith, T Nicholson, D Gowers, F W Gurteen, S Poole, J Bedford; Sitting- W J Backler, Dr Hargrave, F G Smart, P Taylor, F J Mason; Front- D M Gurteen, D Whiffing;

(2) K S Ranjitsinhji, famous batsman for England who played one match for Haverhill while at Cambridge University. Later played for Sussex and fifteen tests for England, scoring nearly one thousand runs.

TOP' (3) Percival Perrin a top Essex batsman of the past who played at Haverhill for a visiting team
BOTTOM.(48) Jabez Gurteen unveiling the plaque on 21 May 1923 as the clubs ground

(TOP (4) An early illustration of a match in progress on the cricket meadow c 1900.
BOTTOM (5) A local match being played on the Recreation Ground c 1901

a foot. The incident was all the more regrettable as it was remembered last season the clubs did not meet as a result of an incident of the same nature the previous season, 1893. After lunch Whiffing and Whiting improved matters, but with two wickets to fall it looked like a Sudbury win but the Haverhill captain F G Smart came to the rescue with a highly valuable forty-one runs and took the Haverhill total to one hundred and thirty and victory. When Sudbury went in again two of their team had already caught the train home and they could only field eight players and the match was called time."

Despite a exceptional beginning to the summer weather wise, when the weather broke it began to disrupt the matches more often than not, and batsmen and fielders were kept busy scrambling into the pavilion or under a nearby tree on many Saturday afternoons. Several games were never finished and some not even started. The Haverhill versus Old Leysians was one Wednesday game which was forced to a halt but not before Haverhill lost the services of one of their best bowlers when Radford badly hurt his side and had to retire from all of the game; this was after slipping on the wet grass when making a delivery. No fewer than nine bowlers were used by the Town eleven in this Wednesday match, which saw the debut of the Rev E J Day who had just moved to Haverhill.

The local newspaper editor then got into the act of promoting a new playing area for Haverhill. He noted "*One cannot help asking oneself how is it that in a town and district such as Haverhill where there is so considerable population of working men, no provision is made for their health and recreation. There is a town cricket club which is seriously handicapped for the want of a meadow or other ground to play in where they could have a 'gate'. At present they play in what is called the Cricket Meadow, but there is a right-of-way through it; consequently they can never recruit their funds by making a charge. This is not fair to the club; it is certainly not creditable to the town. Then the Football Club, the Rovers, tried to make the same terms for the use of the Croft, but I am told a condition was named which the club could not possibly agree to. Strangers coming into the town say what a fine open spot you live in. What room you must have for recreation'. But when you tell them that the streets and the cemetery are the only open spaces to the public, they open their eyes wide. They say 'Why, we have been told you can get land in the country for an old song, that it is going begging'. Well it is not so in Haverhill or near it. I am very far from thinking that ground owners should be asked to part with their land for a mere nothing, but insomuch as the building value has been put into it by the ratepayers, what the ground owners practically ask when a piece of land for public purposes is wanted, is that the ratepayers pay on their own improvements. Assume for a moment that no factory had been built here and no manufacturing undertakings were carried on at Haverhill what would the land on which the town stand be worth? It would be worth very little more than its agricultural value. Yet with the exception of the streets and the cemetery and the school yard the local ratepayers have not an open spot they can call their own"*

The last game of the season in September was a visit to Sawston by Haverhill, but sadly Haverhill were beaten as they were poorly represented, they put up a mere 45, which Sawston easily passed, and at the end of play were 76 for 3 wickets. For the visitors nobody reached double figures nor gave any signs of doing so, and there were seven extras in the Haverhill total which turned out to be the highest individual scorer, which said much for the mediocre performance. As for the averages, Dr Day finished top batsman with an average of 19.9, and A C Beaton best bowler, each of his wickets cost just eight runs. The most momentous thing to happen was at the end of this season when the committee which served both cricket and football agreed that it was for the benefit of both sports that they go their separate ways, and from then on the Cricket Club was on its own. The Football Club calling itself now the Haverhill Town F C did not last very many years before it closed down and the younger Rovers Football Club became the principal one in the town.

One of the opening matches of **1897** was a visit to Haverhill by the Cambridge Idlers who arrived without their captain Mr A G Lawrence, who missed the train. Next to come to town were the Cambridge Tom-Tits which consisted of undergraduates of the University, as most of these strangely named clubs were. But the Tom-Tits had no answer to the bowling of Gurteen (5 for 12) and Dr Day (4 for 16) and reached just 43. Haverhill soon caught and passed that total with Dr Day (62) and P Taylor (58) smashing the ball all over the outfield as they scored 293 for 8 wickets, the highest score made for a number of years. Haverhill were good with the bat this year and in the next few games made 154 against the Cassandra Club, 218 for 8 versus Clare and 155 for 3 against the Idlers. The spectators could now watch the play in minor comfort as a rope was put around the field of play and a number of seats were available on payment of 2d each.

Brilliant weather greeted Clare to the Cricket Meadow, but they arrived with only eight players. After looking round the spectators they were made up to eleven with the help of three Haverhill youths, E Webb, W Thake and T Webb who top scored in a paltry total of 27. After seven matches undefeated Haverhill lost this tag when playing at Newmarket, who had the assistance of two professional players. The season rolled on as the town were rather erratic in winning well and losing equally poorly. However they were unfortunate to lose at Sawston when Rumble was run out which surprised everyone, as clearly the Haverhill batsman was well past the wickets when the bails were knocked off. The Haverhill eleven for most of this year comprised of F W Gurteen, E Day, H Dare, F Haynes, D Gowers, L Kent, J Mann, A Ramsey, H Smith, P Taylor and A Whiffing.

One of the better matches was at Sudbury when the home team failed miserably against the fine bowling of Kent and Ramsey backed up by some excellent fielding, which was often applauded by the home supporters. Kent's batting for Haverhill was then particularly vigorous, once hitting the ball over the pavilion into the gas-works, and then he hit the roof of the pavilion. Gowers and Taylor also gave the watchers a taste of their powerful batting as Haverhill won by eight wickets.

Looking at the statistics nineteen games were played by the first eleven of which fourteen were won and two drawn, quite a satisfactory year. The all-round batting, bowling and particularly the fielding had improved, as had several of the players. P Taylor headed the batting list with an average of over thirty, and Gurteen was the easy winner of the bowling averages taking over forty wickets.

A profit of £11 on a dance in March **1898** which the ladies were instrumental in holding was deemed a success, especially when the balance sheet showed that unlike previous years, the Cricket Club had £10-6-11d in the bank. This year before the AGM everyone sat down at the Rose and Crown to a 'Meat Tea' before the business was started. The President was Alderman W B Gurteen and the Vice-Presidents J Gurteen, F C Christmas, E Ingold, Dr H Hargrave and E Ewart. The Hon Sec (A S Beaton) reported that new teams to the fixture list were Earls Colne, Cambridge Nihilista (the name meaning a belief that nothing is worth while) and Long Melford, and that this season Mr L G Kent who had had a few matches already would be available full-time with his experience and performance. To close the meeting, Mr W A Jarvis, who had recently married, invited all present to join him and drink to his (!) health.

The Cambridge Tom-Tits were the first to visit Haverhill in a match in which G Dare for Haverhill took six wickets for just one run and the Cambridge top scorer was dismissed with a exceptional catch by Taylor. The fielding was certainly much better than in recent years when Beaton also brought off a fine catch. For the home eleven Kent was in great form with the bat, scoring 41, but Whiffing was stumped when he looked well set. Haverhill won by 23 runs. Parkers Piece was the venue for Haverhill when they played Cambridge Swifts, a game which turned out to be an easy victory as Dare took 7 wickets for 15 runs. The oddly named Nihilists from Cambridge included the famous W N Pilkington (Rugby Blue) but could not stop another Haverhill win, this time by one wicket and 95 runs. This was in spite of Whiffing being out first ball he received, and four wickets down before the score reached double figures. Newcomer Kent had already amassed over one hundred runs in the opening games. In view of the bigger turn out of spectators, the collection box was taken round at each match in view of no admission fee being charged. With the early success of the team, the question of new colours for the club was brought up, but after several meetings it was dropped and the old colours were kept.

The Haverhill 2nd XI was also going along nicely with visits to local villages such as Birdbrook, Withersfield, Thurlow and West Wratting, with an eleven which was mainly Mead, Farrant, Haynes, Mason, Hicks, Webb, Thake, J Backler, Arber, A Backler and Allen. Once again the question of running a Cricket League came to the fore, this time it was the Bury St Edmunds club which took issue with a letter to surrounding clubs. But Haverhill sat on the fence by seeking more information before giving their answer and the idea soon died away once more. An interesting incident happened when Haverhill were playing away at Bury Utd at the Cemetery Ground; a shed on Mrs Pavey's premises in Chalk Lane was observed to be on fire. This was next to the cricket ground and several spectators and some players rendered prompt assistance and saved some items but the shed was destroyed. How it came to be on fire was a mystery.

Some more fine batting was seen in the home game versus Earls Colne, Beaton hit a faultless 58, J Mann 35, while Kent blasted 43 including three mighty sixes, one big swipe sending the ball way over the other side of the river. The next game also attracted a large crowd on the Cricket Field on a Wednesday when Mr Douglas Roberts XI came to town. Included in their eleven was the brilliant Essex player Percival 'Peter' Perrin, who went on to play for his county until 1928, scoring close on thirty thousand runs; his highest innings being 343 not out versus Derbyshire, a feat that saw him batting for six hours and hitting sixty-eight boundaries; something the great W G Grace never accomplished in his career. The same season as appearing at Haverhill, Perrin was on 81 for Essex versus Gloucestershire when he was out caught and bowled by W G Grace, but the ball had clearly touched the ground, but with Grace glowering at the umpire with a loud appeal, the Essex batsman was given out. Perrin was known as the best batsman never to play for England. Unfortunately only eight of the visiting team arrived and some local players helped make up the side. Perrin was out for twelve in the first innings but when batting again he showed his skill with a quick 42 not out as the Haverhill eleven won the match. The Haverhill bowlers had achieved what many county players could not do very often, Perrin made over one thousand runs in the 1898 season. When the Town club were playing near enough to home, many followers cycled out of Haverhill to go and watch the eleven play. One week they saw Sawston score 78 all out, to which 'Duke' Whiffing for Haverhill rattled up 75 runs himself; needless to say Haverhill were victorious. There were a few matches when Haverhill reached some three figure scores and in one of these D Gowers reached 92 before being out. The bowlers also had some good spells notably Kent taking 9 wickets for 30 runs against Sawston. When the Long Melford batsman began to hit out when playing Haverhill, the Haverhill captain F W Gurteen put himself on to bowl and quickly altered the course of the game. His first two deliveries saw him capture two wickets and then another one with his fifth ball.

Sudbury could always be relied upon for a good game and sometimes controversy. This years encounter at Haverhill saw a close finish as the home team wanted five to win when Thake, the last man went in. A promising second eleven player, he went on to hit the winning run amongst much enthusiasm. Neither side took a second innings as the visitors had to catch the

5-28pm train back to Sudbury. The Cricket Meadow, being one of the very few places in Haverhill for recreation, was sometimes used for other events. One Sunday evening after divine service about one thousand inhabitants went to the meadow where the Shepherds Brass Band gave a concert. A collection was made amounting to £6-15s which went towards sending a group of workhouse children to the seaside for the day.

The danger of the crossing over the railway was raised once again when one evening the 7-54pm train was nearly made to stop as it approached the crossing leading from the Cricket Field to the Chalkstone Hills. This was on account of some young girls trespassing and standing on the rails. Those foolish maidens had apparently thought it was fun to skip aside at the last moment, but could have had serious consequences. The Great Eastern Railway Company then made it clear they would take steps to punish the offenders if it continued.

The **1899** cricket tea and Annual General Meeting was on 25 March when about thirty partook of a meat tea, and then moved to the Billiard Room for the Meeting where several more members joined them. The Treasurer had a smile on his face as he presented the Balance Sheet which for a change showed a profit on the year of £10-6-11d. This was the second year running that this had happened. The following week the Dance, which had turned into an annual affair, was at the town hall where it was said *"the floor was in an excellent condition"* and the hall exquisitely decorated. The balcony and the orchestra were used as dressing rooms while the lecture and billiard rooms were for supper for the one hundred and eighty attending. The dancing went on until five o'clock the next morning.

The season was opened this time by the 2nd XI with a match versus Sible Hedingham, and the Webb brothers bowled well for Haverhill and they won by 96 runs to 45. The second string also had a large victory over Shudy Camps when they won by one hundred runs. Yet another queerly named Cambridge eleven were due to visit the town, they were made up of Trinity College students and called themselves the Knockabouts. However they lived up to their informal name and failed to turn up, so a scratch game was played instead between the Town and the Factory. This finished Town (112 for 12 wickets) and Factory (93 for 11 wickets). When the Tom-Tits arrived two men short and borrowed two Haverhill lads, Gurteen proceeded to bowl both these out for no runs; nothing is spared in Haverhill cricket!

After some seasons without a Haverhill batsman hitting a century a grand display by H Dare against Long Melford saw 103 written beside his name in the scorebook. Haverhill hit an innings best of 303 that day. Seven Haverhill players reached double figures while six Melford batsmen failed to score at all. The match versus Sudbury nearly produced another three figure score when Whiffing appeared to reach one hundred when he was caught at third man as the ball sped high towards the boundary, and he was out for 96. Haverhill scored 285 before declaring leaving Sudbury two hours to reply but aided by Beaton's work as wicket-keeper, they failed to get anywhere near and the towns victory was applauded loudly.

A match on the Hamlet Croft was beginning to be a part of the August Holiday festivities and this year the Haverhill Victorian CC opposed A C Baldocks XI, the latter winning a low scoring game 28 to 24. The last home game for Haverhill saw them lose at the Cricket Meadow for the first time this season, and they ended the summer with another victory at Sudbury. Only ten matches were played this year and between 15 July and 12 August there were no first eleven games at all. Harry Dare was top of the batting averages with 40.01 and the most improved player was A J 'Jimmy' Mann. Unfortunately A Beaton was leaving the town and would be missed. The bowling honours went to 'Duke' Whiffing with some impressive performances. There was speak of employing a professional but not enough funds were available. Instead more seating for the loyal spectators was on the agenda, but at the lowest possible cost.

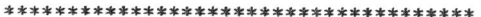

INTO THE 20th CENTURY

In January **1900** it was decided to hold a whist drive unless anything more connected with the War in the Transvaal (Boer War) should occur, in which case the Sec would call a meeting. By March no dance had been held this year, and an urgent meeting was called when it was found that the club were in debt once again and couldn't pay off some officials' expenses. The end of the previous season saw a sum of £17-6-2d owing. A vote of thanks was due to the Haverhill Amateur Dramatic Society for financial aid to the Cricket Club, and it was urgent that the Cricket Club look very carefully into match expenses. Some Vice-Presidents also offered around £2 more over their subs to help out but this could not be the answer over the long term.

The playing season began in May 1900 when Haverhill, who were struggling to raise an eleven, entertained the Cambridge Nihilists with the following team- D Gowers, A J Webb, D Rumball, R Payne, A J Mann, W Mason, J Thake, G Dare, F W Gurteen, A Backler and H B Thake. Needless to say they went down 170 to 59. But Haverhill made up for it the next week by beating another Cambridge eleven, the Pelicans, by three wickets and 89 runs.

It seemed that the local batsmen were slow making worthwhile scores early on, no more so than in the Haverhill versus Linton encounter at Linton, when some remarkable bowling was witnessed. The wicket was as 'dead' as it was possible to be and from this the bowlers took much advantage; thirty-three wickets fell for just 84 runs, both teams having two tries at batting. Haverhill put up 22 and 14, and Linton replied with 17 and 27. For Haverhill A J Webb took 5 wickets for 3 runs in the Linton first innings.

For some reason the Haverhill Club found it hard to get their best eleven on the field of play for several weeks, and it was then the second eleven came to the rescue and new players made their debut appearance in the first team. One of these matches was against Clare at Haverhill where six 2nd XI members were promoted. George Dare appeared in his new role as a slow break bowler, taking 5 wickets for 34 runs, and Clare were out for 77. A J Mann was the only Haverhill batsman to make any prolonged stand scoring 18 as his side were all out for 56, so Clare won by 21 runs. News of a batsman doing well came through when Mr Arthur Whiffing, for several years a member of Haverhill Cricket Club, scored 107 runs playing in Sussex against an Eastbourne team. News of his second century quickly followed - 101 versus Crowborough - he was also heading the bowling averages for his club.

Intense rivals Sudbury arrived to play Haverhill with the help of S D Page the Norfolk County player and an Earls Colne top batsman. A long stand by Dare and Mason for the home eleven - only ending with the score at 191, Mason hitting 90, was the mainstay of the Haverhill innings when they totalled 215. W Mason hit 90. Strengthening their side did not prove best for Sudbury however and they only managed 105 in reply. Haverhill quickly followed this up with a comprehensive victory at Halstead. They scuttled them out for 76 and proceeded to score 156 for 2 wickets. One Tuesday in August saw the downfall of Haverhill wins when Cambridge Victoria, arriving late on the slow train after missing an earlier one, scored 100 before keeping the home team down to a low total of just 27; seven Haverhill batsmen were out for a 'duck' The season came to a close after playing eighteen matches through the summer, A J Mann top of the batting and C McLeod, a newcomer, top of the bowling list.

Haverhill opened the **1901** season with a home game against a Varsity team calling themselves the Cambridge Pelicans, but several of the home team were not playing because of illness. Haverhill's H Dare performed a hat-trick as the visitors totalled 97; T Hawes also captured 3 wickets for 8 runs. D Gowers featured in some lively hitting as he made 53 which included two 6's, four 4's, and three 3's. With Mason contributing 43, Haverhill were the victors as they scored 172. The Cambridge Tom-Tits visit to the town was not a success when they arrived three men short and the match started late, at well past three o'clock. Two local Farrant's made up their side, but there was only two hours cricket on a beautiful sunny day. The visitors were skittled out by the bowling of Kent and Gurteen, and Haverhill soon passed their score of 47. The exigencies of Varsity life meant the Cambridge eleven had to catch the 5-28 train back home.

A visit to Halstead saw the home team score 181 but in an extremely slow time. Haverhill speeded up the proceedings when they batted and had reached 148 for 3 wickets when stumps were drawn. C C McLeod got 60 and W Mason 55 for Haverhill; the former had rattled up 60 runs the previous week as well and looked in fine form. The return game with Halstead was just the opposite with Halstead the winners by 40 to 28, a very low scoring game for such two good cricket teams. The Haverhill 2nd XI had a reasonable season, their top scorer being A Farrant who scored 53 against Halstead Factory before retiring hurt; the best bowling effort came from Stephen Poole, the captain, versus Thurlow with a haul of 6 wickets for 16 runs.

The year 1902 was marked with the Haverhill Cricket Club deciding to affiliate to the Suffolk County Cricket Association for the first time. Another move to form a Cricket League was put forward by Sudbury Cricket Club, and a Haverhill representative was sent to a meeting held at Halstead, but again this move came to nothing. At the Annual Meeting it was resolved to rope off a portion of the cricket field and charge non-members 2d each to watch the matches, an effort to raise more revenue for the club who could not really charge an entrance fee to the ground at this time. Other efforts to make money included a 'ping-pong tournament' in October when the season ended. Mr Coote was elected to be the club's umpire officially, although he had been in this position for some seasons past; this made it authorized.

As with most of the early years the balance sheet showed £18-12-11d in the bank but with the rent of £12 and other bills to be paid, this was cut down to just 12s 11d. On top of this the club were two years behind with the rent and owed £2 for the hire of Farrant's Brake, plus the Echo Office was owed £2-1s. Altogether the Cricket Club was in debt to the sum of £14-17-4d. To improve finances some members agreed to pay double subscriptions, helping in a small way.

This year's fixture saw new clubs from the Cambridge area, Rodney CC, Victoria CC and Cambridge Pelicans as well as the usual rivals from Halstead, Sudbury and other regular opponents. This made fourteen games in all, while the 2nd XI had arranged twelve matches. Came the opening game of the season and the weather was anything but ideal as the rain fell heavily during the morning of the Pelicans visit. As for the play, Haverhill's Farrant had his wickets spread eagled first ball of the initial match. Gowers came in however, and proceeded to hit out at everything, once sending the ball over the pavilion on to the railway track, eventually being caught in the long field. Five Haverhill batsmen failed to score and they were all out for 121. Pelicans had reached 39 for 3 before consistent rain forced the play to end. The 2nd XI lost their opening match 48 to 17 at Weston Colville. Also the ten Haverhill batsmen were all bowled out. The following week Bury United had scored 74 but Haverhill did not have the chance to reply when rain suddenly appeared and the match was abandoned. The Haverhill team was, A Farrant, T Hawes, C C McLeod, C W Bostock, G Dare, H Dare, S Poole, F C Frink, A J Mann, D Gowers and P Taylor, plus F W Gurteen.

After one week of fine weather and a win over Rodney CC, the inclement conditions returned when the 2nd XI played Steeple Bumpstead. The play was delayed until four o'clock and the village side made a quick 51. The opening pair for Haverhill went in to bat but it was raining so hard they were soon back inside and the match ended. After two more week-ends of rain and cloudy conditions it suddenly broke out fine for a match against Cambridge Victoria. The fielding of the Haverhill side was seen as excellent, and F W Gurteen bowled out the last three visiting players for a personal hat-trick. The same player then put up figures of 5 for 15 versus Clare, but could not stop Clare winning the game.

The Haverhill v Sudbury match was declared the benefit for G Coote the Haverhill ground man, and a collection was made during the afternoon. This was an all day match and Haverhill batted first to make 172 thanks to a stand between C C McLeod (45) and G Dare who went on to score 44. Sudbury had four vicars in their eleven - did they pray for more runs? - and Rev King made 52 but Haverhill won rather easily by 73 runs. The 2nd XI then got in on the act and piled up 179 for 5 wickets against West Wratting, the opening batsman Webb being out for nought and the rest of his side making double figures. It was a good day for the Haverhill batsmen who scored most of their runs from boundary hits.

The return match versus Cambridge Victoria saw the new enclosure in operation and the coins were soon coming in to sit in this part of the ground. This was a Tuesday fixture and started at 11 o'clock in outstanding weather. The visitors included in their side six County players which made it a close game before the Victoria Club won by just four runs, to end an up and down season. There were still many matches arranged between scratch teams in Haverhill; the Manufacturing Department versus Ready-made Clothing department (both factory teams) opposed each other while the Haverhill

Nondescripts went to Steeple Bumpstead for a friendly encounter.

Looking at that year's record Haverhill won six and lost six with some games lost to the typical British weather. To be fair, the matches they lost saw below strength teams take the field. C C McLeod finished as top batsman and also top bowler, his best bowling performance being 6 wickets for just 8 runs against Halstead. F W Gurteen, the genial captain, vastly improved his bowling but strangely his batting had gone the other way; his best bowling figures were 7 wickets for 7 runs versus Steeple Bumpstead. In the 2nd XI, T Hawes was top of the batting averages as well as being second in the 1st XI list.

1903, and the usual tea was followed by the Annual General Meeting in March. The committee elected were W Badminton, F Backler, J Bridge, D Gowers, D M Gurteen, F Frink, A J Mann, T P Pannell, A G Smart, S M Silver, H F Thake, and J Sainsbury: Mr H Gurteen and Mr C McLeod were the joint-secretaries. A Jumble Sale brought some extra cash - £28-7-2d - but the dance was deemed a failure when too few people stepped forward to organise this and funds were on the edge once again. A box was placed on a table at the end of the General Meeting for any donations to get the club out of debt. A letter was sent to the Haverhill Amateur Dramatic Society asking for a donation; they were approached because they had highly publicised the fact that they had a very healthy balance in the bank. Only one new player was to play for the club; Mr George Bedford was said to be a decent acquisition, but the players were warned to attend practice and improve their fielding. The club was well placed as there were two wicket-keepers on the books, Mr F C Frink and Mr J Webb. The field was said to be in a good condition but then the first match of the new season versus Pelicans was postponed as the ground was likened to a wet sponge.

Haverhill finally got their first game played but were promptly all out for just 41 and their opponents Rodney CC soon passed this total. Haverhill would probably have been the victors if they had given the ball to G Dare sooner as he proceeded to capture the last five Rodney wickets for only 4 runs in only 14 deliveries. Then after four low-scoring games in which victory eluded them - Haverhill out for just 34 on one occasion - they beat Bishops Stortford when they included the Sudbury professional Mr Machin in the town's line-up. Haverhill knocked up 159 for 8 wickets, but the fielding was nonetheless very weak.

Nearly the whole month of June was washed away when the 'Great Flood' of Haverhill covered the Cricket Meadow together with great parts of the town; this following two days of incessant heavy rain, the like of which had never been seen in Haverhill. The whole of the cricket field was under several inches of water and pictorial postcards of the town under water were very soon on sale in the High Street shops at one penny each.

The Haverhill versus Sudbury match this year was a close affair with Haverhill winning by the slender margin of one run. With the 1st XI not having too much success, it was the 2nd XI who were doing well and it was not until the first week in July that they lost their first match to Halstead Factory. There were many other occasional cricketers in the town who did not join the Haverhill Cricket Club. Twenty-two of these young men got together on the Hamlet Croft for a friendly game, the Old Independent Church playing the Primitive Methodist Church, the OIC winning by eight runs.

Halstead were the next visitors to the Cricket Meadow and put up a score of 111, and left Haverhill to beat that target in the eighty minutes left. Opening bat F Boles, a newcomer, hit 64 as the home team's batsmen started to hit out at everything. G Dare swiped the ball out of the ground from one delivery as they duly won the match. Boles gave a superb exhibition of batting and played with great freedom, his cutting was clean and crisp and his leg-hits were well-timed, and he drove with great force. This gentleman was on a visit to the town and played here for two weeks, scoring 198 runs in four games. At Steeple Bumpstead he hit the ball right out of the ground and it was never found; it was thought to have buried itself in a manure heap.

The season finished on a slight whimper, the only thing reportable was that A Backler made three brilliant catches in the long field against Sudbury. Had the fielding practice been successful? Two interesting matches wound up the season. The G Company of the 2nd Volunteer Corps challenged the Co-op Stores, and the GER Staff took on Mr T Jarvis employees. Haverhill CC managed to win nine of their fourteen games after a poor start, the highest score against them being 243 for 6 by Cambridge Victoria, which had the towns players running all over the meadow one afternoon.

At the **1904** AGM in March, the balance sheet showed just £11-0-1d in the bank, with bills outstanding, a fact that was beginning to be an every year occurrence. When there was a letter in the Essex & Suffolk News about the club being in a bad financial position owing to paying outside players from other towns to play for Haverhill, the Secretary had to reply to this, and to treat the article with the contempt it deserved. He did, however, report to the meeting that it was a job to get subscriptions of five shillings from some members. An application from the 'Shop Assistants' - the Haverhill Wednesday XI - to join the Club and play on Wednesdays on the Cricket Meadow was approved, but the groundsman would have the say on which pitches the different teams would play on, the 1st XI to have the first choice. The Suffolk County Cricket Association then tried to start a Cricket League, but as yet did not state if this was to be local or county-wide, so the Haverhill club decided to sit back and see what developed.

For the fresh season all the players were eager to compete once again with two new additions in B J Hind, an old member of Bury United, plus a former Lancashire League player Mr F R Brown. There were also two new fixtures against Colchester and Dalham Estate, replacing two teams not included this year. Mr W Mason Jnr was to be vice-captain to FW Gurteen while S Poole was to lead the 2nd XI. The Haverhill Wednesday XI, who had been going for a few years now, but not really under the umbrella of the town club, held a meeting in the town hall. Their new captain was to be Mr E W Griggs, the town's post office manager.

It was back to basics after the full-day match against Bury United on Whit-Monday. Bury easily beat the town side, who placed only 56 runs on the board. Once again the fielding of the Haverhill side was reported as *"very weak indeed with several catches dropped, especially in the slips, which any schoolboy would have held on to."* Honours came however for three Haverhill players when F W Gurteen, C McLeod and D Gowers were asked to play for a West Suffolk XI versus the County side at Sudbury. Gurteen scored 2 and 1, Gowers 9 and 0 and P Taylor, who took the place of McLeod who was unavailable, scored 11 and 12. Gurteen had a spell of bowling, and after sending down two wides, he took 2 wickets for 31 runs.

Once again it took a few games before Haverhill hit the winning trail, with victory at Clare was in very windy weather. Gurteen made a great catch off his own bowling when the Rev Highly hit a hard return. Haverhill's Coote then missed a straightforward chance but made a wonderful catch the very next ball. McLeod proceeded to knock the ball out of the ground twice in his innings. Meanwhile the 2nd XI and Halstead Factory ended their match all square at 57 runs each, a tie not seen many times before. Cricket was catching on with the younger generation in the town, games such as Croft Wanderers v Eden Road on the Recreation Ground and Queen Street United v Eden & Duddery United at the same venue.

The Haverhill seconds started on a winning run before they lost their sixth match at home to Hempstead. The 2nd XI were represented by F Whiting, J Webb, A Farrant, W Spicer, W Argent, A Harrington, J Arber, W L Crawford, S Poole, W Cracknell and C Betts. An easy victory came Haverhill's way when Colchester fulfilled their first ever fixture at Haverhill. The visitors arrived with only six players, so they made up with some spectators for a ten-a-side. Considering the conditions of the two teams it was fairly close (186-130). Last man in for Haverhill was F W Gurteen and although he was only at the crease a few minutes he scored eleven - a two, a five, and a four - A J Mann, S A Griggs and W Beavis played for the Colchester side.

The art of cycling suddenly became dangerous in the town, especially for the Haverhill cricketers. While descending Turnpike Hill in Withersfield William Spicer (cricketer and footballer) was knocked down by a horse and waggon. One of the large wheels passed over his leg and his bicycle but he was lucky and received a host of bruises only. Another unfortunate accident befell C C McLeod one Friday when he was cycling towards the Coupals with Mr F W Gurteen, carrying a tennis racket and a pair of shoes. He fell from his bike in the Coupals Road after being troubled by a fly in his eye. He struck the ground with great force and injured his head and one shoulder and had to be attended to by a doctor. It was later reported "the gentleman is now much better."

Batting first at Cambridge versus Rodney CC Haverhill knocked up one of their highest totals for some time, setting a target of 296 for 9 (W Mason Jnr 72 not out, P F Taylor 47, B J Hind 46) and when stumps were drawn Rodney had reached 164 for 4. Mr McLeod was re-appearing for the town after his regretful accident. A side from Walthamstow called St James had taken a late summer tour in the West Suffolk district for some years and Haverhill 2nd XI opposed them this season for a close match, winning 77-75.

The last match of the season proved quite a controversial affair when Haverhill won at Sudbury by 31 runs. Mason scored a well contrived 62 for Haverhill, and then the home supporters saw their best opening batsman bowled without scoring. When Gurteen appealed for an lbw against another Sudbury batsman, the umpire (Backler of Haverhill) gave it as out, and this incensed the home crowd. During the remainder of the innings, the home supporters howled unmercifully when Gurteen bowled. The words of "no-ball" and "how's that" were heard most of the time. The local newspaper had their say *"As a rule an interesting game was when these two sides meet, but it was an unsportsmanlike attitude of the spectators who resented the umpire giving their man out lbw."*

By the time the club was getting ready for the **1905** season the weather was not so good, nothing like cricketing weather, but prospects seemed better with several new players expected to join the club, which was hoped would greatly strengthen it. In addition, the new vicar Rev A C Hair would render some service as the Rev Roberts had done in the past. The new vicar had been at Sudbury and had been connected with that town's cricket club. There had been some bigger attendances at the Cricket Meadow last year but the highest collection taken only amounted to eight shillings, so it was evident that the public who watched and enjoyed the games refused to contribute, forgetting that to carry on such a club a large income was required. By the time of the first match, which was the 2nd XI versus Sible Hedingham, the sun had decided to appear, but not so the visiting team. They had sent a communication the previous day saying they could not raise enough players to carry out the fixture. The Haverhill players decided to indulge in some practice instead. One gentleman who was giving some hints on the game to his children in the back yard of his house in Withersfield Road, slipped on the brick surface and broke his ankle.

Away from Haverhill, the exploits of a former player drifted back to his hometown. Mr A W Whiffing was now playing for Mayfield in Kent and had recently made 102 before he retired from the crease, and then took the ball to take 7 wickets for 24 runs. Then the very next match he went even better and hit a score of 200 before he retired once again - to give the others a chance? - making 37 boundaries.

After a few matches into the season it was becoming clear that the fielding was still a problem for the Haverhill teams. By the time the 1st XI travelled to Colchester neither sides had won a game yet, and this continued when Colchester were the victors. For Haverhill, the batting seemed weaker this time as they only managed to reach 64, which the home team soon passed. The team that day consisted of C McLeod, B J Hind, J Arber, E Mason, W Spicer, P F Taylor, A J Mann, W Argent, F W Gurteen, P Pannell and F C Frink. Others who were in the 1st XI at times were W Mason, D Gowers, W Crawford, J D Rumbold, E W Griggs, A Harrington and G Coote. The 2nd XI, or the Reserves that some people started to call them, picked up their first win at Hempstead who were a very weak team. Argent was in top form and he took 6 wickets for 10 runs; Hempstead losing their first three wickets before a run was even scored. Their score of 24 was all scored in singles and the town eleven soon got these back and went on to register a total of 106, W Spicer making more than the opponents together; the Haverhill bowling was said to be deadly.

The first eleven then showed what they could really do by journeying to Halstead to pull off their first victory, following it the next week by beating Newmarket.

The fact they had managed to win some games now was down to the batsmen doing more than their bit to help gain victory. For Haverhill, McLeod was in splendid form in his innings of 71, hitting his first ball for a six, and he was seldom in any difficulty. He was certainly a good, consistent all-rounder and would certainly have been a valuable player for the Suffolk County. Then came a meritorious victory over Bury United, when there were two brilliant catches by Haverhill fielders. Hind leaned back to catch a ball one-handed that seemed to be going over the boundary, then Frink ran forward to make a great catch almost on the batsman's bat, falling as he did so. The Haverhill fielders could turn it on when they wanted to, but why only in patches!

Cricket was showing a great improvement in Haverhill and it was not just by the town Cricket Club. Other teams were appearing: Haverhill Rose, composed of the younger element were regularly seen. They went on their bikes to play Withersfield School where they were winners with young B Poole the top scorer, and bowlers H Scott taking 6 for 5 runs and B Poole 3 for 3 runs. Another of their games on the Recreation Ground saw an easy win over F Hindes XI, and in the next defeated S Pooles XI by 16 runs to 13.

In the middle of the summer, the Haverhill Club captain Mr F W Gurteen took time out to marry Miss M W Vinter at Trumpington Church at Cambridge. The Cricket Club sent him a letter of congratulation wishing him and his new wife many happy years together. He would not have been so happy with his cricketing pals when during his absence they went down to long-time rivals Clare, and at home too. The excuse was a weaker than normal team, with five batsmen scoring 'ducks' and some feeble Haverhill bowling. They followed this with a loss against Camden on a Thursday evening. Another cricketer to join the matrimonial stakes was A J Mann who married Miss Florence Dunt at Halstead, but was to continue to live in Haverhill at the Hamlet Villas; he worked in the office at D Gurteen's factory.

The poor run of results for Haverhill continued when Bury United gained a revenge for their earlier loss at Haverhill. They rattled up 230 for 4 wickets before they declared; the six Haverhill bowlers all had disastrous results. With the drawing of stumps, the visitors had replied with 141 for 8, but it was a moral victory for the Bury eleven. Then Haverhill had the worst of a draw versus Clare and lost again to Stoke at home. The first two Haverhill batsman were clean bowled in the first over in the latter game. Colchester again arrived at Haverhill as they did the previous year with only eight players this time, picking up three substitutes from the watching spectators; the home side still struggled to win this match even then.

A match at Steeple Bumpstead came to an unexpected end one Wednesday afternoon when a side calling themselves the Haverhill Mixtures went to the village. Bumpstead were declared the winners 161 to 60, the last three Haverhill batsmen were not able to bat as they were expected home for tea at five o'clock. The only other thing of note as the end of the season approached was the bowling figures of S Poole, who took 6 wickets for 6 runs for the Haverhill II's versus Sible Hedingham.

The season saw seventeen matches played by the 1st XI, only one being put off because of the rain. Six were won and eight lost, three ending as draws. The senior eleven relied on thirty-two different players throughout and totalled up 1,903 runs altogether. The only player to feature in every game was J Arber while Walter Mason, the vice-captain, was the top batsman, and F W Gurteen top bowler in the averages. The second team had a worse season than the one before, six matches were won and seven lost. Top bat was A Mason and best average for bowling was from S Poole.

Early in **1906** there was yet another discussion of a Cricket League being formed but Haverhill suggested a league system instead of the knockout basis the Suffolk County seemed to have in mind. Nearby the Newmarket League tried to start up but with little interest it very soon fell through. In Haverhill, Mr H Gurteen took over as Secretary at the AGM, where cheers were heard when it was made known that the club did not owe any money to creditors, and the balance sheet showed £12-13-4d in the bank. A prize of a new bat and a new ball were to be awarded to the two members who were top of the batting and bowling averages each year, these donated by Mr F Sainsbury. In a toast to the Cricket Club Mr R Jarvis said he remembered the Cricket Club since the 1850's. He had watched them in their matches on the Croft in conditions much different from today, and through their sometimes low ebbs. After the business was completed, a gramophone recital was given by Mr W Mason and duets from F W Gurteen and C Gurteen and various songs by club members. A dance was held again and surprisingly made a good sum of cash for the club although it was not very well attended. In fact, there seemed to be more people from Cambridge who danced the night away to the strains of the Blue Strauss Band, and then partook of a supper laid on as well. Other items from the Annual Meeting saw the club call for an estimate to be prepared for the question of laying on the water supply to the Cricket Ground, which was to be sub-let to the Hockey Club of Haverhill for £30, September to March. They had been playing on Greenfields up to now.

The season started with a visit to Long Melford who they had not met for the past seven years, the Haverhill team meeting at the Queens Head to travel by Brake. This proved an interesting game with the visitors successful by just six runs. Prospects looked good but one fixture not on the cards for various reasons. was the visit to Sudbury The 2nd XI met Sible Hedingham at home and won by 54-52, Arthur Whiting starting his first season as captain and top scoring. Harrington was in form and took 5 wickets for 12 runs, but more important was that the fielding had greatly improved. However there were several complaints about not starting on time; two o'clock was advertised but play did not get under way until five minutes to three. It was not fair on the supporters to wait around for such a period. This was actually down to the home players not arriving on time

It was in the Haverhill Wednesday XI that one newcomer shone, G Grand taking 6 wickets for 12 runs at Birdbrook, his deliveries being much too good for the village side. Another regular team in the town was the Haverhill Rose XI who had quite a full fixture list. They included a top Haverhill player in B Poole who hit sixty runs in their win over Haverhill United. There were not many places in Haverhill acceptable for staging a cricket match and even Atterton's Green came into use for a contest between the White Lily XI and S Scotts XI. A few scratch elevens made use of the new Recreation Ground and several times in midweek there were matches there. These included Camps Road United v S Browns XI and Church Lads Brigade v Croft Spurs. This was a busy period for cricket in Haverhill and there were many taking part each week.

One Thursday Haverhill entertained Camden and posted their lowest score for many years when they were all out for 21; of course the visitors won by hitting 95 in their innings. Haverhill then hit back with a score of 161 for 6 declared versus Clare who made 103 for 4 before stumps were drawn; A J Mann getting 64 for Haverhill. However, there had been yet another very late start and if they had commenced on time a result would have been obtained. Another such game was the 2nd XI versus Withersfield when a late start saw the match once again ending as a draw as there was no time to complete both innings.

Shades of the Sudbury match the previous year happened when Saffron Walden came to the Cricket Field and were victors by 5 runs. Jackson bowling for Haverhill appealed for lbw and when the Saffron Walden umpire said it was not out, the batsman grinned broadly. The home crowd showed signs of dissent, and the batsman made several expressions of contempt. Another such appeal was then given as out and the supporters then cheered wildly. Haverhill gained an easy away win at home to Halstead, totalling 167.

At one point the visiting eleven were standing at 7 wickets down for a meagre 8 runs, and were all out for 19, Gurteen taking 5 wickets for 12 runs and Poole 5 for 3. The Haverhill wicket-keeper W Spicer was in top form cutting out several byes.

When Haverhill went to Bury and lost 86-51, it was A Whiting who bowled just three over's and took 3 wickets for only 1 run. C S Gurteen opened the batting and was top scorer, and would have got more when he was out to an 'ill-judged call'. Whiting was also in form for the 2nd XI with figures of 5 for 3 runs when they hustled out Sible Hedingham for only 12 runs. Of the twenty-one matches arranged only seventeen were played. Cambridge Commercial Travellers called off twice while Rodney C C could not raise a team at the last moment. P Taylor was an ever-present for the 1st XI

The only new players mentioned for **1907** were Dr Cole, Mr J S Hill and Mr McGowan. The problem from other years reared its head early in the season when a Thursday match versus Camden was declared a draw as it could not be played right out for a result. This was at Cambridge and it was the visitors who were late putting in an appearance. The following Saturday, Haverhill entertained Newmarket All Saints on a very cold day and with few people watching. Those who did were left shivering as the Haverhill players, some of whom lived very near the ground, strolled in to the meadow as if tomorrow would do. Some were so late that the captain was left looking around for other players to make up the team as it was declared the latecomers were not going to turn up.

After five matches of which two were lost, two drawn and the other one abandoned because of heavy rain, Haverhill suffered another reverse when Halstead were the winners by four runs. Haverhill were all out for 19 and in a second innings, they managed 40 for 3 at the end of play. A good stand between Arber and Taylor ended when a misunderstanding between the two - Taylor didn't hear his partners shout to stay - resulted in the dismissal of Taylor. As the 1st XI were losing most games and the 2nd XI were on a winning streak, the question was asked "Why not give some of the second's a chance to see what they could do," but the two teams seemed to be picked regularly each week and no changes made at all. One thing that was won was the 'King Kettle' offered by Poole's Shop to the first player to score fifty or over; D Gowers was the one to take home this valuable prize after an innings of 53 against Steeple Bumpstead.

The watching spectators then voiced their opinions with a letter to the local press. *"Will you kindly permit me to suggest to the committee of the Haverhill Cricket Club, that in order to add to the pleasure and comfort of the visiting teams and spectators, that they should either change their umpire or make some arrangements to keep him on the field during the half-day matches. It is very annoying to visiting players and spectators to be kept waiting several minutes. Time for half-day matches in all faith is short enough, and it seems ridiculous that from fifteen to twenty minutes should be wasted in the middle of the afternoon. Last Saturday sixteen minutes elapsed and I have been present when over twenty minutes have been wasted in this way. Thanking you in anticipation. 'A frequent visitor'.* Meanwhile, in their eleventh match Haverhill won only their second game as S Poole performed a hat-trick when bowling against Sudbury. Heavy rain showers stopped the game several times but eventually Haverhill got the verdict. The return fixture again went Haverhill's way, but they were struggling until Griggs and Taylor came together and Griggs started to hit out. Griggs was then badly hurt and had to retire from the game; P Taylor went on to score 110 giving only two faint chances as the town reached 225. Not so good in their batting were Helions Bumpstead who came to town for a game versus West End Institute, Bumpstead being all out for 9 runs and seven batsmen failed to score.

Things were looking up for the 1st XI now, and it seemed they could do no wrong after their very poor start to the season. In August, and batting first against Newmarket away, Dr McGowan (59) and S Poole (78) put on a record opening stand of 141 before one of them was out. Poole hit nine 4's and three 3's as Haverhill won by 209 for 7 against Newmarket's 72. A Mason and S Poole bowled throughout the Cambridge Commercial Travellers innings, each taking five wickets as Haverhill were victors once again 140 to 85. Success brings the crowds and a very large crowd was reported at the Meadows to witness another victory over Kelvedon. The sequence was broken when at Halstead it was back to the old late start and slow scoring by both teams in a match called as a draw.

The Haverhill 2nd XI lost only three matches in 1907, two of these to Withersfield, and it was the Haverhill cast-offs who were the main reason for these losses. J Arber hit 52 and S A Griggs 31 playing for the village who also included B Willison. This situation prompted another Echo letter *"Why are so many useful cricketers allowed to play for opponents simply because they have not been asked to play for their home town. It is difficult to understand as non-members were playing in both first and second elevens for Haverhill on the same day. During the present season Jim Arber has only missed one game for Haverhill with a batting average higher than most of the batsmen, Griggs has played for both elevens for Haverhill and a good average of twenty-three. Willison was also playing for the town, but now all three are regular for Haverhill's opponents. If Haverhill wishes to win games, they should always select the best players and not turn them away. If the chief object is to not have a successful playing record then the present policy will be available. One of the chief moans is that they do not like playing in the second eleven. Under such circumstances, it is unreasonable to appeal for more members at the AGM. It is unlikely that members will still pay their five shillings or two and sixpence, when week after week they are not asked to play when worse players are still in the first eleven."*

The next match was a 1st XI loss at Halstead at home 131 to 83, then for the 2nd XI a defeat by Withersfield, who still had in their side W Arber and W Whiting from the town. The last home match was versus Rodney and AH Smith played for the visitors as they came with a player short. The last two Haverhill men came together with nineteen runs wanted to win, and they settled in to score these with good running between the wickets with ten minutes to spare. There was one curious incident when one of Rodney's batsmen was so certain he had hit a boundary that he did not attempt to run, but the sprinting powers of Gurteen got to the ball before he went out of the field and saved four runs. Mason top scored with 60.

Haverhill 1st XI played in all twenty matches of which eight were won, five lost and seven drawn. The rot in the first half of the season stopped as the summer went on, but they did use forty different players during the year. As well as the usual bat and ball awards, Mr AH Long of Steeple Bumpstead donated a new pair of pads, won by P Taylor. The 2nd XI were more successful and won nine of their thirteen games, but ended on a low note with two defeats. W Spicer and AH Smith played in all the games with J Webb finishing top of the batting averages and the bowling. A second team award from Mr W Long of the Greyhound Hotel won D Gowers a new set of pads.

A change was made to the Dance date and this was put on in February **1908**, and on a Thursday, to see if that enticed a larger attendance. This pushed all the right buttons and also included a supper which was down to the Ladies Committee led by Agnes Gurteen. A splendid programme of dances was arranged and music came from one of the areas finest dance bands, the Cambridge Blue Strauss Band. With just under a hundred present, the event went on until three o'clock Friday morning.

Efforts were still being made to form some sort of Cricket League in the South-West Suffolk District, this time convened by Mr FA Graham of Cavendish. Invitations were sent to Haverhill, Sudbury, Saffron Walden, Halstead, Stoke-by-Clare, Long Melford, Clare and Cavendish, but only Cavendish and Haverhill turned up at the Rose & Crown in Haverhill, and Clare wanted more time to think about it. However the other clubs which were contacted were more or less favourable. The invitation to this meeting also pointed out *"It is not intended in any way to interfere with existing fixtures, but to assist in promoting cricket generally in the area."* It was discussed at the small meeting but ultimately left as a suggestion for the time being.

Once again, the first fixture at Clare was postponed as the ground was waterlogged, but the 2nd XI were luckier on the opening match at Steeple Bumpstead. They met at the Market Hill at 1.45 sharp; the match was due to begin at 2 o'clock. This match was a triumph for Haverhill's H Cracknell who took 8 wickets for 10 runs, seven being clean bowled. This was going to be hard to better in the coming season. Haverhill Wednesday XI were again operating successfully and had already beaten Helions Bumpstead and Birdbrook. Another team with quite a full list of games was the Primitive Methodist Club, but their planned opening game - Married v Single - was put off as rain set in just before they were due to start. There was also a remarkable performance in a minor game on the Recreation Ground when B Thake took 9 wickets for 5 runs in the match between Haverhill Church Choir v Eden & Duddery United.

The home programme for the 1st XI started with a visit from Newmarket, but the old problems were repeated when the homesters started their innings half an hour after the advertised start of play. They piled up 186 and Newmarket replied and had reached 150 when the game was accepted as a draw. Some suggested the Haverhill captain should have declared earlier to give the game a chance to gain a result. Furthermore, if the match had started on time there was no doubt that Haverhill would have emerged victorious, but for this match the visitors were the culprits. Nevertheless, several of the home players came strolling to the ground well after the time of the commencement. In addition, there were not many members at the ground and they were reminded that the cricket club could not survive without their help; gate money could not be charged so the collecting box was the only way to operate. Another item, which seemed to be always present, was the sloppy fielding of the Haverhill Cricket Club's two sides. It was suggested that extra time be spent on this during the week, but this did not materialise, as the players were once again late in turning out for the extra sessions.

The team were again soundly beaten in the trip to West Wratting Park. The Haverhill score of 75 was quickly passed and eventually ended at 280 for 6 wickets as the Haverhill 'trundlers' were attacked without mercy. Langthorne for the Park side hit 117 as six bowlers were tried by the visiting captain, but there was not one maiden over in the thirty-nine bowled. Haverhill carried their inadequate form into their next match and were beaten on their own ground by Cambridge Commercial Travellers. Questions were asked if Taylor was really out lbw as he stood for quite a while before walking to the pavilion, while C S Gurteen made one or two wild strokes as did F Backler; all-round a poor showing.

When Rodney C C (Cambridge) came to the Cricket Field, Haverhill batsmen were encouraged with the words "*Hit at everything.*" The game started forty minutes late yet again, and one home batsman was still putting his pads on when he was needed quickly as wickets fell rapidly. Helped by F Boles, the opening bat who notched up 95 not out, Haverhill won but only by the slender margin of one run - 166-165. Just as if things were beginning to look better, Griggs had the ball bounce up and strike him over one eye leaving a nasty gash. He was led away and treated by Dr Walker. A high scoring match versus Walthamstow Wanderers ended 278 to 185 in the London team's favour. It was not often that both Haverhill elevens won on the same day but the 1st XI were successful against Halstead while the seconds won at Withersfield who only managed 20 all out. W Spicer hit a hasty 101 not out in Haverhill's total of 162 for 2. The season saw nineteen games played, eleven of which were lost and five won. The 2nd XI fared a great deal better and lost only one match out of their twelve matches. Mr F Boles was another fleeting visitor to the town and played five games while he was here; in three of his innings he scored 112 twice and 95 not out. This year saw the Hockey Club playing their matches on part of the Cricket Field, but the agreed rent was proving hard to collect from this venture. They were given another year on the ground and asked to pay both annual rents

---

Before the Haverhill team could start their **1909** season a letter to the local newspaper read, *"One hears about the duty of spectators towards the cricket club and while that duty is not recognised to such an extent as it ought to be. It must not be forgotten that the cricket club has also a duty to perform, to provide the best possible sport they can. What I refer to is the short period during which play is actually in progress. Drawn games have been seen more and more and when games are played to a finish the more people would come and watch, and the attendances are dropping away quickly."* As well as this voice of a critic, the weakness of the team, in both batting and bowling was seen once again this year. However, it was not until the fourth game against Newmarket that Haverhill lost a match. By this time the talk of being feeble in all departments had made the players determined to improve, which they did. Winning for a second time in succession drew another comment *"By playing good cricket in every department and followed by some very smart fielding Haverhill were triumphant.*

July proved a good month for Haverhill batsmen S A Griggs (67 v West Wratting and 54 v Sudbury) and F W Hinde (53 v West Wratting and 69 v Sudbury). However, J Arber 77 and A Mason 101 then outscored them both, both for the 2nd XI, but this eleven's winning run came to an abrupt halt when Stoke-by-Clare thumped them 200 runs to 54. A Wednesday match was arranged for Mr FW Gurteen's XI against Mr A Sainsbury's XI; the wealth of cricketers included a top professional in C C Page of Middlesex. This resulted in a delightful free-hitting and rapid scoring game; the like had not been seen at Haverhill for quite a while. After Mr Gurteen's team was dismissed for 110, Tubbs and Page began batting and the fielders began leather hunting in a big way. 73 runs came in just twenty minutes and the 200 mark was reached in seventy-five minutes, the final total being 272.

Owing to the many wet days throughout this summer the first team won six and lost four, and the only player to turn out for every game was S A Griggs. Seven players scored over fifty. J Arber and A H Smith played in every game for the seconds who won eight and lost two of their eleven matches. The first match ended with Mr G W Coleman's XI 207 for 5 declared and Haverhill replied with 42 for 6. Haverhill lost heavily at Newmarket, then on Whit Monday they beat Bury Utd, followed by another big defeat at West Wratting Park. An improvement in playing results was seen afterwards for an up and down season. They used 25 different batsmen and 13 bowlers, and scored 1,942 runs altogether. The team for most games included S Hinde, J D Rumbold, S A Griggs, Dr McGowan, W C Spicer, A Mason, P F Taylor, S Poole, B Willison, W Mason, A J Mann, A H Smith, F W Hinde, A Mason, F W Gurteen and H W Badcock,.

After the season had drawn to a close, Mr W Poole came forward to suggest that a new pavilion should be the target in the next year. He suggested a Grand Concert or something as extensive as this to start the ball rolling for this project; the yearly Dances had not been so successful cash wise for the last few years. Letters were sent out to solicit donations for the project. The old pavilion had been just an old hut before this date so Mr W Mason was to prepare a plan and estimates. The old fence on the ground was to be removed and Mr Mason offered to add a portion to the present meadow. Also a new fence was to be put up at a cost of £8. It was suggested that a quoits pitch be laid as well but this was not followed up. The estimate for new facilities was put forward at £125. Because of subscriptions and donations coming in early, it was decided to start work on the new building almost immediately.

The weather interfered with the second eleven's matches. Their highest score was 222 for 7 v Halstead and lowest was 43 v Hedingham. A Mason top scored with 101 v Halstead St Andrews, and B Poole ended top of the averages for bowling. Some players in 2nd XI were J Arber, F W Hinde, A Mason, H Cracknell, G Webb, D Gowers, A Whiting, A H Smith, W Argent, J Brown, B Poole, S A Griggs, J Mizon and C S Gurteen. W Arber played in four games and never troubled the scorer at all. In spite of the wet summer the groundsman George Coote was praised for his efforts to provide a reasonable wicket, he was employed at fifteen shillings per week

Throughout the season, some youngsters had been seen on the Cricket

Meadow on more than a few occasions and the cricket club secretary had obtained the names of boys playing hockey on the Meadow. Subsequently the fathers were advised that future offences would mean prosecutions and a notice to be put in the Echo newspaper to this effect. There was an application from the Hockey Club and Old Independent Football Club to use the cricket ground. The Hockey Club was offered the use at £3 rent but refused the OIC unless the Hockey Club did not take up their offer. At a meeting in October the Hockey Club were relieved of the hire of ground and the Football Club used the ground for their season.

For **1910**, the Shop Assistants Cricket team were given use of the ground as usual subject to the guarantee as last year. So far the cricket club had twenty new members at 2s 6d each. All labour on the meadow when erecting the new pavilion was to be insured, and all buildings on the ground to be insured against fire. The new structure was to be insured for £200. Alderman Gurteen was approached to open the new pavilion Whit-Monday at 11am. The nets were ready by the first week in April for practice, and amongst the adverts in the newspaper was one for the Haverhill Fancy Bazaar, next to the Town Hall, offering a well-assorted stock of boy's cricket bats, balls and stumps. There was no sign of any new blood in the team for the next season, only a couple of players who had not been able to play regularly the previous year.

Building operations had been in progress to get the new pavilion ready for the proposed opening date. The new structure had a frontage of 31 feet and contained a room 20 feet by 16 feet and two dressing rooms 9 feet by 8 feet. Two windows overlooked the field of play and there was a window in the side of the large room, and one in each dressing room. A veranda seven feet wide ran the entire length of the building and on to this two doors opened. Access to this veranda was by three steps from the ground, and on the roof there was a bell turret. There was a flagstaff at the south end. The building was weather boarded outside and match boarded inside and stood on brickwork two feet high. The roof was covered with felt and galvanised iron and the whole pavilion enclosed by a 4 feet six-inch 'un-climbable fence'. The scoring box remained as before.

Mason & Sons erected the new pavilion for the Cricket Club per plan and

specification at an estimated £130, which included the following:
Fitting new seats in dressing rooms £2-10-0
Six new seats £6-12-0
Erecting new fence and gates etc £36-7-6
WC and urinal- scoreboard- new window £2-10-0
Notice boards & new forms to sit on and painting £2-2-6
Clearing old pavilion mess £1-0-0
New galvanised 250-gall tank £6-10-0
New drains - 500 new bricks.
This plus all carpenters and bricklayers time
The full account for the pavilion was finally put at £187-12s, which was approved, and after collecting all promised monies, a deficit of £8 was announced. A whist drive was planned to help get this bill settled. This was held in November and cost 2s 6d to attend, and a supper by Mrs Sparrow took place as well at this whist drive at 8d per head. The result was a profit of £6-13-8d. It was still being thought that if any cricket leagues were to operate in the district, Haverhill should be involved and the club captain was to keep an eye out for any news on this front. It was afterwards felt that it was not in the club's interest to enter a cricket league but to hold a Dance in January 1911. As for the playing days, the first XI met all the usual opponents plus Clare College Unemployed, Harston and the Regent CC from Cambridge; no fresh teams were on the 2nd XI list. A visit to Long Melford was the opening match and was won 69-42.

The weather was brilliant for the opening of the new pavilion in May and the crowd was such that had not been seen on the cricket meadow for many a long year. A new pavilion had been talked about for more than a few years and was sometimes referred to as Haverhill's answer to the Loch Ness monster - talked about but never seen. Mr H Gurteen said, *"For many years we had been laughed at for what had previously been their pavilion, but this is a very pleasant accommodation for the visitors."* However, it was rather a quiet gathering, owing to the death of King Edward VII just being announced. Alderman W B Gurteen, an old cricketer for the town, turned the key in the door and Jabez Gurteen recalled the poor little shed when he was playing. A new flag was run up the mast for the opening but then returned to half-mast. The flag was a blue and white sectional flag with HCC on it. Mr J Gurteen remembered the times as a lad they would creep under the flaps of a tent that was the only cover on the ground. The 1st XI then celebrated the opening with victory by 164 against Bury United 70, and to end the day it was made known that the 2nd XI had also won their game 121-58 at Stoke-by-Clare.

Following the sunny day for the grand opening, the weather suddenly changed for the worse and rain prevented some matches to even begin. The Haverhill versus Sudbury match was to be an all-day affair but owing to Sudbury arriving extremely late, - the game started at 2-30pm. Haverhill batted first, and made 137 for 6 wickets before the rain fell heavily and the match was abandoned. The next week there was sparse attendance due to the wet and very cold weather, and after Haverhill were all out for 218, Melford were skittled out quickly for a meagre 14 runs. They were given another chance and had reached 24 for 3 when time was called. Bowling for Haverhill, newcomer C Keenan took 7 for 9 and S Poole 3 for 2, while the two Haverhill opening batsmen ran up 109 before one of them was out. It was Keenan who notched up 103 not out versus Newmarket as Haverhill scored 220 for 6, but Haverhill could not bowl their opponents out and the match was drawn. Then the new man helped the 2nd XI at Hedingham and was man-of-the-match with 148.

In the match at Haverhill against Saffron Walden, the visitors went in first and made 126. For the Haverhill bowlers, Keenan's performance was exceptional and very much appreciated by the spectators. He commenced bowling towards the town but had limited success and changed ends where he quickly started to puzzle his opponents. Twice he took two wickets in succession but was denied a hat-trick both times. He got the last two batsmen out in two balls to the applause of the watching people. Unfortunately, when Haverhill went in to bat Keenan had to catch an early train and could not bat, and Haverhill lost the match, all out for 47. Keenan's performances were not forgotten quickly and if he came back to the town on another visit, he would be welcomed in the cricket circles.

Of the seventeen games played in 1910 only six were won with all the victories coming in the first nine matches, and only one game was affected by rain. In spite of the wet start to the season Haverhill scored over 200 runs in five games, but their lowest score was all out for 47. The captain, Mr F W Gurteen, was the only one to take part in every match. For the second year running, B J Hinde was the winner of the new bat. During the season W Spicer scored 103 v Bury, C Keenan equalled this against Newmarket, and

Hinde scored 100 not out v Roding. Several players made fifty or over during the year. The winner of the 'King Kettle' offered by W Poole for the first fifty of the season went to P F Taylor. Fielding was good and overall very smart. Some of the fresh players were G Bedford, R C Barnard and A Backler, while G Coote the groundsman also played in six games, his highest score being five. R Etheridge took part in five matches registering four 'ducks' and a two. The 2nd XI were very successful and only lost one match out of fourteen, this being at home to Saffron Walden, W Arber playing in every game. The second XI used only six bowlers and G K Keenan scored the teams only century 143 against Hedingham. Usual players included A Harrington, J Brown, W H Challis, A Farrant and W Argent.

For the **1911** season, the bowling strength looked to be greatly reduced, as the unexpected death of Mr T J Mason Jnr shocked all the townspeople. He had topped the bowling averages the previous season, and H Cracknell, who was second best bowler had left the town, and no significant newcomers had arrived at the club. After winning their opening match Haverhill visited Halstead and scored 53 for 3 when the match was abruptly ended by a severe storm. The 2nd XI lost their first match at Steeple Bumpstead by a rather big margin, and the Wednesday XI also tasted defeat at Helions Bumpstead, who were the victors by 94-11. All the local grounds were reported as being dry and hard. At home to Sudbury, Haverhill won more easily than it was suggested. The wind was very keen and this was the excuse put forward when the visitors' fielders missed several catches. Away from the pitch the Cricket Club entered a decorated car for the Coronation Day parade in May; Mr Sainsbury provided the car.

Came June and the Haverhill 2nd XI, for the first time in many years, found it impossible to raise a team and were forced to scratch a game for that reason. Then they put out an extremely insubstantial team to face Steeple Bumpstead at the cricket meadow. They were fortunate to escape with a draw as they were far behind when stumps were drawn at six o'clock, with plenty of light left. This solicited cries from the onlookers of "play it out" and "be sportsmen." With victories being overtaken by losses, the spectators began to be fewer and fewer. To try to entice them back, a Married v Single match was arranged, the Haverhill Brass Band marched through the streets on the way to the ground, hoping many would follow them. However, there were only a few spectators more who saw the Singles win.

The 2nd XI went to Castle Hedingham and, as in previous years won easily with bowlers H V Scott (6-14) and C Freeman (4-9) in better form. The 1st XI posted up two wins, versus Bury on Whit-Monday and at Saffron Walden when R Mallinson hit 80 to top score. In a quite indifferent season, Haverhill wound it up with a home victory over Bury United to complete the double over these opponents. This brought to end a season to forget, but J D Rumbold won the bat prize and S Poole the new ball. The annual Dance was held as usual plus a Whist Drive and a Jumble Sale (raising funds apace now).

The highlights included the best match at Camden (Cambridge). They scored 141 for 6 declared and in reply, Haverhill lost the first two wickets for no runs, and with four wickets down their total stood at 14. Nevertheless, at the call of time Haverhill had won with six more runs than their opponents with one wicket in hand. Vigorous play was seen from McGowan, Griggs and Gurteen. Then came a severe thrashing at West Wratting Park and this was followed by another appalling beating by the Colne Valley Ramblers. The 1st XI got past 200 just once and scored 198 on one occasion, but no player played in every match. New names appearing were G Pond, H V Scott, R Mallison, D H Unwin and Rev Newberry. The 2nd XI lost three matches out of the eleven played. Several games were called off, some not because of the weather; mainly an eleven could not be raised by both Haverhill and their opponents. J Arber and C Claydon played in every 2nd XI match. In with the usual names in this eleven were newcomers E Butler, J B Ashard, B Poole, W A Waters, S Hill and S Willis.

The Annual Meeting of **1912** elected the same officers as the previous year, then fifty members sat down to an excellent meal thanks to the admirable attention paid by Mr and Mrs Elles. The loyal toast and musical humour made up the rest of the evening. Mr T J Mason resigned as Treasurer at the AGM as he was moving away from the town. Some bills were unpaid as the bank balance was in the red but by only a very small amount. There was to be more recognition paid to the Wed XI players who thought they were not being praised as much as the Saturday players, as they were still the same club. It was agreed that the Wednesday XI be recognised as full members of the club, same as the 2nd XI. There was a presentation to the Secretary (Mr H Gurteen) on his marriage; this was a marble clock and a pair of ornaments purchased from A G Carter's High Street shop, also an Illuminated Address. A toast, 'Success to the Haverhill C C was followed by several others - 'Kindred Spirits' and 'The Donors'. Then suddenly the gas went out, leaving no lights, but candles were on hand ready for such a break as the gas supply in the town was going through an unfortunate spell at the time. Mr Elles also entered with a steaming bowl of 'Punch'. Regarding the unpaid bills, several members came forward to give donations to help clear the debt. The harmony of the evening continued with Messrs Gooch (piccolo), violin solos. W Mason (gramophone selections) and ended with the National Anthem and Auld Lang Syne.

Estimates had been invited for painting the new pavilion but E Goldsmith's £13-15s estimate was not accepted. This included burning off old paint from the building and flagpole; repainting with best quality paint, and preserving fluid applied on all wood surfaces. Gilt was to be treated with 'gold leaf', and the metal roof rubbed down and painted with best quality oxide paint etc. The estimate of £6-18-6d by Mr A Basham was the one selected.

After the opening match which was a draw, Haverhill won versus Clare College Unemployed at Haverhill in most unsuitable weather. Stephen Poole's work with the ball was excellent and judging by this game he would be the mainstay of the teams bowling once again; he took 7 wickets for 18 runs. His first two wickets came were in his first over, two more in his second and then two more in his sixth. Only one batsman failed to score in the Haverhill total of 111. There was one new addition to the opponents this year, the King Edward VII Grammar School from Bury St Edmunds. In the home fixture with Halstead S Poole performed a hat-trick, but the visitors smart fielding kept the Haverhill score down to 55 and they lost by 12 runs. The 2nd XI were doing well again and upholding the reputation of the town. At Birdbrook, they amassed 169 for 6 before declaring and when the village side batted, they were much slower in making runs than the Haverhill side had been. Their opening batsman, Pell was particularly long-winded as he tried the patience of the bowlers and the onlookers. During his first forty minutes he scored just two runs and during the hour and ten minutes he was at the crease he only scored ten, although the Haverhill bowlers tried to tempt him with some easy deliveries. Quite a sigh of relief was heard when he was finally caught out.

When Bury United could not fulfil their fixture on Whit-Monday, the 1st XI played against the 2nd XI in front of a large gathering; the firsts played with ten men and the seconds had twelve, to help. The result was 2nd XI 95 and the 1st XI 209 for 6, A Mason scoring 97. An interesting fact was that opening for the seconds were B J and F Hinde, who were father and son. The next week saw Haverhill at Cambridge facing the Regent Club. The visitors were said to be most feeble in batting and bowling, and they tasted defeat by over one hundred runs. When fielding, F W Gurteen hurt his knee and could not bat; he was housebound for quite a while after this game. Half the Haverhill side did not trouble the scorebook at all. It was certainly not the town's day as the 2nd XI playing Linton also went under by 95 runs in a match where both teams were very poor in the field and many catches were put down. Time after time, the ball was allowed to go to the boundary without as much as a token effort to stop it. Must have been something in the water that weekend.

The Haverhill School was beginning to take cricket seriously and formed a competition with four teams named 1, 2, 3 and 4. It was hoping that this arrangement with the young boys would help the town Cricket Club in years to come. The only downside for some of the most promising youngsters at school was the lack of decent pieces of grass to play their matches. The teachers were doing their best and hoped some kind landowner would come forward with help in that direction.

Haverhill had a weekend off when the new team King Edwards School called their game off, as they could not raise a team. However, when Haverhill did play they were on the end of a defeat at Halstead where once again the fielding was noted as very poor. They then went on to surpass themselves when they won by no fewer than 99 runs over Saffron Walden, Unwin and Mason putting together a stand of exactly one hundred. In consequence of his injury when playing at Cambridge, F W Gurteen was not able to play any more in the current season, Mr W Mason taking over as captain. Another good cricketer to go missing was P F Taylor who decided to sever all links with the club after twenty years as a player. He was always a favourite with spectators and scored as many runs as most people in the team. He was also a fine footballer and an excellent athlete, running in the Haverhill Gala each year. However, Mr Taylor had said something out of order, against the welfare of the Cricket Club, and his name was to be struck off the list of members; it is not known what was said.

There was a novel event at the cricket club one Tuesday when twenty-two ladies representing Haverhill and Kirtling played each other, the two umpires being men though. Many watching were surprised at the knowledge the fair sex had of the rules of the sport. Brotherly tuition was noted for several players, and the manner in which the ball was thrown in after a hit shamed many male cricketers of the town. Batting produced several boundary hits and it was a delightful afternoon. As the Haverhill ladies eventually lost, a return match would see them in better form. However, the men seemed to have their form back with the bat and in one week-end, high scores were seen in the matches, W Spicer 60, A Mason 58, Dr McGowan 51 and D Gowers 42. For the 2nd XI versus Cowlinge, R C Green took 8 wickets for 25 runs. Wretched weather curtailed several matches towards the end of the season. No player scored a 100 for Haverhill this year and W C Spicer was mentioned as one of the best wicket-keepers in the area. One highlight was that the 2nd XI was unbeaten throughout 1912.

At an early meeting in January **1913** to discuss what fixtures were to be accepted or not, everyone was unanimous that the club did not play West Wratting Park, as they were getting too strong for the likes of Haverhill. However, it was resolved to play a Married v Single match, as this had proved popular and also a crowd puller, and some all-day matches. As for the spectators, they were to be looked after more, and some more benches were purchased for their benefit. As for the players, a cupboard was to be put in each dressing room.

The cricket ground was enlarged by moving the ropes back a bit, and in doing so they had enclosed the public footpath for a considerable distance. The public were not inconvenienced to any great extent, but the path was diverted for a distance of a few yards. It was stated that it could prove quite awkward if members of the public made an active protest and cause the rope to be set back to uncover the old path. Various points of view were put forward as to the encroachment on to the path, and although nine out of ten saw nothing serious in the near future, the tenth could have taken it into their head to upset the arrangements. Some extra trees to be planted in the Cricket

Meadow.

Just when everything was in place for the beginning of a new campaign there was a measles epidemic in Haverhill with many, especially children, going down with this contagious illness. It also affected the sporting life of the town and the 2nd XI and Wednesday eleven had their games cancelled because of this; they could not take a chance to spread the outbreak. Thanks to the heavy rain, the ground was not in any condition the following week to entertain any cricket at all, but on the Monday, the match against Camden went ahead. After the Cambridge side had batted out their innings, many spectators decided to go home, as they had been tired of the long wait for the Haverhill team to come out to bat. The few left kept shouting for the players to get a move on. For the record Haverhill did win the game, but only in front of a very insignificant crowd. The second XI started with a home match versus Earls Colne and lost 88-36. It was a poor show by Haverhill with the bat with six batsmen failing to trouble the scorers in any way.

Showing how much the cricket relied on transport, the game between Haverhill and Regent at the cricket ground was advertised as starting at 2-30 or as soon as the train arrives from Cambridge. Regent duly arrived and took their time in bringing up a total of 169 which left Haverhill not time enough to even try and win, and the watching public another game with no result, not what they wanted to see. For the first time since 1910, a Haverhill batsman scored a century, Dr McGowan scoring 104 at Halstead. Following this, the 2nd XI's G Webb made 84 against Yeldham.

Visiting Witham for the first ever match between these two sides, Haverhill decided to strengthen their line-up as their opponents had a reputation as a good all-round team They brought in J Vallient from Saffron Walden and W A Smith of Halstead. Witham put up 184 but Haverhill were the victors with 227 for 7. W Spicer got 65 and A J Mann 52 not out for a surprising result. With Vallient still in their side, Haverhill went to Parkers Piece in Cambridge to face Camden. A Mason and Vallient opened for Haverhill and were not parted before they had 190 on the board, Mason 90 and his partner 96. They declared at 218 for 4 and as Camden were 167 for six when play closed, it was deemed a draw.

The summer was mostly dull and cold but Haverhill scored over 200 on four occasions. Fielding was slowly improving and at times was very good as they won six of their seventeen matches and lost five, the rest being left as draws. Regular players were J H Clarke, J Valiant, G Pond and J H Hill although thirty-eight different players were tried in the first team. R C Green was in the 1st XI on four occasions this year but not called upon to bat in any of them. Although Mason and McGowan got over three hundred runs each, the top of the averages was J H Clarke. The 2nd XI had a poor season from the playing point of view, with only three wins in eleven games. One match versus Linton was tied at 109 each. The 2nd XI lowest score was 18 all out at Stoke-by-Clare.

1914. At the cricket ground, which consisted of some four and a half acres, several new trees were planted along one side and called 'Doctors Avenue', and shutters were made for the pavilion windows. Once again, the weather was not exactly the best for cricket when the season opened and a practice match between two sides from the club members was cancelled as it was decided it was too cold for such a game. The visit of Yeldham to Haverhill was also cancelled and the 2nd XI's fixture versus Halstead II was a victim not of the weather but because they could not raise an eleven for the match. A start was eventually made when the 1st XI travelled to Cambridge to face the Regent Club on what was the coldest May Day for thirty years; the game was declared a no result. Haverhill made 187 for 3, J Clarke 68 and W Spicer 63, to which the home team reached 109 for 6 when time was up. There were three fresh faces amongst the players, S Ketteridge, A Humphrey and R Goodman.

The weather was just the opposite the next Saturday when the sun shone brightly as Haverhill faced the Bury & West Suffolk side for an all day match starting at 11am. The town eleven did not match the weather and were defeated. The rain was back for the visit to Saffron Walden and after the Walden team had nearly completed their innings, the heavy showers ended the day's sport. The return match with Regent at the cricket meadow was notable for the bowling of Haverhill's Mason whose trundling was so effective that he claimed nine victims for 19 runs, a surprise as he had not been very successful so far that year. However, he could not help as Haverhill lost once more. A large turnout then saw Haverhill lose at home 146 to 130 to Camden on the Bank Holiday Monday. So far, the Haverhill supporters were beginning to expect their team to either lose or draw their games.

The losing spell continued, including a severe trouncing at Camden, also the wet weather which caused some more postponements. The Wednesday XI were doing slightly better; this was strange as most of this eleven were regulars in the Town's first and second teams also. The 1st XI lined up mainly, W Spicer, A Mason, A J Mann, D H Unwin, J Ashard, G H Pond, R C Green, D Gowers, G Bedford, W Arber and G Coote. The 2nd XI was usually, J Arber, J Brown, C Clayden, J S Hill, B J Hinde, S Hinds, J Hoffmann, A Humphrey, S Ketteridge, G Webb and G C King. Then after several defeats, the 2nd XI claimed a victory at Stoke-by-Clare. There was one week-end when there was no cricket for the three Haverhill teams. C Claydon probably wished there was not a match the next week when, whilst batting for the seconds against Earls Colne, one delivery flew of the edge off his bat, hitting him over one eye. He needed medical attention and took no further part in the game.

At last in late July the tide turned and how! Facing Clare at home, Haverhill suddenly found the form expected and hammered 243 for 4 wickets, to which Clare were bowled out for merely 39 runs; only one of their batsmen reached double figures. Top Haverhill scorers were J Clarke 96 and W Spicer 65, while G Pond was in stump-stirring mood and took 7 wickets for 6 runs in his ten over's and Mason had only 4 runs scored off his 8 overs, and took one wicket. Wicket-keeper Spicer caught out three Clare batsmen, all off Pond's bowling. A J Mann scored 111 not out v Newmarket; Spicer and Mann played in every game.

In an effort to fill the money bags, the Cricket Club being once again in dire straits, the club put on a Fete in the gardens of the Coupals House, the home of Mr J Gurteen. The two town bands straight away offered their services. The Rope Works erected a large tent and some small tables while two police constables were asked to attend. 200 teas were served and there was a tennis tournament of mixed doubles; together with quoits and bowls: all the fun of the time was on offer. From 6-30 dancing was indulged in on the lawn until darkness ended the proceedings. A profit was made on the Fete of £20-12-2d, but the club was still in the red by £46-9-7d when the season finished. To help this deficit a pig was promised, to be sold to benefit the Cricket Club.

This was held on 15 August 1914, eleven days after Britain had declared war on Germany. The First World War then put everything on hold as countless young men of Haverhill went to war. No fixture list was made, but it was decided just to play the occasional scratch sides. No annual Dance was held this year either, nor for the next couple of years. The Cricket Club's secretary was one who saw duty in France with the Red Cross; while back home, the vice-captain W Mason entered the wedding stakes.

****

LET'S START AGAIN

In July **1919**, after no meetings of the Cricket Club since April 1916, it was agreed to start operations once again. The pitch had got into a poor condition as it had been left unused for the majority of the war years. The ground and buildings were in bad shape, with plenty of work needed on them. Many Haverhill soldiers failed to return from the conflict and it was soon realised that more youngsters of the town would be joining the Cricket Club. It was agreed to double up the subscriptions from 5s to 10s; this was to try to wipe out the shortfall at the bank, which had increased to £78. D Gurteen's factory gave £25 towards this. Other things were hurriedly arranged, a Jumble Sale at the Corn Exchange and then the ever-reliable Whist Drive, the latter leading to a Dance after the whist playing had finished; this raised £3-3-8d.

The meeting of the Cricket Club was held in the Council Room at the Town Hall when forty people turned up. As well as beginning cricket once again, the question of forming a Junior section of the Club was discussed, but nothing further came of this as the most promising of the youngsters would be given some outings in the 2nd XI. As it was, there were not many matches arranged this year as more than one cricket club in the area were having trouble in reforming after the war. It was middle June before the first game was played in 1919 when Haverhill renewed acquaintances with the Regent Club from Cambridge, the final scores being Haverhill 142 (A Mason 37) and Regent 149 for 8. This was followed by a victory over Saffron Walden. The 2nd XI also began with a win over Castle Hedingham with W Spicer top scoring with 81. Then D Gowers rattled up 80 in the return fixture. The Sunday XI had one outing versus Stanstead, winning by the slender margin of three runs. Re-elected President was Mr J Gurteen, and the captain of 1st XI was Mr F W Gurteen.

For the **1920** season, the early meetings of the club were being held in the Bell Hotel, but no music of any kind was allowed. One such meeting was held to discuss the formation of a Wednesday XI, and for this eleven F Backler was elected as the captain and R W Scott the vice-captain. Arranging matches for this and the other Saturday teams was still hard as many other towns were in the act of getting their cricket up and running once again after the war. Two new fixtures for Haverhill were versus Boby's C C and New Chesterton Institute CC.

Weather conditions then made preparation of the pitch for practice quite impossible, and there were several days before it was playable. Fortunately the opening match was away at Cavendish. On that village's pretty little ground Haverhill were victorious by 70 runs, but when the ball dropped into the long grass in the outfield it did not go much further, so most of the boundaries had to be hit way into the air. In fact, in the Haverhill innings of 118 there were no less than 83 singles. The team for this first game of the season was A Mason, J H Clarke, D H Unwin, H Poole, J Mann, J D Rumball, P F Taylor, G Coleman, W Arber, A H Smith and F W Gurteen; others coming into the team were S Poole, W Spicer, C C McLeod and F Poole. The 2nd XI first match was at Thurlow where the following represented the Haverhill side= D Gowers (capt), J S Hill, R W Scott, W Arber, H B

Hinde, S A Hinde, H Poole, W Wallis, B Newman, J B Ashard, A Baldock and B Webb. The village side were poor and were bowled out for 23; Ashard and H Poole both took 5 wickets for 10 runs.

Perfect weather on Whit-Monday saw Haverhill ending as victors over touring side Walthamstow Wanderers. This could be noted as H Poole's match as he came to the wicket when Haverhill were looking in danger of losing, but he proceeded to have other ideas and was severe on any loose bowling, and played with great conviction. He batted at number nine and ended with 55 not out. The match at Newmarket was expected to see some high scoring, as both sides were good with the bat. However, it ended 54-43 to the home team, who included fast bowler Leek who played for Suffolk. Several balls moving quickly produced some knocks for the batsmen. Unwin was the only player to reach double figures while Ashard hit a six right out of the ground and S Poole made two great catches in the slips. At this time, three sons of S Poole were playing cricket for Haverhill, also playing together in the Football Club as well.

Meanwhile the 2nd XI got their third successive victory at Halstead, as S A Hinde made 69 out of the Haverhill total of 103. His favourite stroke was a forceful drive over cover point and he included twelve boundaries in his innings. S A and H B Hinde were brothers, and S J, another younger brother, was playing for his school aged fifteen, lately taking 6 wickets for 4 runs against Sudbury Grammar School. In the midst of a flaming (!) June, the Halstead v Haverhill match was continually interrupted by rain but was eventually finished with the visiting Haverhill eleven the winners, 90 - 113 for 4. Both teams plus the umpires and scorers were then invited to a fine tea by Mr H Radford, a Haverhill man, who had recently opened a shop in Halstead.

One week after suffering a big reverse at Camden, the Haverhill 1st XI returned to Cambridge to face New Chesterton Institute on the Trinity Hall ground. They put up 207 for 5 and then bowled out the home team for 64. Brothers B and H Poole both got half centuries as the ball came off the hard ground quite fast; wicket-keeper W Spicer was also in superb form. Another large score was made at Sudbury by the 1st XI, 263 for 5 declared, with really good batting and not many signs of faulty strokes. D H Unwin 92 and H Poole 68 were Haverhill's top scorers, one of Poole's hits clearing the pavilion.

Bad news for the sporting efforts of Haverhill was when the nineteen-year-old George Alec Bedford passed away. The son of Mr and Mrs Bedford of Little Bradley Hall he had been in hospital following an operation for two months. He had played football and hockey as well as cricket for the town. The season ended with a special match between Mrs F W Gurteen's XI and Mr A H Smith's XI, the latter being mostly the young boys who were showing promise. The Cricket Club however had refused the Sunday Schools to play on the meadow but did say yes to the Elementary School.

Before the next season opened (1921) a silver salva was presented to Mr F W Gurteen to mark his 25 years as captain of the Club, and the meetings were back once again at the Rose & Crown. Although the Wednesday XI held a separate meeting, they were still part of the Haverhill Cricket Club. In some of the opening games, there were some close finishes. On Whit-Monday, Walthamstow Wanderers came to play Haverhill as usual and scored 245 for 9 and Haverhill 212, a record number of runs scored on the ground in one day. This was a good match for the Haverhill wicket-keeper Spicer who let only one bye past him in the big score. For one game Haverhill borrowed the Suffolk player H Leek, who proceeded to top score with 68 versus Bury & West Suffolk. Bury made 35 and 23 from their two innings, with Leek taking 13 wickets in these two innings. Haverhill were worthy victors as they also included the well known Essex player Walter Mead, although he was coming to the end of his career.

Haverhill broke new ground when they included Braintree on their fixture list, the first time these two sides had ever met at cricket. Haverhill went in first and made 135 to which their visitors reached 134, a tight match indeed. The final match was against Newmarket, but rain during the game stopped play after Haverhill had reached 124 and Newmarket had not been able to take the bat. The 2nd XI had trouble raising enough players for their last game against Linton and it was called off. On the cricket meadow a boys match took place between Mrs E Unwin's XI and Mrs F W Gurteen's XI; this was becoming an annual event. Another boys match was Mr Gurteen's XI versus Mr A H Smith's school XI.

In summing up the season, it was B Poole who was top of the batting and also the bowling averages for the 1st XI, and D Gowers the best with the bat and S A Hinde with the ball for the 2nd XI. The best of the Haverhill teams were the Wednesday team who lost only once, although they did not have as many games as the Saturday teams did. The 2nd XI only lost two encounters, the second one being the last match of the season, while the 1st XI won and lost an equal number.

H W Hinde started the **1922** season well with a sweet innings of 90 in the Whit-Monday game against Walthamstow. It seemed practice in the nets on different days of the week was paying off for both elevens. Newcomer H J Ingle was prominent for the seconds starting with 100 not out against Hedingham; he went on to top the batting as well as the bowling for the 2nd XI. A number of evening games were played by the Haverhill Idlers mainly on Thursdays, this team consisting of shopkeepers and other such like, L Simmons, F Mitchell, A J Hill, and P Green included. Some already played for the town club. Versus Camden, three Haverhill batsmen scored highly, Spicer 61, B Gooden 61 and B Poole 64, to help their team to a win.

For one of their games the 2nd XI were missing several of their regular players but still played the match. They probably regretted this after the substitutes were 'not very good', seven being clean bowled, making strokes hardly according to the book, and the other three were all run out. Two week-ends were lost when rain decided to stay about all day, but the Cricket Club Dance at the Hamlet Croft one Wednesday evening, was fortunate with the weather. A special enclosure with the grass cut very short and rolled flat was for the dancers and music was from the Co-op Band. Admission was 6d and three hundred attended. There were also other amusements such as Bowling for the Pig and 'Racing Frogs'. The green at the cricket meadow was still unplayable so the bowls fixtures were played on Mr D M Gurteen's lawn at the Mount. Mr Gurteen also offered to buy a new set of bowls for the club. The Council School were also given permission to play on the meadow and Athletic Club, permission to practice there too..

The Wednesday XI saw A Bowers notch 96 against Stansfield followed by P Taylor making 99 before being caught on the boundary. For the same eleven the next week Ingle made his 1st XI debut versus Braintree and proceeded to get a useful 47 not out as the opponents were beaten. A report towards the end of the season said that there were some very sporting games this year, some of the best since the club was formed in 1883. There were 22 matches, some with exciting finishes, and B Poole scored over five hundred runs and took over fifty wickets during the season. Mentions were made of the valuable service of Mr C Claydon as the scorer and Mr Coote as umpire; Mr Coote had also been the groundsman for nearly 25 years.

The 1922 season was one of the most successful ever experienced by the 1st XI, eleven games won and just four lost (six were left undecided). No away match was lost. The 2nd XI statistics were, ten won, four lost and two drawn. They used 32 players, 12 playing in only one game but D Gowers and S Ketteridge in all games. Newcomers included Rev S J Pearce, P Green, H H Farrant, E Wiseman, and A Baldock. Of these, the Rev Pearce was a useful bowler and ended with figures of 7 wickets for 17 runs versus Braintree. The Wednesday XI won six out of the eight played (P F Taylor at 99 the highest scorer). Altogether there were 89 members of the Cricket and Bowls Club plus 17 juniors (these included five Poole's and five Gurteen's).

An end of season pleasant surprise was an announcement by Mr Jabez Gurteen the Club's President, saying he was in the process of buying the cricket meadow from Mr W Mason and presenting it wholly to the Club. On top of this, it was proposed that the Council lay on the water supply to the meadow. The expense of a fence around the ground was also met by the executors of the late Mr W B Gurteen. The opportunity to buy the ground came up, the President bought it, and had the pleasure of handing over the deeds, for as long as the Club continued. The Deeds were to be held in trust for the club by F W, W & C S Gurteen, the president's. A commemorative tablet was to be put up in the pavilion regarding the gift.

Monday 21 May **1923** was the date the cricket meadow became the property of the Haverhill Cricket Club without any restrictions or conditions, the club being obliged to pay just the rates and tithes. Mr Jabez Gurteen unveiled a commemorative plaque at the ground at 11am in front of a large crowd. The tablet was placed on a wooden support just inside the main entrance of the ground, a brass tablet surrounded by an oak frame bearing the words:

"Haverhill Cricket Club founded 1861. This tablet was erected as a token of gratitude and appreciation by members of the club in commemoration of the magnificent gift of the ground by J Gurteen Esq JP, and of the fencing provided by the legatees of his late brother W B Gurteen JP 1923"

In his speech the president mentioned that in younger days he had played cricket and got better as he got older. He became a member of the club as soon as he left school and in turn was Secretary, Captain and Treasurer at different times. In those early days, the club had no home and the home games were played on various pitches around the town. His three sons were the Trustees of the ground, with no special conditions on the lease. It was a red-letter day for the club and although it was assumed the club had been formed in 1861, the records before 1893 had been lost. A Grand Promenade Dance followed with the Co-operatives Society Band, followed this ceremony on the cricket meadow.

At the same time as buying the meadow for cricket, Mr Gurteen also purchased another plot of land not far away called the Camping Close, where the original Haverhill Football Club had played its first games, now the site of Aldi Supermarket. Although the cricket field was just over four acres, the land bought consisted of just over seven acres. Before Meeting Walk and Mount Road were built, the entrance to this cricket field was by way of Manor Farm, over the river and along an official cartway across the present site of North Street Garage to the meadow. The field belonged to Manor Farm and the early address of the cricket ground was given as off Hamlet Road.

The cricket meadow (246 on the 1841 Tithe map) and the Camping Close (38A on the map) were originally in the hands of the Lord of the Manor, the Beaumont family, then bought by Mr George F D Spurling who paid £30-4-8d for the redemption of the tithes before being purchased by Mr Walter Mason in 1917. The field then was described as bordered on the north by the railway, on the south by the River Stour and the east and west by lands of Arthur G Smart and small lands of Abraham Pannell, H W Farrant and S G Wiseman; the last three had allotments on what is now the cinema complex car park. After Meetings Walk was constructed, it was the best way to the cricket meadow; the main entrance was at the bottom of Meeting Walk and bridge, and straight across the path along the meadows. This was all subject to any rights of way, and there was a footpath cutting across part of the cricket meadow and up and over the railway on the way to Chalkstone Hills.

At this time (1923), it was stated that the ground had been used for cricket for the last forty years, which gave a starting date of cricket on this particular field from 1883. No mention has been found anywhere as to the first cricket ground in Haverhill, although it once was stated that they had to thank Mr W W Boreham for the use of his meadow for playing the cricket matches. One old member of the cricket club also mentioned that "In the old days we had to play our games in whatever field we could and there was no stated meadow where cricket was played on a regular basis. Odd reports of cricket matches mentioned playing on the Croft; this was not the Hamlet Croft but the meadow at the end of Chauntry Road now part of the Recreation Ground.

With the ground now enclosed, a nominal amount was charged for admission to the home fixtures, that is to those not members of the club. A membership ticket at a price of ten shillings carried free admission to all the cricket matches played on the ground; ladies were welcomed at a lower rate of three shillings. Admission to the ground was fixed at 3d (including tax), children under 14 at 1d, pensioners and the aged incapacitated free. The full list of games meant that there was a game on every Saturday of the season, with the teams now journeying to away matches by motor vehicle.

Everything seemed to take off now the ground was in the club's sole ownership, with several people in the town coming forward to make donations. Gifts of forms for seating came from D M Gurteen (2), Mr Thake (1), J Sainsbury (1), Mr Mann (1), C T Boardman (1), W Claydon (1) and F W Gurteen (2). Mason & Son offered to provide two comfortable seats for the use of the older people. Two tenders for painting the fence were received, one was £77 and the other £226, but the second was so high that painting was let go at the moment, to be reconsidered in one year's time. The Secretary was given a special job when the tea tent was left in his hands. Some longer wooden benches of fifteen feet were to be bought for ten shillings from Butchers at Heybridge. A brand new urinal had been planned, and a drawing and estimate of £12 was accepted;. Mr Mason was to build this. No word on the new screens had been received but the old canvas ones were to be renovated.

A site was selected for the bowling green and everyone agreed to engage an expert for preparing the new green. This new green cost £12-5-7d to get ready and bowls players were advised to wear rubber-soled shoes. Attention turned to the cricket pitch and it was marked out at 40 yards by 40 yards. Now admission was to be forthcoming, the important position of gatekeeper was taken by Mr J Arber who had offered to help in this job. Water supply was finally laid on for the wicket, pavilion and bowling green, and was completed at £33-15s. Conclusively the cricket team's colours were agreed to be 'blue and white'.

An early fixture at Halstead was put in doubt for an unusual reason; there was a frost in the morning, then two hailstorms followed by some more showers that kept stopping play. The two clubs decided to end it all by declaring the match a draw, to let everybody go home for a warm beside the open fire. Another unusual event at a cricket match was the presentation to Haverhill Rovers Reserves Football team in the cricket interval between innings, of the Bury & District League Two trophy which they had won in the recently ended football season.

There was an unfortunate mishap which befell Mr F W Gurteen, captain for the 28th year, when he sustained a fracture of the leg in a match v Bury Utd on 16 June 1923. He was soon back watching the matches as B Poole took over as captain for the remainder of the season. B Newman was the top batting and F Mitchell in the bowling averages. The 1st XI record was 11 won and 4 lost with 6 undecided. With a quite settled team, three players played every game and only twenty players were used in the matches, but the fielding was still quite poor. A collection was made at one game for painting the fence, and although much money was collected and promised, there was not enough; the collection was to go into the club's main fund.

The **1924** season saw matches with the usual teams being met; Teams met- Bury and West Suffolk, Halstead, Newmarket, Witham, Braintree, Camden, Bury Utd, Thurlow Hunt, Saffron Walden, Sudbury, New Chesterton Institute. The opening match was a visit to Halstead, and after Haverhill had put up a total of 83, the home side decided to go slow; when stumps were drawn they had only reached a meagre 39 for 7 and the match was declared a draw. Against Sudbury B Poole turned in an exceptional bowling performance by taking 7 wickets for a mere 2 runs in his eleven over's,

Haverhill winning by 41 runs. Not to be outdone, the 2nd XI skittled Steeple Bumpstead out for 16 with S Hinde capturing 7 wickets for 8 runs and J Scott 2 for 3.

The first century of the season was put up by H Poole against Sudbury for the 1st XI; he wrote up 119 not out as Haverhill defeated one of their long time rivals. In the return match at the cricket meadow, the spectators saw one of the biggest hits of the season when H Poole scored a mighty six. He sent the ball over square leg as it went on to clear the fence on the river side of the ground. It was a short while before the ball was found and returned to the match. This match saw an opening partnership for Haverhill of 108 featuring Spicer and Gooden. When Bury and West Suffolk met Haverhill, the town's reputation saw the Bury eleven strengthened by the inclusion of Walter Mead, the old Essex and England bowler, and R G Evans, a Cambridge University 'blue'. However, Haverhill still ended up victorious by 182 to 147.

Haverhill then put up their highest innings score when they entertained a team brought together by Mr E H Farrant. They had scored a good 177 for 6 before declaring, but then Haverhill ended with 232 for 7 as most of the batsmen scored over double figures. The 2nd XI's S A Hinde had the best set of bowling figures this summer when he finished with 9 wickets for 23 runs versus Clare in August.

A familiar face, Bert Poole, was again top of the batting and the bowling, and W C Spicer excelled this year behind the stumps. Out of the twenty-two games played only two were lost by the 1st XI, and the other twenty were won. The highest total for an innings was 232 for 7. Reliable batsman H Poole started the season off with four 'ducks' in his first four games then came out of his shell to crack 119 not out against old rivals Sudbury.

Keeping a check on the attendances at matches, 2,557 people paid to see matches over the first season in 1923 and the club soon raised the prices to see the games to one shilling with juniors at sixpence. Small programmes were also printed and sold. Mr Sainsbury had offered the use of a large roller for the pitch, and a pristine notice board was placed on the left of the admission gate. On the playing side, some more players were coming in from the surrounding villages to try to get a place in the Haverhill sides. The club mourned the passing of Mr Walter Mason, for many years an official and prominent member of the club. A further look at the Members List saw it now contained seven Gurteen's, and eight Poole's and 111 members altogether, twenty-two juniors and twenty-four ladies, more than enough to enjoy the Dance to Tommy Turner's Band and frequent whist drives.

The Annual General Meeting for **1925** began on a sombre note as all stood in memory of the late President Mr J Gurteen. The new President elected was Mr F W Gurteen who had been 28 years in the post of captain of the Haverhill Cricket Club. This year drew the largest attendance for any Annual Meeting. The business and after meeting activity ended with songs by a gentlemen's sextet led by P C Kibble, and finally closed at 11-30pm. New to the first eleven's fixture list was the 3/5 Dragoon Guards who were based at Colchester, and the North Essex Wanderers. Haverhill were without the Rev S J Pearce who had left the town.

In the return match with Newmarket, it was the turn of F W Hinde to shine as he took 5 for 14 with his leg breaks and other spinners.. B Poole made two good catches in the slips and one at square-leg, while W Spicer stumped a couple of batsmen who were enticed by Hinde's spin bowling. H Poole then made a very quick 100 not out as Haverhill won easily. The match versus the Dragoon's at Colchester was called off as they could not find a suitable ground to play this match. Haverhill did face a forces team when they played the 1st Suffolk Regiment, which they won.

After a promising start to the season that saw plenty of runs being scored, Haverhill 1st XI faltered, began to register some low scores and were beaten too easily. However, they perked up again towards the end of the summer. The Wednesday XI were also getting in more games with the following being the nucleus of the team - Rev N Armstrong, H B Newman, P F Taylor, J Smith, F Starnes, F Miller, J S Hill, A Alston, R T Hammond, S Levett, A Whiting and T Sizer.

Summing up this campaign the 1st XI won twice as many games as they lost, but a longer than usual list of games were victims of the weather. They managed over 200 in an innings five times, the highest score being 271 for 9 at Witham. There were three individual centuries, two from H Poole and one from new captain B W Hinde. In all, over three thousand runs were scored.

The second XI's up and down season saw their highest score 217 for 9 versus Clare and their lowest just 17 at Castle Hedingham. A young D Gurteen played one game (61 v Baythorne End). Top of the batting list was H Poole once again, having been there in 1920, 1924 and 1925. His brother B Poole was top in 1921-22-23. The best bowling performance was put up by J A Scott when he took seven wickets for eight runs in the match against Sudbury who were all out for an embarrassing 23, their lowest score versus Haverhill. The absence of A Bowers after four years with the club was felt in the bowling strength; he had bowled over 340 over's and taken 84 wickets in his time with Haverhill. The best news was that some younger players were being given games in the 2nd XI as the club realised this was the only way to progress. The Bowls section had twenty matches on a fine new surface, but the year ended sadly with the death of an old and valued member, Mr W Poole.

The Annual Dinner in April **1926** saw a presentation made to Mr H Gurteen for his twenty-five years as the Secretary of the Cricket Club. One of the oldest players present commented, "This club is one happy family." Mr H F Thake presented Mr Gurteen with a solid silver salva and an illuminated address; 120 members donated for this. Looking to progress, the engagement of a professional was agreed on, but at a later meeting this decision was changed and no-one appointed. A new flag and flagpole were purchased and erected at the ground.

The Haverhill batsman to make an impressive start to the season was H Poole who scored 111 not out at Newmarket, hitting 15 fours in his innings. D H Unwin was given a chance to show what he could do with the ball and proved very effective, delivering seven over's, giving away a measly two runs, and taking three wickets. After these two performances, Haverhill were within sight of the winning post when time-up was declared. However, it was a moral victory to open the season. It was disappointment all round the next week when only three and a half over's were bowled when Haverhill entertained Sudbury, and the rain saw the game called off. This match would have seen the brand new sightscreen in place having been bought for £9-14-8d. An interesting match was anticipated when the town eleven had a visit from Mr F Hawkins XI from London. He brought with him Patsy Hendren, the Middlesex and England cricketer, but the weather again closed in and no play was possible, nor the chance to see an England batsman in Haverhill.

It was another up and down season as the first team started out with some big scores, then faded away and lost games towards the end of the summer. Twenty-two 1st XI matches were played; ten were left undecided while they were the victors in eight games. The last game provided an exciting finish as in reply to Mr E H Farrant's XI's 204 for 8, Haverhill scored 205 for 6; winning in the last over.

Once again, the year (1927) started with a sad scene as former Haverhill stalwart cricketer Mr Stephen Poole passed away in January. He lived in Duddery Road, the fifth son of the late Charles Poole. He became a playing member of Haverhill Town Cricket Club in the 1880's. He was also a member of the Haverhill Brass Band and later the Co-op Brass Band which came into being by the amalgamation of the Shepherds and Town Brass Bands. He was 60.

Posts for the season were D R Gurteen, 1st XI captain with B Gooden vice-captain. H B Newman was to captain the 2nd XI with vice-captain R C Poole, and the Wednesday XI captain was J Mann. For the away matches the members would be given expenses of 2s 6d. There was again a record membership of the Cricket Club this year. After some deliberation at a special meeting, the Haverhill Men's Hockey Club were allowed to use the ground, the Ladies team as well, but a fee was agreed for each club. A letter in the local newspaper asked, "What about the very poor condition of the Recreation Ground, no game of cricket could be played there, and local teams were searching around for a suitable field, so why not clean up and sort out the Rec."

It was beautiful weather to start the season and the players had been getting in some practice on matting for the first time. Runs came freely in their opening game at Saffron Walden who put up 134 for 8 declared, to which Haverhill passed at 137 for 1. There were 91 runs on the board before the Haverhill opening pair were parted, B W Gooden ending with 69 not out. Back in Haverhill on the same day, the 2nd XI saw half their side out for 'ducks' as they lost to Yeldham. The seconds put this behind them and travelled to play Wickambrook & Denston who were all out for 14. This was on a meadow which was not in very good condition, the cows having to be chased off before the game could get underway. One week later the fixture versus New Chesterton Institute was played but players were in short supply when the 2nd XI could only raise ten players on each side.

The Wednesday eleven were operating again but with very few matches. The team usually consisted of H B Newman, H J Baylis, P F Taylor, L Simmons, B P Sadler, S Levett, T Sizer, S W Grove, W Beer, R T Hammond and W Hammond. Fresh players for the 2nd XI were J Morrell, C Nunn, R Offord and A Thake. The Haverhill Club Juniors were given a few fixtures including a local 'battle royal'. when they opposed a side titled Haverhill Juniors. The young Haverhill C C Juniors were composed of D F Offord, S Hammond, F Morley, D Poole, P Spicer, M Chandler, P Heath, W Thake, N Pryke, C Suffling and S Albon. Some good Haverhill names in there, possibly sons of 1st team members? Their local opponents lined up with E J Unwin, J E Rumball, Henry Farrant, J E Clarke, Harold Farrant, R Webb, J Richardson, S Cornell, R Dare, E Brewster and E Siggs; players of the future? B W Craddock, a seventeen-year-old, played for Haverhill first team versus Mr Scott's XI and scored 26. He was a pupil at the illustrious Charterhouse School, and he timed the ball excellently and hit very cleanly, and was also smart in the field. He was the son of Colonel Craddock, now in India, formerly captain of his regiment the 20th London when they were quartered in Haverhill during the first war.

Now we see a new match on the calendar when there was a Ladies versus Gentlemen game. Some villages had tried this and it had gone down well, so now it was the turn of the Haverhill Cricket Club. The men used a baseball bat instead of the usual bat, and had to bat and bowl left-handed. It ended with the ladies scoring 146 and the men 145; or was it not the thing to bring defeat onto the females of the town? Dr Sunderland was in the male eleven, just in case. All except two in the ladies team were unmarried; Mrs Unwin, run out for 15, and Mrs Borrowdale bowled by W V Gurteen for 4, were the exceptions).

In the seasons summary, the 1st XI played 19 games, won 6 and lost 1 with the remainder being declared draws as time and weather moved in. The so-called summer hit the cricket scene rather unfavourably in 1927 and it was not until the fifth week that any kind of result was obtained. Thirty-three players were used by the Haverhill 1st XI of which nine only appeared once. Seventeen different bowlers were given a chance but the mainstays were D Unwin, J Scott and B Poole who got through over one hundred over's in the season. The 2nd XI fared a bit better with only one of their matches postponed, losing 5 and winning 7. C H Cutmore was top of the batting averages and M Grover the bowling.

The 1928 summer was late in arriving, and it was some time before the groundsman was able to do anything like his usual job on the pitch. The rails needed creosoting and the lean-to shelter bought for £11 was to be erected in its position. Allotment holder Mr Farrant was asked to clean out the ditch on the west side of the cricket meadow, and the Haverhill Urban District Council was asked to make up Meeting Walk for wheeled traffic, although cars should not use it, but enter by the north-west gate. The club decided to buy a hand-roller to take the place of the winter ballast roller on loan from the Council. As it was, the HUDC said they were unable to undertake the making-up of Meeting Walk and the matter was then dropped. A tree falling from Mr Smart's property had broken part of the fence, and Mr Smart had paid the cost of repairing the fence.

With beautiful weather to start for a welcome change, the Haverhill sides looked to be strong in batting for the season, but in the very first match they suffered a defeat on their home ground by Walthamstow Wanderers; not the way it was planned. The 2nd XI did much better with an opening stand between R C Poole 53 and C H Cutmore 68 giving them the edge over Steeple Bumpstead who were the losers on this occasion. In the victory over RAF Duxford, it was the 1st XI bowlers who did the damage; B Poole (2 for 0 runs) Scott (2-4) and D H Unwin (2-6). A high scoring game followed, with D R Gurteen 72 not out and Ambrose 54, securing a draw against long time opponents Camden. Two other high-level performances came from J D Unwin with 98 for the Wednesday XI versus the East Anglian School, and W Spicer 86 not out against Halstead.

With a charabanc at their disposal, the teams were now travelling a bit further for their matches. The last game was lost against Chelmsford, the first fixture between the two clubs. Over the season, the 1st XI played 25 matches, winning 6 and losing 8, the first time for many years that they had lost more than they had won. Bowling had fallen off rather badly as had the fielding which seemed to have returned to its old pattern of giving away too many simple runs to the opposition's batsmen. Five times their opponents scored over 200 runs while Haverhill only once passed the two hundred total. The 2nd XI were not that much better as they won 6 and lost 6.

The General Committee in **1929** consisted of G Bedford, C T Boardman, J W Pearson, D S Gurteen, D Gowers, C Claydon, W Hodges, A Mason, Wm Poole, A Smith, E B Sunderland, F W J Simmons, H F Thake and E W Walmsley. Other items coming out of the Annual Meeting saw that the umpires at each match were to be paid one shilling for home fixtures and two shillings for away games. Transport for the team was in the hands of Mr A Baldock who charged halfpenny per mile and if the game was cancelled, twenty-five per cent of the fee was to be paid. To help offset travel costs it was decided to charge the Hockey Club £3 each year for using the cricket field, and one shilling admission for the planned Whit-Monday Dance at the ground. Mr Underwood had asked if the school team could practise on the ground, the answer was yes, between 3 to 4-15 for two days each week; this could provide the stepping stone from schoolboy to youth cricket play and so benefit the town's cricket. Towards this aim, some junior matches were to be arranged for the next year.

On the playing side of this season after seven matches had been played, only one had reached a definite conclusion, that being the Whit-Monday clash with Camden, which the Cambridge side won by 64 runs. Time was often the factor, and had it been agreed, extra time could have produced a result to either Haverhill or their opponents. The town eleven had saved some games with last minute stands and a few more minutes in other fixtures could well have seen them winning a proportion of the games. One second eleven match was particularly low scoring; both Haverhill and Denston could not stack up a hundred runs between them. It seemed that the bowling of most clubs in the district was not up to standard, and the batsmen were mainly on top. The match versus Chelmsford at Haverhill was typical as the visitors ran up 202 for 9 wickets and left Haverhill two hours to overtake this total. The home team started well and scored quickly, the first wicket putting on seventy-seven runs, but at the appointed time for closure Haverhill were within sixteen runs of victory, and the match was declared yet another draw. Top scorer Unwin

TOP.(6)1921-Back,H Gurteen, S Hinde, A J Mason, H Poole, W Arber, G Coote. Sitting- D Unwin, B Poole, D M Gurteen, W Spicer, A Smart' Front- C Clayden, A Mason:
BOTTOM (7) 1927. Back-F Backler, H Poole, W Spicer, G Coote, R Hammond, A Mann, H Gurteen. Middle- P Taylor, B Poole, B Goodden, F W Gurteen, D R Gurteen, A J Mann.

(8) Ladies versus Gents 1930; Back- W V Gurteen, Jim Unwin, ? , George Unwin, Maynard Gurteen, ? , Phil Taylor. Centre- Dr Sunderland, Peggy Taylor, Wendy Bedford, Grace Gurteen, Di Taylor, F W Gurteen, Katherine Unwin, Nora Bedford, G S Gurteen. Front- Babs Emson, Phyllis Boardman, Joyce Taylor, Sam Taylor, Joan Gurteen, Freda Emson, J T Boardman:

(9) 1937 1st XI; Back- N Pryke, H Farrant, W Sephton, J Rumball, J Chapman, F Rowlinson, A Dickerson. Middle- G Coote, J Thake, F W Gurteen, H Poole, H Gurteen. Front- A Willis, E Mason, R C Poole, C Levett:
(10) BOTTOM: 1937 2nd XI:

(11) TOP; 1930 Haverhill 1st XI
(12) BOTTOM. The Old Pavilion c1930

TOP.(13) Informal; Tim Ralling, ? , David Pryke, Harry Farrant, ? , Geoff Herbert, Ken Kitchener, Ray Rogers, Henry Sephton; Front- Mick Farrant:
BOTTOM. (14) Captain Bill Scrivener & Tim Ralling.

(15) Haverhill from the air, showing the cricket ground on the right.

(63) was exceeding the half-century for the third time in the season. The seconds meanwhile were registering their third win of the season when they visited newcomers RAF Duxford, Haverhill's Hammond accounting for 6 wickets at the cost of only 16 runs.

The report at the conclusion of the 1929 season remarked on the feature that out of the 25 games the first eleven played, no fewer than 15 were left undecided, and of the ten remaining, six were won and four lost. The latter four were all at Haverhill when Camden, Colchester & East Essex, Newmarket and Mr H Ruffle's XI went home victorious. Three players turned out in every game, H Poole, W C Spicer and P F Taylor, while seven players appeared in the first team only once. Haverhill realised upwards of two hundred runs on four occasions with the highest being at Colchester, which was 244 for 6. In this fixture the Poole brothers (H & B) were associated in a stand which added 160 runs for the fourth wicket, their batting during this partnership was spoken of by some older club members as about the best they had witnessed for many a summer. H Poole made a record 736 runs this season including an innings of 121. J D Unwin also got 130 not out. Despite this record total of runs, it was B Poole who topped the batting averages with 33.6; if his brother had scored four more runs then he would have taken the leading position, it was that close. A newcomer was R A Willis, a youngster who quickly became a regular in the team and got over 1,000 runs in the 1st XI (Saturday and Wednesday teams). Top trundler was T B Ambrose who took a record 57 wickets in this season. One game that was not played was the second's match with Baythorne End, when both sides were left waiting on their home grounds as they both got the venue wrong.

The Wednesday XI played eleven matches this year, their highest number of games so far. For their usual line-up, we take the match versus the East Anglian School (Bury St Edmunds). This was R A D Willis, L G Simmons, H J Baylis, H B Newman, P F Taylor, B Sadler, R T Hammond, H Shanks, E Thake, B Jobson and S Levett, shopkeepers making up nearly half of this team. It was questionable whether the improved fielding of all three Haverhill teams was maintained this year, but over all it seems to have averaged itself out. The distressing circumstance under which the team was deprived of the services of its captain (the late D R Gurteen) was still fresh in their minds, and the leadership was taken over by the vice-captain B Poole with some authority. It was a tragic end to a young sportsman when Mr D R Gurteen lost his life in a motorcycle accident mid-season. A group of young men who had been at a tennis party at his home the Mount went on their motor-cycles to Baythorne Hall to collect a tennis racket taken by mistake, and on the return journey the accident occurred at dusk, about a quarter past ten in the evening. He had been captain of the cricket for two seasons and was a good hockey player, among his many other interests.

The Haverhill second eleven managed to complete all their matches of the summer when they won ten and lost six. Although they reached over hundred in most matches they also put up two very low totals; 36 and 41 in the games at Cornish Hall End and Wickhambrook. Newcomer D F Offord was the only member to appear in every match, and another recent fresh player C H Cutmore was the top batsman in averages. Haverhill rounded off their season with a new meeting, a two-day match against Beaumont Pilgrims, a touring side; both teams had two innings and which the Haverhill eleven ended up the winners.

****

THROUGH THE THIRTIES

During the winter, the pavilion was painted and repairs carried out to the wooden floor fitted on the veranda; the scoreboard would be the next to receive attention, as it was getting rather shabby. Insurance was also taken out against fire for the pavilion (£500 for the building and £100 for the furniture and fittings). After two dozen new balls were purchased at 18s each, the **1930** season was up and running. Had the whole of the season's programme for the first eleven been carried through, there would have been twenty-four matches but four became victims of bad weather. Of the remaining twenty, ten were won and five lost, the others again undecided. It was wicket-keeper W C Spicer who took part in every game and W V Gurteen was the new captain with H Poole as his deputy. Had it not been for an absence during all July with an injury to his hand, H Poole would have been near the top of the batting yet again. After his return to the team, he was not the same batsman but still returned some good scores.

Batting was a feature for the first eleven this season as the team were dismissed for under 100 on only two occasions, both being against Crittalls. In the home match with Halstead, the Haverhill innings was declared closed at 237 for 2 wickets, B W Gooden with 100 and H Poole, with 81 carrying their bats when their partnership had reached 136. Even this outstanding performance was put in the shade three weeks later when, against Newmarket, Goodin and J D Unwin put up a record for the Haverhill ground that looked unlikely to be extended in the near future. These two batsmen opened the innings and obtained a mastery over the opposing attack, scoring at a very fast rate. They actually put on 223 for the first wicket with Unwin's share being 122 not out. His partner seemed certain to follow suit before being bowled out for 94.

On the 9 July 1930 the Cricket Club held a Grand Fete at the Coupals, home of W Gurteen. One hundred posters were displayed all over the town, this after some people had expressed not knowing what was going on in the town this summer. The Club made every effort to impress and engaged the Co-op Band to play for them. To dispel any thought of youngsters causing upsets, a constable was on duty throughout. The ladies were in their element running the tea tent in a large marquee hired from the Haverhill Rope Works. All the usual games were provided - Bowling for Pig, Treasure Hunt, Clock Golf and Kill the Rat - plus a tennis tournament for mixed doubles. The Fete made a profit of £66-2-9d, a welcome boost to funds.

On the playing side of the season Bill Sephton appeared for the first time in the second team, then soon in the first eleven where he ended the season as runner-up in the batting averages to Goodin. During the summer, some outstanding bowling performances were seen, including T B Ambrose 7 for 24 against Colchester and East Essex, W Sephton 7 for 41 versus Crittall, E Thake 5 for 15 versus Halstead and A Bowers 6 for 24 in the win over Braintree. Another new bowler, F St G Unwin, later played for Essex, he lived at Baythorne End. Three Haverhill bowlers sent down an amazing 510 overs between them, Sephton, Ambrose and B Poole, also accounting for rattling opponents' stumps on 87 occasions. Although not on the playing staff, the efforts of Mr A Willis as umpire and Mr G Coote, the groundsman were voiced, both being in their respected positions for quite a number of years. For the second eleven the unfavourable weather affected their season, but 7 games were won and 5 lost out of those that survived the weather conditions. There were some very good bowling efforts including H Newman's 5 wickets for 6 runs versus Halstead II, and 4 for 13 against Saffron Walden II. A Sephton put up 7 for 13 at home to Withersfield and W Humphrey 4 for 15 over Saffron Walden II. Top of the batting averages was J

Jobson with N Pryke in second spot, and Newman easily top of the bowling. P F Taylor got 100 for the Wednesday XI and ended their best batman. This team only managed to play seven matches this season, winning two and losing three of these. The last two late fixtures for Haverhill were both called off because of the unfavourable weather.

Towards the end of the season, a Ladies versus Gentlemen match was contested on the cricket meadow. Some nearby villages had played a Ladies v Gentlemen game. Mr F W Gurteen captained the men and Miss Di Taylor was in charge of the ladies. The Ladies batted twice and totalled 102 and 36; Miss Joyce Taylor scored the most hitting 49 not out. The Gentlemen, with Dr Sunderland in their midst in case of accidents or mishaps, eventually won by nine wickets. The Ladies eleven consisted of Misses P Boardman, F Emson, J Taylor, V Bedford, P Young, J Gurteen, G Gurteen, K Unwin, N Bedford, P Taylor and D Taylor. As the Echo reported "A good time was had by all." At the November Committee Meeting, the President reported certain unsatisfactory conduct on the part of the proprietor Mr F Baylin in regard to the catering, and other members voiced concerns that a change of headquarters was advisable.

LADIES.
1st Innings.

Miss P Boardman run out	10
Miss F Emson c F M Gurteen b J Unwin	0
Miss Joyce Taylor not out	49
Miss V Bedford b G Unwin	14
Miss P Young run out	3
Miss J Gurteen b G Unwin	9
Miss G Gurteen c J Boardman b G Unwin	2
Miss K Unwin c and b G Unwin ...	2
Miss N Bedford b W V Gurteen ...	5
Miss P Taylor c and b G Unwin ...	1
Miss Di Taylor b W V Gurteen ...	1
Extras	6
	102

In January 1931, a Sub-Committee met at 11 High Street to discuss the Whist Drive scheduled at the end of the month. It was also decided that all committee meetings were then to be held at the Town Hall and the usual AGM at the Rose & Crown. Mr G Coote, the reliable grounds man, was given a rise in his wages and now received thirty shillings per week, and Mr C Claydon was to be the new gatekeeper. There was also the question of a clock being placed on the ground, and estimates were to be invited for this. Other ground improvements to be carried out before the new season began included new wooden screens to be made by Mason & Son (12ft by 15ft high) at a cost of £12-10s each. These were to be fitted with wheels for easy movement. Permission was first required to cut down some of the poplar trees in one area of the ground, but Mr Farrant refused to have these trees cut down, and it was difficult to place the new screens in position accurately for quite a time. During the summer, Mr Frank Backler took over the duties of gatekeeper from Mr Claydon who was unable to get time off from his work to carry out the obligation. The conveyance for away games would now leave from the Market Hill, which was a more central meeting place. To try to keep on good terms with the village sides, the Haverhill C C sold two used cricket balls to the Sturmer and Kedington clubs. The Secondary School were also allowed to play some matches on the cricket meadow as the town club tried to entice more young lads to become members. Subscriptions for joining the Cricket Club were reviewed and resulted in Vice-Presidents costing 15s, Adults 15s, Juniors (17-20) 5s, Juniors (under 17) 2s 5d, visitors (for the day) 6d (for the week 2s. Subscriptions for both cricket and bowls included admission to all games on the cricket meadow.

The first match saw Haverhill travel to Colchester & East Essex the 1st XI captain being B W Gooden and the team including three Sephton brothers, two Thakes and two Pooles; the rest were J Chapman, E Pryke and W V Gurteen. Time was up in this encounter before a result could be decided; there was always a strict time limit to games. The 2nd XI under R C Poole met Great Yeldham with the team of H J Baylis, R Bigmore, W Humphrey, J Hoff, R T Hammond, H B Newman, N Pryke, P Spicer, Rev B Barton, W Spicer and P E Baldock. When the Wednesday XI got going, they visited Hawkedon and won by 18 runs, C Crompton taking 8 for 14 and in his fourth over, 4 wickets in 4 balls. Then the same bowler performed a hat-trick for the 2nd XI, in his first over against Helions Bumpstead for Haverhill 2nd XI to dismiss their last three batsmen.

A scratch side calling themselves Burton End were arranging some matches. One versus Shudy Camps saw the Haverhill side all out for just four runs; nothing else was heard about this team in the future. At home to Chelmsford, Haverhill clean bowled all their opponents batsmen, but they did reach a respectful 160. The 1st XI bowler J Chapman had a fine spell and against Halstead, he took 8 wickets for 22 runs, following this up versus Bury United with figures of 5 for 10. H B Newman went even better for the seconds with 5 Halstead II wickets for 6 runs.

Haverhill 1st XI encountered some wretched weather at various times and of the twenty-two games arranged, five had to be abandoned as they won ten and lost four. One of the losses was away but three were on their own ground. As in some previous years, H Poole headed the batting list, scoring over 400 runs in the process. J Chapman took 66 wickets. Unfavourable weather affected many games during the 1931 summer and the 2nd XI only managed to play thirteen of their eighteen matches, of which they won seven and lost five. Overall, the scoring had been low and only J Jobson hit over fifty; he did it twice and finished top of the 2nd XI's batting averages. Their best bowler was H B Newman. Mention was made of the two umpires in the seasons round up; A Willis and W Thake were there for every match and were most reliable.

At the beginning of the 1932 season, another important member of the cricket club passed away, this being the pony which was used to pull the roller, and it was quickly voted to get another pony as soon as possible. There was also a change in proceedings when the Annual General meeting was held at the Town Hall, but with no sit-down meal or entertainments afterwards, this being seen as a way to entice more young members to take part in the running of the club. It was certainly a break in tradition. Gate returns had been studied over the past ten years or so, and it was seen that in 1923 around 2,557 attended all season, and cash taken was £24-13-1d. This was the highest during the period looked into, while 1931 was poor with only £7-12-9d taken on the gate all season.

The season should have started on the last Saturday in April, but the 1st XI had its first two matches cancelled through the weather and the opponents not able to raise a side. It was clear the batsmen were short of practice but heavy rain on the wicket in the game versus Crittalls saw Haverhill win by 58 runs.

Many strokes which should have brought boundaries produced just singles, the outfield being very slow. The opponents were all out for 22 with J Chapman starting the season as he had finished the last, taking 7 wickets for 7 runs; his first six over's saw the batsmen struggle to score any runs at all. His fellow bowler E W Pryke took 2 for 7 runs. The 2nd XI finally got started when they won by 49 runs over Crittalls II at Haverhill, R T Hammond doing his share with bowling, taking 3 for 12 and top scoring with the bat, making 46. The usual Whit-Monday match with Camden saw Haverhill reach 12 for 2 wickets when heavy rain caused the match to be abandoned. Lunch was taken but no more play was seen. It is interesting to find that in this Haverhill eleven were six sons of former first team players, these being W V Gurteen, the brothers Poole, C P Spicer, J E Rumball and E Thake, quite a young team. F St G Unwin from Baythorne End, who had assisted the Haverhill side on a few occasions, had been on trial with the Essex County side. He created a favourable impression and was given some games; later he was taken on full-time by the County side.

The brothers B and H Poole knocked up 68 and 58 respectively against a team called the Carabiniers in a mid-week game, then H Poole was in great form in the game with Braintree scoring 53 with some characteristic batting, including 7 fours and 2 sixes; in one over he plundered 17 runs. In the game with Halstead II, the young Haverhill wicket-keeper E Thake dislocated his thumb and had to leave the field, but was not going to bat; fortunately Haverhill had won the game before it was his turn to take the bat. W Sephton helped towards this with 82 before running out of steam and being run out. Walthamstow were touring again and met Haverhill on a dead wicket caused by all the wet weather; this year they triumphed by seven runs.

Other notable successes with the bat were B W Gooden with 84 versus Ely City, while H Poole's 89 against Colchester & East Essex contained three3 sixes and 10 fours, and Haverhill were the victors. He followed this up with 78 against Saffron Walden. With the dropping of the Haverhill Wednesday XI, some mid-week matches took place between a Haverhill XI and one or two of the village teams, the Haverhill side being a mixture of 1st, 2nd and players who were not getting many games each weekend.

Some 2nd XI players were being drafted into the 1st XI which was good for the future. Newcomers into the seconds were J Collis, C W Poole, R Felton, S

H Preston, S Willis and B Sadler; two of these were from Thurlow. When short of players for one week-end in August, the team announced in the Echo newspaper included A Player and A Fielder in the 1st XI and A N Other for the 2nd XI, not very original. For Haverhill this summer, it was some unsatisfactory fielding that let them down when the batting was going strong.

For this season, the cricket fixtures continued well into September and for a while the football and cricket clubs fought it out to get players, some resisted until the cricket had finished while others turned to football straight away. The other thing was that September was often getting colder, though not always so. Once again the weather interfered, five fixtures were abandoned, and these were not re-arranged. Eleven of the 21 played were won and four lost. The downside was that on seven occasions Haverhill managed fewer than one hundred runs in their innings, but were lucky in some when their opponents were also low scorers. A more pleasing feature was that a good proportion of quite young players met with some success, both with bat and ball.

From the beginning of the summer of **1933**, the running of a Wednesday XI was uncertain and an appeal was put out for more players for this side. For the 1st XI's opening game, they won handsomely against Colchester & East Essex by 111 runs. B W Gooden, who went in first for Haverhill was top scorer on 67, and E W Pryke was among the wickets, continuing his promise as a proficient bowler. Haverhill seconds unfortunately lost their first match by thirty runs at Castle Hedingham, but a Thursday match with touring Gidea Park found Haverhill swiping up 241 for 8 in their victory. Haverhill continued this run of batting with 253 for 2 declared against Halstead with E Thake 101, Gooden 79 and H Poole 59 in some fast scoring and the whole team batting with confidence. Taking their place at the wicket, the Halstead batsmen seemed to give up on trying to overtake the Haverhill total and settled down to some very slow scoring; that was until the rain interrupted play and the match was abandoned with Halstead stuck on 65 for 3 and holding their nerve for a poor drawn match.

After going three years without advertising the cricket games in the local newspapers - a possible reason for low attendances - it was decided to place an advert each week in the Echo to try to entice spectators back to the cricket meadow. To this end, the seating arrangements at the ground were extended and some more comfortable seats put in. These were at the Meadows end and all of these were said to have very comfortable backs. These seats replaced the old uncomfortable wooden benches which had been on the ground for as many years as some could remember.

By this time, the Wednesday XI had floundered and was not operating this summer, except for an odd mid-week game at the Cricket Meadow, but the week-end sides were going well. The first ever fixture versus Royston found Haverhill winning with W Sephton getting 68, and then his brother A Sephton got into the act with 64 against Exning. Another new fixture was versus Broomfield when Haverhill went for a victory after their opponents left them one hundred minutes to score 176 runs. H Poole reached 100 and Rumball was 50 not out, and Haverhill won by one run in the last over. Meanwhile the 2nd XI had a new find in W N Encliffe who had already scored a fine 65 in the match against Courtaulds. Towards the end of the season however, Haverhill suffered their biggest defeat for some years when St Giles (Cambridge) trounced them. Haverhill were all out for 25 in only seven and a half overs and then saw their opponents make 201 for 5. The St Giles pitch was the best ever played on but the Cambridge side was superior in nearly every way; they scored freely while only W Sephton got 19 of the Haverhill total. This was Haverhill's lowest score since 1900 when they made 27 against Cambridge Victoria. In mid-season the 1st XI had their best spell with a run of six successive wins.

As with the previous season, the summer of **1934** started with another death. This time it was the ever reliable gatekeeper for the past season Frank Backler, who in his younger days had been a useful all-rounder for both the Wednesday XI and the week-end teams. The clashing of the cricket and the football season then had an effect when the Haverhill 2nd XI had to cancel its first game at Clare as they could not raise a side; some of the members were still on the football field. The 1st XI did not have to travel to Colchester as heavy rain made their ground at the Garrison unfit, so a group of town cricketers sat around twiddling their thumbs. The Haverhill cricketers had tried to start the season one week earlier this year to try to avoid clashing with the football at the end of the season. However, this did not happen as these two postponed games showed. When the 1st XI went to Braintree the opening batsman B Gooden was out first ball, not a good omen. However, the next pair, W V Gurteen (75) and Rumball (65) made up for this, Helped by J Chapman's bowling - ten over's, eight maidens - he claimed 8 wickets, the visitors tasted victory in their opening match for the first time in several years.

Into June and Haverhill batsmen were showing some good early form for a change. B Poole registered 84 against Colchester & East Essex, his innings including 9 fours and 3 threes, before he was run out. Meanwhile W Scrivener was scoring freely for the seconds. Offsetting this, the Haverhill fielding was definitely not up to standard in some of the games, and it was thought that not having men out deep to stop boundaries was the thing that mattered. The team had also lost a good batsman for a while when W Sephton had an operation, and taking time out to recover his form with the bat. B Sadler came into the 1st XI late one week, and despite going in low down the order, he hit a worthy 33. There was also a boys match at the cricket meadow one weekday evening when East Haverhill opposed West Haverhill. This match ended East 79 (E Barrett 55) and West 140 (R Dawson 90).

Haverhill continued to set records however, but not of the right kind. The 1st XI at home to Ely one Saturday in July gave a sorry display of batting and were dismissed for only nineteen, the lowest ever total by them. Ely batted comfortably so the wicket was not to blame. It all started badly when B Gooden had his stumps scattered with the first ball of the Haverhill innings, and B Poole was sent back to the pavilion in the following over. W V Gurteen then gave a simple catch and they were left struggling when H Poole was clean bowled for nought. The Ely fast bowler was the one to do the damage, and his side showed how it was done by scoring 108.

Entering August, the 1st XI and the 2nd XI both won their games against Saffron Walden, with the seniors following this with a mid-week drawn game with Cambridge College side the Jabberwocks. The town was then treated to a very competitive game on the school playing field when the Old Independent Church played the Methodist Church, the OIC ending victors 47-38. When B Poole made 113 in Haverhill's total of 232 versus Broomfield, he remarked he had hit the same score versus Rodney CC at Cambridge in 1909, a long serving batsman indeed. In this season's game he treated the Broomfield bowling all the same and made his runs at a very fast rate with some high-quality strokes.

As the season moved into September the Haverhill 1st XI were once again struggling to raise enough players when the football season began once again, but the 2nd XI finished their games early this year. Haverhill again lost heavily to St Giles who were in danger of becoming the town's bogy team. On the other hand, the return match with St Giles saw Haverhill rattle up a much better score than the previous season's match at Cambridge, 205 for 3. 101 of Haverhill's runs came from B Poole, who was reported as *"showing nearly every scoring stroke in the book and gave no chances."* A light then appeared on the horizon when F E Rowlinson, who had been playing his cricket for Withersfield, his home village, came to play for Haverhill. Although he could bat as well as bowl, as the future would show, his first game saw him as a bowler, taking 4 for 25 in his match for the Haverhill 1st XI. The town eleven ended their summer with a visit from Courtaulds and had scored 94 for 1 when rain stopped play for the day and the season. B Poole rounded off a fine season for himself with 68 not out.

Of the 22 matches played, Haverhill 1st XI won 7 and lost 7 with 8 left undecided as the weather or the clock was against a firm result. They also called upon twenty-eight different players, more than the previous few years. The only player to appear in every match was E Thake, who was a very capable wicket-keeper. The most outstanding batsman however was H Poole who topped the century mark twice and made over fifty on three more occasions. But his brother B Poole beat him to the top spot in the batting averages, scoring 635 runs altogether for an average of 39.6, an outstanding figure. Although absent through injury until June, E W Pryke was the best bowler. R T Hammond finished top of both batting and bowling for the 2nd XI who won 10 and lost 7 of their matches.

The opening match of **1935** was against Colchester & East Essex who put up a score of 175 for the home side to try to overtake. When it was the turn of Haverhill with the bat, everything was dwarfed by the display of B Poole, who came in when the first wicket was down for just five runs. Of the 103 runs scored when he was at the crease, all but 18 came from his bat, his 85 including 13 fours and 4 three's. Haverhill managed to hold out for a draw when time was called with them still 30 runs behind and one wicket to go.

The first eleven consisted of H Poole, J Chapman, E W Pryke, N Pryke, J E Runball, W J Scrivener, H Sephton, R Smith, C E Suffling, J Thake and B W Gooden. The 2nd XI lined up for a start with R C Poole, H Farrant, R T Hammond, S Hammond, W C Humphrey, J Jobson, C Levett, E Mason, H B Newman, B P Sadler, K G Smith and A Pannell.

Then came another draw followed by a heavy defeat at Braintree by 115 runs, being all out for a meagre 57 runs. The season did not start very brightly for Haverhill; they had to wait until well into June for their first success, a convincing victory over visitors Broomfield by 48 runs. The weather on this occasion was ideal for cricket and the Haverhill batting was well in advance of recent years. For Haverhill B Poole, a reliable batsman, hit his first ball to the boundary and was clean bowled with the next. Nevertheless, F Rowlinson came to the rescue with a fine knock of 60, aided by H Poole's 46 not out to guide the town team to their win. The 2nd XI visited Glemsford for the first time ever and brought back a win as well; R T Hammond's figures of six wickets for nine runs came as his deliveries were too smart for the Glemsford batsmen. The opposing sides in a Monday evening match at the cricket ground were styled R C Poole's XI against R Bradnam's XI but could well have been Haverhill II versus Withersfield, the latter winning. Rowlinson followed up his score versus Broomfield with a well constructed 74 not out.

Into July and the 2nd XI won at Cornish Hall End by one run (88-87) while Stoke-by-Clare set a record in local cricket when they were skittled out for four when playing Poslingford. It was a much better occasion for former captain and player W V Gurteen when he was married in Surrey to Miss Mary Adeline Cooper from Epsom, and received a smoker's cabinet as a present from the Cricket and Bowls Club. Mr Gurteen was an all-round sportsman in the town as he also played hockey, served on the committee of the Swimming Club and enjoyed tennis as well. He had followed in the footsteps of his father and grandfather in playing cricket for Haverhill.

Haverhill managed to rouse themselves as the year progressed, and on the same day in August both the 1st XI and 2nd XI scored over two hundred runs to win their games against Saffron Walden's two sides. H Poole added to his laurels with 103 that saw him strike 5 sixes and 11 fours. R C Poole was the 2nd XI's top scorer in their win, getting 63. Keeping it in the family, H Poole then got 94 against J Miller's XI from Cambridge who included in their ranks

E L Jessup, son of England batsman Gilbert Jessup. Then the 2nd XI's J Jobson topped them all with an innings of 105 not out versus Thurlow. However, it was in a lower innings that an unusual thing happened. E Mason included an eight in his innings at the cricket meadow against Halstead. This happened when he ran four after his hit to the boundary was fielded just short. Then the throw in was wild and went through for four overthrows; hence eight being hit off one ball.

Getting the batsmen and the bowlers doing their best in one match was the aim of Haverhill, and when it did happen, victory was in their grasp. Haverhill were increasing in strength as September approached and were winning some games, E Mason taking 6 wickets for 16 runs to help defeat Bury Utd when his bowling was said to 'nip off the pitch a bit snappish'. At the seasons end the 1st XI had won seven of the twenty matches played with C P Spicer the top of the batting averages E Mason the best bowler. For the 2nd XI, J Jobson was the top bat while A Thake was the best bowler. They had won ten of their seventeen games.

For the **1936** season, it was quoted "From the playing point of view the position is as good or as satisfactory as well as could be and the club is in a fortunate position to be in possession of a well appointed ground with capital accommodation for both players and spectators. It is concerning finance that matters are rather disturbing. A special appeal was set up for £150 for improvements to ground and buildings." In spite of this, the club made an accomplished start at Broomfield when they beat the home side by the big margin of 186 runs. This was down to the superb bowling of R T Hammond who took 4 wickets for 10 runs and H Farrant who went one better with 4 wickets for just 5 runs. The top innings was from J E Thake who scored 109 before he retired not out. In spite of this the very next week they lost at home to Cambridge YMCA by exactly one hundred runs. Two new players, A P Dickenson and D Freeman, made their debut in At Cambridge in the return fixture, Haverhill forced a draw with the best performance coming from J Chapman who ended with bowling figures of 5 for 8 runs in five overs.

In June W Sephton make a reappearance after missing nearly four years recovering from an serious operation. The Wednesday XI were again in operation and introduced some newcomers, R Dawson, E Orris, E Iron, Jim

Baker, H Peverett, E Loveday and S Sparrow, who were all in the side for the first match against Withersfield. The Secondary School were also playing some matches on the cricket meadow. The 2nd XI made their customary appearance versus Thurlow, which was always an added attraction at the annual Thurlow Flower Show. The Haverhill eleven were victorious that day mainly through their bowlers, E Mason 6-13 (all clean bowled) and H B Newman with 3-4 in five overs.

Rainy weather then put paid to some games over two more weeks, and in August two Haverhill Club players, J E Rumball and C P Spicer, had a week touring the Midlands with the Old Colonians, past pupils of Earls Colne Grammar School. They played six matches including against Stratford-upon-Avon. Rumball was rewarded for his prowess when he was included in the Suffolk XI to play Surrey; unfortunately, they went down by an innings and 61 runs. He did, however, keep his place for the County's next game against Cambridgeshire, scoring 41 for Suffolk as they drew the match.

The wretched so-called summer of 1936 saw a curtailment of several games, and of the twenty-two arranged no fewer than five had to be abandoned. In another game away at Newmarket, play was possible for only about an hour. However, of the games played, ten were won, three drawn and four lost; three of these losses were at home, not so bad in all. With the ball, J Chapman performed a hat trick versus Newmarket. There were not very many batting scores above the fifty mark, the best being J D Unwin's 91 against Saffron Walden. After topping the bowling in the 2nd XI for the past two seasons, J Chapman stepped up to finish top of the 1st XI bowling. H Poole was again the top batman's averages. C Levett was the 2nd XI's best with the bat.

Haverhill made a blistering start to **1937** beginning at Sudbury, who had not been on the fixture list for several years. Haverhill were the victors and then went on to register wins over Bury Utd, Camden and Newmarket. Against the last named side, F E Rowlinson and J Chapman troubled the home side, Chapman getting three wickets in his first two over's and Newmarket were soon reduced to 7 for 5 wickets. They eventually made 43 while Haverhill got the win with 86. The 2nd XI were also in form with a win at Courtaulds, R C Poole scoring 80 not out of the total of 213 for 7, which the home team could not reach. The first defeat for the 1st XI came in their sixth game at Saffron Walden, even though F E Rowlinson was beginning to show good form with both bat and ball. Haverhill were then at home to Sudbury, who they proceeded to skittle out for a meagre 21. It seemed that there was something in the wicket, but when Haverhill went in, they showed nothing out of the ordinary and knocked up an impressive 235. Two other stirring scores came from J E Thake, 50 versus St Giles and 77 against Ely.

A delay in starting the game versus Camden resulted in both sides agreeing to face only eighteen overs, not a new thing but not entered in for many seasons. Haverhill made 142 for 7 and Camden 80 for 7, so with the arrangement, the win was for Haverhill. Up until the first Saturday in July Haverhill looked all set for their best ever season with eight wins and one draw from the ten games played, but after this they lost three and drew three of the next six encounters. The season ended with two matches on successive evenings (Wednesday and Thursday) between R C Poole's XI and the soldiers of the Royal Army Signals Corp, who were encamped at Boynton Hall at the time. Each side had half-an-hour's batting, R C Poole's scratch side winning both games.

An interesting item came in the local 'Echo' newspaper when their reporter had been looking at an old copy of the Haverhill & District Magazine dated December 1883. *"From investigations it seemed that cricket matches have been played in the town under various auspices for at least seventy or eighty years hence, but a properly constituted Cricket Club came into being in 1883 in conjunction with the Town Football Club."* The next year (1884) the magazine reported as follows, *"The opening game for the Haverhill Cricket Club for this year was played on Easter Monday at the Club's ground, after which a social tea was provided at the Rose & Crown by Mrs Fell. The Club commences its second season under favourable auspices, and it is to be hoped that it may have a prosperous time, and the young of the community especially much helpful and pleasurable recreation."*

Cricket is a game associated with blue skies and warm sunshine, with the players sweltering in the heat, and the watchers sitting preferably in the shade. This was far from the picture when Haverhill entertained Bury in their last match of the season. A biting north-west wind was blowing,, accompanied by cold shower, and the light was sometimes poor. The match started with only a very few spectators, some with winter coats on. Bury proceeded to win, their first triumph over Haverhill since 1934. The season finished with the 1st XI winning 9 of the 21 games played and losing 6, the rest were down as draws and some unfinished. J E Thake was the best at batting, scoring over five hundred runs altogether. The 2nd XI played sixteen games and won 8 and lost 8, a medium season for them.

The first two matches of the **1938** campaign resulted in wins for Haverhill over Newmarket and then Bury St Edmunds. The 2nd XI began just as well with victory over Newmarket Ramblers, who were all out for 34, which the Haverhill side overtook quite comfortably. In the 2nd XI side were newcomers F Parker, C Crompton and W L Morris, while the 1st XI included C Levett, A Bishop and L Pearson making their debuts. The Whit-Monday encounter with seasoned visitors Camden resulted in a Haverhill win, making it the fourth on the trot. A breakdown of the 101 scored in this game by the very capable Frank Rowlinson saw 1o fours, 4 threes, 13 twos and 23 singles. Following their worthy display for Withersfield R Bradnam and F Bradnam were also given some games for Haverhill.

The return fixture with Camden at Cambridge again resulted in a Haverhill victory, the first time for many years that they had done the double over this illustrious cricket club. Haverhill declared their innings closed when they reached 200 for 9 and then bowled the opposition out for 91. The usual spell of inclement weather which appeared regularly each summer saw two games being put off, but when the sun appeared once again, both the first and second eleven of Haverhill beat Courtaulds. The 2nd XI put up the biggest score of 208 for 6 in their game. However, the next game brought the third defeat for the 1st XI when they were second best to Cambridge YMCA.

By this time J Chapman and F E Rowlinson had taken 120 wickets between them, this was up to the beginning of September. The 1st XI were still chalking up the runs and Bury United were the latest and last to feel the brunt of the hard-hitting town batsmen this summer. They could only muster 84 against the Haverhill score of 236 for 9. The season ended in nine wins in the twenty games played, four being lost and the other matches declared draws or abandoned because of rain, 2,579 runs being scored over all. Four of the players appeared in every game, the captain H Poole, J E Thake the vice-captain, H Farrant and L Pearson, while F Rowlinson and Rumball were absent only once. Victory in eleven of the sixteen played was the lot of the Haverhill 2nd XI, losing just three with two left as drawn matches.

For **1939** the first game was a visit to Bury where Haverhill were all out for 68 and subsequently lost; the team was H Poole (captain), J Chapman, A P Dickenson, H Farrant, E Mason, A J Norfolk, L Pearson, N Pryke, F E Rowlinson, J E Rumball and W Webb. To offset this, most of the players went to the Club's Dance where two hundred turned up to while the night away to Tommy Turner's Band. A special buffet was laid on by the Ladies Committee, and the MC was Mr W V Gurteen. A new team was faced early in June when Haverhill journeyed to Soham, but there were familiar faces on Whit-Monday when Camden were the visitors. It was quite a surprise however, when they proved to be very weak in batting, not like former years, and Haverhill won easily. However a visit to Newmarket saw Rumball (22), N Pryke (26) and L Pearson (8) being the only scoring batsmen for Haverhill in a match which contained fourteen 'ducks'. Even so the 1st XI managed to scrape a low-scoring victory.

The 2nd XI had a reduced fixture list and when they did not have a match, it was often an R C Poole's XI versus local villages to fill in the gap's. An away match against Clare saw the 2nd XI bowl them out for 17. The Wednesday XI were also in action with games against Cambridge Farmers at Babraham and Stradishall RAF and West Suffolk Police. The latter game came to a sudden halt at 74 for 9 when a message was received that the Police were to return at once to their respective stations; war was imminent. A last minute cancellation was also received from Honington RAF for their match against Haverhill II. Both Haverhill teams' matches were then called off ending the season owing to the state of emergency.

It was a strange season with sixteen games completed with only two defeats for the 1st XI and twelve games won. The 2nd XI were not so good and won just five of their fifteen games and lost six. The scoring was low with only one innings for the 1st XI over fifty but the opponents also found runs in short supply. The highest innings by a 2nd XI batsman was only forty, this happening twice from Freeman and Hammond.

NEWMARKET v. HAVERHILL
At Newmarket on Saturday. Scores:—

HAVERHILL.

J E Rumball lbw b Puddicombe	22
F E Rowlinson b Pask	0
D Freeman c Hopkinson b Hunt	0
N Pryke run out	26
H Farrant lbw b Puddicombe	0
H Poole b Kefford	0
A J Norfolk b Kefford	0
L Pearson not out	8
E Mason b Puddicombe	0
M Webb b Kefford	0
J Chapman st Young b Puddicombe	0
Extras	5
	61

NEWMARKET.

L V Pask b Rowlinson	8
G R Hopkinson b Chapman	6
F Brooks b Chapman	6
B Mingay lbw b Rowlinson	6
M Kefford lbw b Rowlinson	0
A Claydon b Rowlinson	0
R J Waugh b Rowlinson	0
A Hunt not out	1
A Fuller b Rowlinson	0
H A Young b Rowlinson	0
F C Puddicombe b Rowlinson	0
Extras	10
	37

A PERIOD OF WAR

Many cricket clubs suspended their 1940 season when war was declared in September 1939, but some, Haverhill included, decided to operate in 1940, but with a limited fixture list and running just one team. There was, however, another sport being catered for in the town when the new public tennis courts in the High Street were declared open on 4 May 1940. Sudbury, Exning, Newmarket and Soham were played against, but for most of the summer, the opponents were either 'an Army XI, RAF XI or scratch team set up for just one day. The Wednesday team managed to squeeze in some matches. The Whit-Monday eleven consisted of W J Scrivener, D W Wright, R Orris, S Clarke, R C Poole, B Jobson, H B Newman, A L Webb, J Brother, W H Turpin and A Wombwell.

It was decided that in matches, play would cease at 9-30pm as double summer time was in force, and that members of the Forces were let in free. Sunday games would be arranged if there was enough opposition (Forces XI's) and if they wanted to play on this day only, but in the end just one match took place on a Sunday. A War Sub-Committee was formed to see to Sunday Concerts on the ground. Over half the sides that Haverhill met in 1940 were service teams from the RAF, Army and others stationed nearby. The best bowling performance was by F Rowlinson, 7 for 12 versus an RAF XI.

In August, a match came up when Haverhill Juniors took on Saffron Walden Wanderers at the cricket ground. The scores ended Haverhill 24 and 30, and the Wanderers 47 and 56. The juniors on show were L Backler, J Mizon, G Baker, P Thake, M Poole, R Harding, C Jones, E R Starnes, D Wordley, J Parken and R Farrant. Another interesting encounter was the Searchlight XI versus an Army XI. The cricket ground was then closed down on 30 August 1940. During this season, the death of Dr N McGowan was announced at Southsea. When based in Haverhill, the doctor had played some very good games for the cricket club with many double figure scores, his last season being 1914. He was born in Scotland, was an all-round sportsman, playing rugby, and was a member of the Haverhill Golf Club.

Twenty players were called upon to play for the club and H Poole top of the batting averages and E Mason top bowler. One newcomer was A J Williams, a school teacher, who came from his North London school with the evacuees. E Mason was top bowler in 1940

Early in **1941**, Grey Pullman Coach's announced that they were unable to take the team to away matches, so the Club put out an advert that they were open for matches only on the home ground in Haverhill for this summer. The military had also been granted use of the nets on Thursday and Sunday each week, and the War Weapons Entertainment Committee had use of the ground for a dance on Wednesday 23 July 1941. This was from 7-15 to 10-30 to music by the Regimental Band of the Royal Fusiliers. This summer saw members of the Ex Servicemen's Club being allowed to join the Bowls Section of the Cricket Club for 5 shillings as the ESMC Bowls Green had been taken over by the military.

It was a very successful season for the Haverhill elevens who were undefeated playing, 17 of which 15 were won and 2 drawn Fourteen games were contested at Haverhill and the other three at Exning, Newmarket and Saffron Walden. Eleven matches were against servicemen, mainly RAF. One was advertised versus Fusiliers XI from Shudy Camps. They were stationed there for quite a time and played several games against Haverhill and other local sides, usually attracting a good attendance at each game. The Wednesday XI also got in a few matches, again versus service elevens from local RAF stations and army camps. Haverhill used forty different players during the season including F W Binks who made just one appearance, scored 100 and then retired. In War Weapons Week, there was a cricket match of some sort every day of that week. The cricket ground was also hired out to the Irish Pipers who were stationed in the town for an extended period.

The season ended with a match between Haverhill First Aid Party and Haverhill Auxiliary Fire Service. The teams were 1st AID; W Scrivener, G Farthing, D Sparrow, S Boydon, J Stratton, D Brown, A Skelton, E Barber, W Newman, W Nunn and N Pryke. The AFS side consisted of C Ives, A Clarke, R C Poole, R Hammond, F Calver, E Wimpress, T Jarrald, W Farrant, H Farrant, J T Boardman and A Basham. The latter ended as the winners 95 to 60. Other such games were Aid Raid Volunteers v Haverhill ATC, and Military Police v Home Guard. The season came to an end with Haverhill against the Kings Royal Rifles who were resident in Haverhill on the Hamlet Croft at the time.

Knowing the English love of cricket and the rivalry on many a village green and cricket meadow, a bright spark came up with these scores in the War game.

Germany v The Rest

| A U Stria | run out | 0 |
| C Slovakia | c & b Hitler | 0 |

P O Land	c Stalin b Hitler	10
D Enmark	run out	0
N Orway	c Quisling b Hitler	1
H Olland	retired hurt	2
B Elgium	st Leopold b Hitler	3
Luxe M Burg	b Hitler	0
F R Ance	c Mussolini b Hitler	23
G B Ritain	not out	20
	Total 59 for 8	
A Merica to bat		

It was becoming nearly impossible to play away cricket matches so Haverhill put up an advert in **1942**, inviting all teams to arrange a match with the town, but only on the cricket meadow. As it was, games were arranged against the RAF who sent several different elevens to town, probably from various airfields in the district, it seemed at one time that the airmen were in town every Saturday. Newmarket were the only regular side to play Haverhill in this season. Once again, such diverse matches as the Air Raid Wardens versus First Aid Party, and Haverhill Literary Institute against the National Fire Service were seen. The young Air Training Corps were also in action for a few arranged matches. The cricket ground was again hired out to the Irish Pipers, and further cash came the Cricket Club's way as the War Charities Club were holding regular dances and donated a sum to the cricketers.

Showing his prowess in **1943** in another sport, H Poole won the Bowls Challenge Cup for the third year running. As a result it was deemed his property outright, but he gave it back on the condition it would not be claimed as such in the future. This summer also saw cricket matches being played on Sundays for the first time ever in the town. These were not the Haverhill Club games but Fire Service versus the Home Guard and others such as these; they only had time for sport on Sundays. Units of the Local Defence had use of the meadow during the summer months for practice drills and other activities, and the ground was at last given a catering licence, but only for the serving of tea to the players.

The cricket meadow was becoming the favourite site for events in the town as the Hamlet Croft had been taken over completely by the military, but the Grand Open-Air Holiday Dance in June had to be speedily transferred into the Town Hall when the rain appeared. This building was packed when over three hundred came along, with a big crowd in the balcony. Jimmy Trail and his full RAF Band provided the music. For Red Cross Week, the local branch had the loan of the meadow for the whole week and tents were erected everywhere to the consternation of some Cricket Club members.

FUSILIERS' XI

Sec.-Lieut. Turner c H. Poole b R. C. Poole	71
Sec.-Lieut Lowe lbw. b Scrivener	60
Fus. Pendelbury not out	30
Fus. Howarth b Williams	10
Fus. Rushton lbw. b Newman	0
Col. Whowell c Pryke b Williams	4
L Sgt. Maund b Newman	2
Extras	25
for 6 wkts. decld.	202

Mr. Atkinson, Cpl. Whalley, Cpl. Horsfall and Fus. Smith did not bat.

HAVERHILL WEDNESDAY

A. J. Williams c Atkinson b Rushton	19
C. P. Spicer c and b Whalley	41
N. Pryke b Lowe	22
H. Poole b Whalley	13
R. C. Poole b Rushton	15
H. B. Newman b Rushton	3
W. J. Scrivener not out	5
D. Poole b Rushton	0
A. L. Webb lbw. b Rushton	0
Sgt. G. Howard b Whalley	6
H. Hartop b Rushton	8
Extras	4
	136

However, the most upsetting news came when R T Hammond of Recreation Road, who had played regular cricket for the town, passed away in Addenbrookes Hospital in Cambridge after a short illness; he was just thirty-four. He had worked at D Gurteen's factory for many years. Better news of another Haverhill cricketer was from D Freeman in Kenya. Corporal Freeman wrote, "Ever since I came to this station I have longed to play cricket in Nairobi, and at last I have succeeded. We played against the best team in this area who had some top County players from England; we lost but the game was exciting. Up to this match our team had played fifteen matches without being on the losing side."

The Bank Holiday Monday in August, usually the Gala date, saw a 'Grand Show' on the cricket ground, being arranged by the Haverhill Amalgamated Produce Association, as part of Victory Gardens Week. There were classes for fruit, flowers, vegetables, poultry and rabbits. The band of the Oxford & Bucks Light Infantry provided the music for this show. Haverhill was lucky in musical events as various regiments of the forces were stationed in the town throughout the war period.

The season was wound up with a Ladies match when the NFS (Females) took on the JWAC, which drew a larger attendance than usual. The game between the A Company Home Guard and the B Company Home Guard attracted another sizable crowd. In all, the Haverhill Cricket Club took part in eleven matches in 1943 and were unbeaten; all matches were at home. During this limited season they met a side from Sewards End near Saffron Walden for the first time.

At the Annual General Meeting in March **1944** the Cricket Club were congratulated for keeping the game alive in the dark days of war. On theBowls Green side, Mr Mason considered work on the ground had not sufficed, and members needed to meet and sort out how to do this better. The Bowls Challenge Cup had resumed and was won this year by Mr C H Benton while the Bowls Championship was won by Mr C J Webb and the runner-up, Mr J Ives. A committee meeting of the Cricket Club was held in the Pavilion for the first time, while Mrs H Poole and Mrs H Hawkes served the teas at each match. The Club played fifteen games against the usual Forces teams and won 10 and lost 3, the highest individual score of 129 came from F

Rowlinson; this player headed both the batting and bowling averages. With soldiers billeted in the town it was thought that some would play for the town club, but only once this has been recorded when Lt Wisdon played four games for Haverhill during 1944. One stalwart was Mr A Willis the Haverhill umpire.

The Club's balance sheet of **1945** presented at the Annual General Meeting showed a loss of £125-2-4d, plus expenses still to be paid for a fresh motor mower. The Supporters Club (formed 1927) had handed over £1,028-7-5d to the Cricket Club in the past few years to help reduce the yearly deficit. Subscriptions were increased again up to thirty shillings for vice presidents and members twenty shillings while the youths paid ten shillings and the juniors (13-16 years) two shillings and sixpence. A silver cup was presented to the Bowls Club by Mr Herbert Webb, for the 'best pair' tournament while another cup passed on by the Gala Association was to be sold for twenty guineas. The Ladies Committee was going well in their activities which included serving teas for players and onlookers.

Up to this time, the forces teams opposing the cricket club throughout the war had been largely anonymous as they came to Haverhill for matches. Now in 1945 the full titles were given as Haverhill entertained RAF Chedburgh, RAF Castle Camps and RAF Wratting Common amongst other local airfields. They even took on the Searchlight Company one Sunday, and a RAF Band played for a Cricket Club Dance. While it was proposed to run two teams this year, there is no mention of a second eleven except the Wednesday XI which had been taking part in a few matches during the war. As a finale to this season, L E Mayes XI took on Newmarket Town Cricket Club.

Now that hostilities were over, the Cricket Club concentrated on the ground itself, which had taken quite a pounding when used by other organisations for purposes other than cricket. A list of 'to do's' was drawn up by the committee and included painting the two pavilions (cricket and bowls), the shelter and other huts with not less than two coats, and this to cost not more than £80. Mr R Gowers & Son were given this task. There were also quite a lot of repairs to the seats, those on the south side to be repaired and painted, plus the west side where necessary. With paint in short supply, an appeal was made for anyone with some paint, or even half a tin, to donate it to the Cricket Club. The moveable forms were patched and repaired and the boundary fence, especially the corrugated part, was given the once over and the wooden supports repaired. Mr D M Gurteen gave an illuminated record of bowls champions over the years to be framed and hung in the pavilion.

Fire insurance was looked at and the sum insured was increased to £1,050 for the old pavilion, the new pavilion on the cricket meadow, the old tin office and the shelter as well as for other effects in each mentioned building. Some used bats and balls were purchased for £3, and it was agreed to give a rise to the long-serving groundsman Mr G Coote, he was to be paid £3 per week. The ground was let out once more to the Haverhill Homecoming Forces Fund Committee.

****

FRESH BEGINNINGS

Things were now getting back to normal and the Cricket Club decided to run two teams once again starting in **1946**. As H Gurteen had relinquished the post of club captain to take over as Bowls Club captain from D M Gurteen, R C Poole was the new 1st XI captain. The bowls section was also holding its meetings separately from the cricket side and to this end, they had entered the Steeple Bumpstead Bowls League. On the Cricket Club side, the fee for the umpires was increased to 3s 6d each match. The transport for away fixtures saw Mr Burgoin's terms accepted, being 1s 6d per mile with a minimum of £2. Twenty-five per cent would have to be paid if cancelled within three days and members to pay fifty per cent of the costs for each away game. £50 was also given to cricket club from the Supporters Club, which meant that nearly £200 had been given since the Supporters Club had been formed.

An attractive fixture list had been drawn up for both teams, including more clubs who had been regular opponents before the war, plus a new works side from Sawston. As they had been for several years, F E Rowlinson and J Chapman were the top bowlers, and H Farrant, now returned from being in the forces, was looking forward to his cricket once again. A familiar face missing though, was H Poole who had been connected with the club for twenty-six years as a player, and as captain for the previous ten years. The new Haverhill 2nd XI was led by pre-war stalwart H B Newman.

In their first match of a new season, the 1st XI faced Bury United, and after they had posted a total of 85, Haverhill were the victors with a score of 192 for 9. Haverhill were represented by the following eleven, F Rowlinson, H Farrant, A Pannell, J E Thake, J Chapman, R C Poole, A Thake, W G Smith, A Hinton, P Rowlinson and C J Corkindale. The team from RAF Wratting Common were the opponents for the 2nd XI's opening game, the scores ending 63-44 in the airmen's favour. The seconds team consisted of, R Nunn, L Felton, W J Scrivener, C Farrant, L Mayes, H B Newman, G Nunn, R Smith, C Thake, D Steed and L Farrant. The 1st XI also faced an RAF side, this time from Stradishall, victory going to the town club.

Haverhill Cricket Club were testing the water by putting out a Haverhill Junior side as well. They had a match versus the Old Independent Church Juniors one Monday evening, the Club's boys being victorious 83 to 26. *".... promising form was shown with the ball by Vaux and Fox for the OIC, while Knopp behind the wicket was very good."* Also on the school playing field, the Haverhill Secondary School met the OIC Juniors on a Monday in July, the pupils winning by eight runs 79-71.

The opening four matches gave Haverhill 1st XI three wins and one loss, the same record as the 2nd XI. However, when the West Wratting team failed to arrive for a fixture with 2nd XI, a game was quickly arranged with H B Newman's XI playing W Scriveners XI instead, as everyone was keen to get a game of cricket going. Even some spectators who had settled down to watch found themselves taking part. New opponents were Poslingford who were not quite strong enough for the 2nd XI who won by fifty-eight runs. The Haverhill opening pair made 93 between them while H Sephton took 8 village wickets for 34 runs. When a strong RAF XI took on Haverhill, four town batsmen were back in the pavilion without a run being scored, two more wickets fell for a meagre ten runs and the Haverhill XI only managed to creep to an all out score of 23, which the RAF passed with 45. It was in the Haverhill side that the best bowler was seen, J Chapman showing excellent figures of 5 wickets for 9 runs although on the losing side.

During August the Haverhill 1st XI made the long journey to Hemel Hempstead to meet and defeat the works side of John Dickinson in an all-day match. Captain R C Poole certainly enjoyed the trip with a top score of 53. Back to an afternoon fixture at Halstead which was declared a draw when time ran out on Halstead who needed 24 to win with two wickets remaining;

this also happened when Haverhill were in sight of the winning post when their time ran out, as matches were played to a strict timetable. A friendly fixture from before the war was also revived when the Rev Barnes XI took on a mixed Haverhill side at Thurlow.

The bright summer that had greeted the beginning of the cricket season was not on show when the next match had to be cancelled. When Hedingham were visitors to Haverhill the following week, a start was made, but after the visiting team had completed their innings, Haverhill were prevented from batting when the rain started to put the damper on matters. Everyone retired to the pavilion, and no more play was possible.

A Sunday afternoon match was contested by S Dedman's XI against L E Mayes XI, resulting in good-humoured banter between the two sides, plus a good-sized crowd to watch proceedings and sometimes join in the fun. Mr Dedman's team was first to bat and made a healthy 60 for their opponents to aim for. When they batted, Mr Mayes XI started off with a disaster; their captain was out, caught in the slips when the ball rapped his knuckles. Wickets tumbled in quick succession, and seven men were back in the dressing room for only six runs. Then V Pannell and W Wiseman came together and mastered the bowling, taking the score along to the final 51. We can safely say everyone spent an enjoyable time.

It was a summer of ups and downs. Haverhill 1st XI were all out for 25 against Saffron Walden, who went on to win quite easily by knocking up 123, despite R C Poole's tempting slow bowling. Then the 2nd XI visited an accomplished village side in Birdbrook one Sunday to register a victory of 176 to 91. The Ex-Serviceman's Club in Haverhill were also putting out a cricket team on occasion and making a round of local villages on Sundays. As it was, the weather played a part in the fixtures again, and the Haverhill public were not attracted to the cricket meadow in any large numbers throughout this season. Of the fifteen matches played by the Haverhill 1st XI, they won eight, and only one score topped fifty (R C Poole 53). The captain was also top of the batting averages and Rowlinson was the best bowler, although J Chapman registered a hat trick versus Mildenhall.

The **1947** season began in the first week in May with a low scoring game for Haverhill at Newmarket, but one which Haverhill came out on top 83-47. New players included K Dodd (no not that one), D Poole, R Mills, F Mason, S Clarke and C King. The second game of the season was quite the opposite when Halstead visited the cricket meadow. After the town side scored 186, Halstead proceeded to top that with 203 for 4; so one victory and one defeat. With plenty of lads looking to have a game of cricket, a Cricket Club 3rd XI was put out for a friendly encounter with the Haverhill Rovers Football Club to wind up the football season with a match in their whites instead of red shirts and boots. The Rovers asked to use the cricket meadow until such time the Hamlet Croft became available; this was granted until 15 March 1947. This was on a 'Gentleman's Agreement' with no charge but the Rovers were to make good any damage. In addition, the Rovers put forward an idea for uniting the two clubs (cricket and football as it was way back in the past). A sub-committee did meet and talk this through, however, they could not reach a decision, and the amalgamation of Haverhill Rovers and Haverhill Cricket clubs was finally abandoned. With all the talented cricketers in the younger generation, it was agreed that junior members (13-17 years) to be accepted in the Cricket Club, but only allowed in the pavilion when accompanied by a parent. This rule was set because as a licence was to be obtained for catering at the Cricket Meadow which was also to sell ale and spirits in the future.

The Whit-Monday match versus Camden was extended to an all-day affair. The Haverhill innings was a reasonable 70 due to D Poole, for although he only scored fifteen, he stayed long enough to make Camden hurry their game. In the end, Camden did grab the victory, but only by seven runs. The adverse result came mainly from some misfiring on the part of Haverhill batting which proved costly. The 1st XI seemed to do better away from home and chalked up another victory at Hoffmanns at Chelmsford, 100-49. The 2nd XI gained a narrow victory (106-103) over Sawston II on their ground. Again at Saffron Walden, Haverhill 1st XI put the home side in to bat, but they were so slow that their innings was very late in finishing at 125 for 6. This left Haverhill with a small amount of time to make their reply, but all the Haverhill batsmen pitched in with some astonishing big hitting to help the score along. With five minutes to spare, they had reached and passed the Walden score to end on 142 for 7.

There were two exceptional games in mid-week during July. First, N G Prykes XI versus E W Prykes XI on a Wednesday, led by two brothers from

Haverhill and Colchester who tried to get this family challenge in each summer. But it was a Thursday game when H B Newman's XI played Weston Colville that one of the bowling feats of the season was seen; W Sephton captured 9 of the villagers wickets for only 11 runs. Of course the scratch eleven won the game.

The cricketers of Haverhill were gradually getting back into the groove after the second war, but it had taken time to re-adjust to the peacetime sporting scene. The 1st XI had taken part in nineteen matches, all completed for the first time that anyone could remember, of which they won eleven and lost eight in mostly excellent weather. Their highest total for an innings was 285 for 6 against A Bowers XI on August Bank Holiday Monday. H Farrant played every match and R C Poole was only absent once. D Poole finished top of the batting averages and F Rowlinson the bowling; the latter also scored the only century of the season, 112 not out. A F Thomas, a Cambridgeshire County player turned out for Haverhill for a few games and as a bowler took 18 wickets at a cost of 6.7 runs per wicket each, but did not figure in the top averages, as he did not play enough games. The ground had also made a good recovery from its use by the Haverhill Rovers as their football pitch, the Army still occupying the Hamlet Croft.

At the end of the summer Mr G Coote retired as grounds man. Age 73 he had held this post for 47 years Mr Len Jacobs was elected as the new groundsman at £5 per match. A presentation was made to Mr G Coote at a special meeting. This meeting also had a few more issues to discuss at the same time that needed attention before the Annual General Meeting. Mr W C Blake sent a letter, from the Haverhill Memorial Committee, suggesting a new playing field be built on the Meadows, of which the cricket ground would form a part. A sub-committee was to investigate for the cricket club. The cart used for removing the grass cuttings was beyond repair, and the pony harness wanted renewing. To bring the cricket club into the modern era, the purchase of a motor mower was discussed if a cheap one came up for sale; Atterton & Ellis were also asked to submit some prices of these. The Motor Mower Sub-Committee met at the Bell Hotel, and with the help of the Supporters Club decided to order a 30 inch cut mower from Atterton & Ellis.

At the beginning of the **1948** season, a cheque of £100 was passed to the

Cricket Club from the result of a successful Dance which had been organised by a special committee selected for that purpose. This saw the summer underway with a healthy figure in the Bank. Gate receipts had risen steadily since the war years; one year a single match topped £22. More much needed cash came from a Dinner arranged at the Rose & Crown at five shillings per ticket. Mr Farrant, on behalf of the Supporters Club, also handed over a cheque for £30 plus the gift of a motor mower and trailer which had cost £312-13-8d. Offsetting this, the groundsman had asked for a rise and his wages were increased to £5-10s. Later on, the new mower was not working satisfactory and was returned to the makers; a report was expected.

The first match was against Exning which Haverhill won by scoring 111 for 2 wickets in reply to their opponents 99. G Fairey (52) and N Pryke (51) were the two not out batsmen who proved the winners for Haverhill. In the game between the two 2nd XI's, the result was Exning 54 Haverhill 112. This early season form did not last however, as the 1st XI promptly lost their next game to Sawston, but the 2nd XI made it two wins on the trot when ending victors over the Sawston 2nd XI. This set the 1948 pattern, a win over Westgate Brewery and a loss to Camden and another defeat at Braintree. In the latter game, the home bowler G West captured all ten Haverhill wickets.

The Haverhill bowlers took the honours in some matches including the defeat of Saffron Walden when R Mills took 5 for 19 and F E Rowlinson 5 for 31. The 2nd XI's H Sephton also got among the wickets with 6 for 33 in the clash of the 2nd XI's. Up to July it was the seconds who were doing rather better out of the two Haverhill sides. In bowling out Sawston II, it was H Sephton once again who shone as he sent down eleven overs of which six were maidens, and ended with the really exceptional figures of 7 for just 8 runs. He followed this with 5 wickets for 5 runs versus Braintree II who were all out for 29. Meanwhile August was ushered in with the Haverhill 1st XI losing a low-scoring match at Newmarket 63-62.

Despite these performances, it was H Sephton's brother W Sephton who topped the bowling averages for 1948 with some steady performances. Newcomer H Fairey played in fourteen games and was top in the batting averages, second being N Pryke. The year ended with the club thinking of installing a concrete wicket on the ground that would be used mainly for practice sessions, costing in the region of £100.

Once again, the balance sheet presented at the 1949 Annual Meeting showed dire details, a loss of £125-2-4d over the previous season, and to this was to be added the expense of putting the newly bought mower into a proper condition. It was thanks to the Supporters Club, which was formed in 1927, that the club had kept its head above the financial waters, with £1,028-2-4d being handed to the club over the years. As it was, the subscriptions were increased to thirty shillings for the vice-presidents, twenty shillings for members and ten shillings for the younger members. The idea of a concrete wicket was abandoned and instead a concrete floor was put into the Bowls pavilion

The opening match of 1949 was at Westgate Brewery where Haverhill suddenly found themselves 7 wickets down for only 36 runs, not a good way to begin. They managed to double this when they were all out and reduced the home side to 22 with half the side back in the pavilion. However, before the next wicket was taken they had passed the Haverhill score. The team was G Fairey, A Thake, F E Rowlinson, N Pryke, H Fairey, W Sharples, R C Poole, W Sephton, R G Mills, P Ralling and P Rowlinson. The Haverhill 2nd XI entertained Halstead II for their first match and had an easy win when their two bowlers R Smith and H Sephton did the damage to put Halstead out for 24. Their eleven consisted of S Nunn, W J Scrivener, H Sephton, D Poole, A Sephton, B Jobson, C Farrant, H B Newman, R Smith, L Mizon and G Herbert.

Visiting Courtaulds at Bocking, Haverhill gained their first victory of 1949 and again it was their bowlers who wreaked havoc in the home batting order. As Sharples was taking 3 wickets for 8 runs, F E Rowlinson sent down eight over's of which six were maidens, and ended with figures of 7 wickets for 5 runs, truly a remarkable performance. At the finish of this game a challenge was accepted by a certain Haverhill cricketer (not named) to a single game of darts from a Courtaulds player, of 501 up; this also resulted in a Haverhill victory, so the team travelled home in a gay mood. At the start of June the Haverhill 2nd XI had a poor result versus local rivals Thurlow when they were toppled out with a measly 14 runs in just ten over's. In addition, the clock denied the 1st XI a win over Newmarket; having totalled 147 they had reduced their opponents to 59 for 9 when time was called. Haverhill 1st XI carried on their good form in the return match against Courtaulds when they won 150 for 6 (declared) to 44. Meanwhile the 2nd XI were at Courtaulds II where a heavy downpour delayed the start until 3-45pm but they scored 123 for 5 before time ruled out a result, as the home team stood at 29 for 3.

It was one Sunday that the best match of the season (an all day encounter) took place on the cricket meadow when R C Poole's XI entertained Mr B H Belle's XI which consisted of Suffolk County players, but even these men were soon in difficulties against the Haverhill bowlers of Rowlinson and Sharples. Nothing was given away in the field, and the visitors total was 86 when all their wickets were down. J Blewett from Cornish Hall End and D Game of Exning opened for Haverhill, but with two wickets down for 52 runs, N Pryke faced just four balls before the heavy rain prevented any further play and the game was unfortunately brought to a close. A few weeks later R C Poole took a side to Dulwich in London to play Griffin Athletic, a Sainsbury's sports team. They travelled there by Burton Coaches and the Haverhill Bowls Club went along to play their counterparts from Griffin. The cricketers lost narrowly while the bowls club were the victors in their game.

Very often, the two Haverhill teams met their respective opponents' elevens on the same day as when Haverhill I went to Sawston and won 180 to 150, and the Sawston and Haverhill II's met at Haverhill and this ended in a draw. On the cricket ground one Sunday a team made from Haverhill's 1st and 2nd team and playing under the banner of Mr A Thake's XI entertained Willesdon Postal Sports Club. After putting up a low score, the visiting eleven soon found themselves on the losing side as Thake's team passed their score of 48 before the second Haverhill wicket had fallen.

J Blewett was now appearing regularly for Haverhill and was the top scorer in the match versus Camden, but ended on the losing side when Haverhill could only muster 104 for 8 to Camden's 186 for 4 when stumps were drawn. Making a first appearance for the 1st XI were C P Spicer and W Baker, and in the 2nd XI there were debuts for F Sargent, M Brown and A Sadler. When Horseheath won the championship of the Weston Colville & District League, they were invited to come to the cricket meadow on a Sunday to play H Farrant's XI, which was composed of mainly Haverhill II's with added players L Mayes, G Nunn, G Barrett, V Gurteen and E Alderton. The village side won by 98-92 watched by a larger than usual crowd.

On the August Bank Holiday weekend, as well as the two matches on

Saturday, a Haverhill side played host to Hadleigh & Thundesley in an all-day encounter. In reply to the visitors all out total of 98, Haverhill made a mediocre start, but recovered enough to make 155 for 9 to win the game. They were unfortunate to lose W Sephton to an injury before many overs had been bowled, and he was unable to bat or bowl for the rest of the game. The cricket season went on until the last weekend in September and was now overlapping the football season by a considerable period. This was beginning to stop those who played both sports from making a start of carrying on with the football or cricket each year. This also meant it was the end for many of those who wanted to take part in both cricket and football for Haverhill.

Thirty-one matches were played in 1949, and more or less the games won and lost equalled themselves out, with newcomer J Blewitt top of the batting averages and W Sephton the best in the bowling department. With repairs to the surrounding fence where twenty-eight posts were found to be broken and other groundwork to cost over £80, plus new netting and posts, an appeal to the National Playing Fields Association was to be made for financial assistance. On top of this the talk of the concrete wicket was raised again, and one was laid with new nets and posts, for practice, at a lower than anticipated cost of £31. For some reason, possibly financial, a silver cup given to the cricket club by the Gala Association was sold off for twenty guineas.

The **1950** summer began with a whimper as the first cricket week-end of the new season was washed out by some un-summery weather. Haverhill managed to get away the next week with a visit to Courtaulds at Bocking who were restricted to 37 all out, eight of their batsmen being clean bowled. This set the tone for the afternoon as Haverhill themselves were then all out for 48 to win a very low scoring and short match, the spectators going home early. With the Haverhill II also meeting Courtaulds in the battle if the second elevens, Haverhill were also victors, 90 to 70; again many of the batsmen were bowled out. Must have been something in the air! Sawston however, piled on the runs at home to Haverhill the next week, setting the visitors 181 runs to win. Haverhill reached 116 for 9 and managed to hang on to their last wicket to force a draw. Once again, the second teams of the two clubs met at Haverhill with Sawston II proving winners.

For a special match at the Cricket Meadow the weather was on its best behaviour when the sunshine brought a large crowd out to see R C Poole's XI (mostly the 1st XI) do battle with Suffolk Club & Ground. B H Belle, the Oxford 'Blue' and the Suffolk county captain captained the opponents. The visitors also included their top bowler in J N Stevens and a host of top county and university players. The Haverhill team was strengthened by the playing of W J Blewett, the Cornish Hall End opening bat, and had their own two county players in W Sharples and F E Rowlinson who had been in the Suffolk team versus Essex II at Clacton. Altogether an opportunity for all lovers of 'King Willow'. The Suffolk side eventually gained a comfortable victory, making 182 for 3 before declaring at the tea interval, Haverhill trying several bowlers. R C Poole's XI replied with 114 as the County players gave a strong lesson in fielding. Perkins, the Suffolk professional, took 3 wickets for no runs in 2.4 over's. One thing remaining was the winner of the lucky programme number, who was urged to claim his prize of cigarettes as soon as possible.

The first Sunday game was W J Scrivener's XI v Castle Camps winning 90-45 against the village side. On the same Sunday the 1st XI went to Exning and lost narrowly by two runs. Pat Kearney, the player-coach of Haverhill Rovers, was now quite a regular in the Haverhill Cricket team. W J Blewett, who was now playing most of his cricket for Haverhill as an opening batsman, knocked up 66 not out in his first innings versus Halstead. Halstead totalled 147 and Haverhill 141 for 8, forcing another drawn game. The 2nd XI batsman A Pannell then followed suit with 76 not out against Broomfield, opening casually before hitting out quite lustily with 1 six and 11 fours.. He followed this the next Sunday with 61, playing for N G Pryke's XI against Fina Sports Club (London).

Two Haverhill cricketers were selected and played for Suffolk Club & Ground at Culford School. In their team's 218 for 4, F E Rowlinson hit 21 while R C Poole did not have a chance with the bat. Rowlinson also played for the Special Constables v Regular Police in a special fixture at Haverhill. Another interesting match was on the cricket ground in July when Eastern Electricity (Haverhill) pitted their strength against the Eastern Electricity Board from Bury St Edmunds one Sunday afternoon. The Haverhill Modern School were also in on the act with two matches versus Sudbury School, the main bowler for Haverhill was D Levett (7 for 26) who had already had some games with the Haverhill 2nd XI.

As with last year, a team of Haverhill cricketers visited Dulwich in London for a match against Griffin Sports Club. Haverhill were the victors by 184 to 102, but everyone said it was the day out which was most enjoyed. It was C W Poole, the brother of R C and captain of the Bowls Club (who also had a game v Griffin), who had arranged this match, and the visitors were entertained to lunch and tea as well. Burton Coaches provided the comfort of the journey stopping on the way at Epping for refreshment on the way and returning to Haverhill at well past midnight.

Entering August a fresh team faced Haverhill when the 1st XI went to Bury St Edmunds to play the Beds & Herts Regiment, the soldiers winning. The Haverhill versus Halstead fixture saw Haverhill declare at 219 for 7, W J Blewett hitting 100 not out. Halstead could only manage 59 to give Haverhill a big victory. For the winners, R G Mills took 4 for 25, which included three wickets in one over. This was on the Bank Holiday Saturday, and on the August Monday Haverhill took on E W Prykes XI and Blewett was clean bowled for 14; you can never tell can you? Willesden Sports Club were also visitors to the Cricket Ground to face A Thake's XI. He was the 1st XI's opening batman at this time and a regular in the team.

It was common to see old veteran bowlers, darts and billiards players but not often elderly cricketers. Haverhill, however, boasted of such a cricketer in S A Griggs (Doc Griggs to everyone). At the age of sixty-six he was amongst his works team of Atterton & Ellis when they played a game against the Eastern Electricity Board on the cricket ground one Sunday. In his side's win, Doc scored 15 not out in an innings in which he played very confidently. When his team went out to field, Griggs was already waiting with his pads on to keep wicket. Cheers were heard all round the ground when he caught one of the opponents out - between his knees. He afterwards remarked, *"I feel as fit as a fiddle and my eyes were never better and I could see the ball as big as a football."* Doc Griggs was also a fine footballer with the Rovers for many years after being in the Rovers team at sixteen years of age; a true sportsman of Haverhill.

One of the last matches of the season - m which went on well into September this year, overlapping the football season by several weeks - was a Sunday match starting at 11-45 between Barclays Bank (Cambridge & District) and Barclays Bank (London). Mr R D D Collie, the manager of the

Barclays Bank in Haverhill, captained the home team. The two sides had some very good cricketers in their elevens. The London side reached 169 for 6 declared in two hours, then the Cambridge team fought back with a higher score of their own to become the winners. For the Cambridge side, T Brooks, who had not played during the current season, gave a chanceless display of attractive cricket in his innings of 102 not out.

In summing up the season, the Haverhill 1st XI played twenty-one games, winning nine and losing seven, the top batsman being W J Blewett who made some heavy scoring when he came into the side. W Sharples headed the bowling. The 2nd XI took part in sixteen matches, winning six and being on the losing side eight times. Their top batsman was A Sephton and bowler, H Sephton, his brother. One thing still causing some concern was the debit over the season of £154-18-3d. During the year, the concrete wicket was completed for £31 to serve for net practice, while a place was found in the meadow at Wilsey Farm for the pony that pulled the roller.

At the Annual General Meeting of **1951**, serious steps were taken by the Cricket Club to introduce Sunday cricket matches, but one member asked, *"Will the pitch take all of this use?"* The most significant business of the meeting, however, was the resignation as secretary of Mr Horace Gurteen. This was after fifty years of unbroken service, which saw the club envied by visiting teams as to the set-up and friendly nature of all involved. Appointed to this post was Mr F W Gurteen, while the new treasurer was to be Mr R D Collie. There were now twenty-one committee members plus the officers.

This season began with an uninspiring match away at Bury St Edmunds team Westgate Brewery. Not one Haverhill batsmen got into double figures and their all out total of 37 was not enough, they lost by 48 runs. One newcomer to the Haverhill team, John House, was looked on as a good member, as it proved over the next few years. On the Whitsun weekend, Haverhill posted their first victory of the summer by 135 runs over R L Speck's XI with. the early batsmen behind this win. The 2nd XI gave a top performance when captain H B Newman skittled out four opposing batmen in one over, all clean bowled for a win over Courtaulds II, with figures of 8 wickets for 17 runs. At Sawston, a last wicket stubborn resistance earned Haverhill I the victory. On the same day the two club's 2nd XI's met, and this encounter was won by Haverhill who only used two bowlers during their stint in the field. This game saw the very low figure of just three boundary hits in the entire innings of both sides. The first matches of 'flaming June' were called off due to a miserable wet weekend.

With younger boys becoming members, a match was arranged one Monday in July between the Cricket Club Boys and the Haverhill Scouts, on the cricket ground. The Scouts were beaten by 13 runs; bowling for the Club Boys G Sizer took 8 wickets for 13 runs, which included a hat trick. The teams lined up, Cricket Club Boys; D Levett, A Fuller, G Sizer, J Burgoin, D Fitch, P Deeks, B Parker, N Haylock, P Allen, T Iron and C Cliff. The Scouts paraded, D Coote, J Coote, T Parkin, D Kiernan, J Kiernan, G Phillips, J Benton, P Kerswell and G Herbert. Yes, that is only nine players for the Scouts but to compensate for this, Parkin and J Kiernan went in to bat for a second time in one innings to make the number up, probably a record in itself.

What was becoming an annual event was the match between R C Pooles XI (Haverhill's first team) versus Suffolk Club & Ground at Haverhill. Even the veteran spectators, who had sometimes found it a good place to doze on a Sunday afternoon, had to snap out of their meditations and applaud the efforts of the Haverhill bowler W Sharples.. He produced an action without warning when attacking from the Haverhill end and bowled three batsmen straight away for an astonishing hat trick, and before the applause had died away, he rubbed it in by wrecking the stumps of another Suffolk batsman. The visitors were then 113 for 8 but made some more quick runs to declare at 151 for 8. Poole's eleven had a good go at knocking off the runs but against a strong Suffolk attack they fell short by 78 runs, mainly due to not being very happy against slow bowling.

Sharples continued his skilful bowling into the next weekend and took thirteen wickets in the two matches played. But it was a mixed bag for the club as the sun shone brightly, and the ground was hard and played some tricks. This was ideal for the fast bowler of which Bill Sharples was one, and at Braintree he took 8 for 27. Then in front of a large Haverhill throng on the Sunday, he skittled four County batsmen out in four balls in one over. Despite this, the Suffolk Club & Ground were victors over Haverhill (R C Poole's XI) 151 to 73. In the Braintree game Haverhill were successful by 55 runs. Special mention in this match went to young P Kerswell who took two fine catches, one on the boundary line. Meanwhile the 2nd XI were not up to standard in their match versus Braintree II. They were without their captain H B Newman and the opponent's bowlers registered two hat tricks in the match.

In July, one of Haverhill's top sportsmen passed away. David Gowers was 79 and a life-long resident of the town and a leading light in sport, religion and the industrial life of the town. He began his sporting days at an early age as a playing member of both Haverhill Rovers Football Club and the Haverhill Cricket Club and continued with the latter club's 2nd XI until he was in his fifties; he was noted for his prolific batting. He also turned out for the Suffolk County Football team, and carried on when he retired to serve on committees of both clubs in Haverhill. He also worked his entire life at the factory of D Gurteen's, retiring in 1939.

The 1st XI were having a good season and setting up several good victories, the 2nd XI following suit. One of their games produced an exciting ending when opponents Sawston II needed just four runs to win from the last three balls, and H Sephton clean bowled their last pair of batsmen to win the encounter. Two town players, R C Poole and J House, were selected to play for Exning & District against Suffolk Club & Ground, showing that Haverhill cricket was being noted in the highest circles of county cricket.

What was becoming an annual event was the visit to Dulwich to play cricket and bowls against Griffin Sports Club. The cricket saw a very high scoring match with both sides scoring over two hundred runs; Haverhill edged ahead to claim the victory. The Bowls Club made it a double in their game. The Haverhill 1st XI ended their winning streak when they only managed a draw versus Broomfield, where they were said to be *"very weak in the field."* This, however, was a good match for Mr Extra who made a total of 28 runs for Haverhill.

Of the other cricket teams in and around Haverhill, the Haverhill Electric Sports & Social Club were in action at the cricket ground, winning their match in midweek against Premier Travel. They had further matches with Atterton's Iron Works, the Works putting on 92 for the first wicket, the Ram and Kedington. The Electric team sparked two more wins. This raised talks once again of a Cricket League in Haverhill to see teams from factory and social club elevens. On the school playing field in Wratting Road, the School

XI were opposed by the School's Old Boys XI one Monday evening, attracting a substantial following.

Although the Haverhill 1st XI were having a very good summer they ran into trouble when visiting St Ives, and by the skin on their teeth they hung on to stop being beaten. With one wicket remaining, they needed over forty runs to win but with this nearly impossible task. Harold Fairey (22 not out) and Pat Kearney (0 not out) batted out the time to save the match. Haverhill had made 89 for 9 when play ended. The 2nd XI had a creditable victory over old rivals Clare on the same day 160-73, with the following team; S Nunn, W Scrivener, G Barrett, E Orriss, G B Thurman, H Farrant, D Levett, S Robinson, H B Newman, H Sephton and R Smith. Levett took two first-rate catches behind the stumps in an impressive performance. Second highest scorer for Clare was Mr Extras who totalled 42. Also worthy of note was the bowling of H Farrant versus Stoke-by-Clare for the 2nd XI the following weekend, when he took 4 village wickets for a mere 4 runs. Stoke had been going well until Farrant took the ball in his hands.

What should have been an attractive fixture, the game between the 1st XI and RAF Stradishall at the air base, ended in the way some other games did that Saturday, by rain. That the game reached the stage it did was quite a surprise as the wet weather set in early. The airmen made 114 for 3 in ninety minutes and Haverhill started their reply when it became impossible to continue. Haverhill had reached 19 for 0 wickets when the match was abandoned. It was now September and the next game was stopped early on when a heavy storm washed out further play in the game versus Hoffmanns. The town's Sharples, one of their top performers, was making a return to the team after some time off, when he was unavailable to play.

In summing up the season, the 1st XI were unbeaten for the summer after losing their opening game to Westgate Brewery, and even the spectators were not voicing the opinion that 'the cricket it not up to how it used to be'. They had 2,760 runs in total, averaging over fifteen for each wicket lost in their nineteen matches. W J Blewett was again top of the batting averages, Archie Pannell running a close second and scoring the most runs (350). Bowling saw Bill Sharples the finest with Frank Rowlinson also near to his best again. Although there were a good total of runs scored in most of the matches, neither Haverhill nor their opponents managed to top the two hundred mark in any of the games.

1952 started with some sad news when Mr F W Gurteen passed away in late April. He was a member of the large Gurteen family who provided work for a greater part of Haverhill, and a member of the Urban District Council for many years. He was very active in sport of which cricket was undoubtedly his favourite, for which the Haverhill Cricket Club had much to thank him for. He was captain of the first eleven of the club from 1896 to 1924, and a popular figure with both home and visiting teams; then he became President from 1925 up to his death. It was planned to erect a memorial somewhere in the ground to commemorate the late Mr Gurteen, or a plaque in the pavilion in view of his lengthy service to the Cricket Club. In his place Mr Horace Gurteen was voted as President

For the beginning of the 1952 season, Haverhill visited Westgate Brewery and managed to hold out for a draw after a tight finish to the game In reply to their opponents 142 for 5 Haverhill were 99 for 9 when stumps were drawn. This was not the start they wanted, and when Bury St Edmunds came to Haverhill for the second game of the summer, they inflicted the home team's first defeat for almost a year, thus a long run was ended. The worst thing, however, was that very few spectators were on the cricket meadow to see this match. This season saw the official start of regular matches on Sundays, this after some games had been on that day over the past two or three years and the club decided to make it official. The opening Sunday fixture was against West London Indoor Cricket Club and some 'brighter cricket' was seen, especially from veteran F Rowlinson who entertained the watching crowd with his hard hitting and fruitful bowling as Haverhill easily ended victorious.

There were different secretaries for the Sunday XI, Bowls Club, the Saturday sides of the Cricket Club and the Supporters Club. There were also several different sub-committees formed to deal with such matters as holding a dance and looking at the clubs insurance. To raise the profile of the club and increase the finances, a 'Carnival Ball with Len Copsey's Music, was arranged for the Town Hall for Whit-Monday evening. A bus bringing in people from the surrounding villages to increase attendance.

It was four weeks into the season before the first win came for the Saturday

1st XI, this over Sawston, thanks to a bowling performance of merit from A Thake with 4 wickets for 8 runs. The Sunday side were mostly on home ground each week, and visitors came from works teams who could not play on weekdays. The first century innings was by J Blewett in a Sunday fixture, with his 106 versus Northcote CC. The Whit-Monday game saw Haverhill and Newmarket oppose each other. After Haverhill had put up a reasonable score for their visitors to aim for, Newmarket crawled along. The Haverhill captain R C Poole tried to entice them with some slow bowlers, to try and get a result, but Newmarket held out for a uninspiring draw. More well known names were appearing in the team now, J House, A Pannell, N G Pryke, G and H Fairey from Horseheath. In addition, the Rovers FC player-coach Pat Kearney was playing cricket as well.

The return match with Sawston provided a one-run victory for the Cambridgeshire side, 99 to 98, but rain prevented the now regular match of R C Poole's XI v Suffolk Club & Ground from starting. Poole also played for the Club & Ground on two occasions. One or two games on Sundays were under the banner of the club's captain R C Poole, although it was made up of most of the first eleven Haverhill side. Other Sabbath games were against the likes of Aviation Developments Ltd from Welwyn Garden City, St George's Hospital, the Daily Mirror and the London Transport Passenger Board. Two week-ends were spoilt by rain but the Haverhill 2nd XI managed to play against Braintree II, when 65 by G Barrett gave them the win.

July brought better weather as the temperature rose to over 80 degrees in one ten day period. This meant the swimming bath in the town was the favourite spot, some saying it was too hot to enter the water; surely not! Unfortunately, Haverhill's cricket did not rise as high and they promptly suffered their biggest defeat in the sun at home to Hoffmanns, who won by hitting 250 in reply to Haverhill's 68. The next day, the Sunday XI were winners versus Fina Petroleum Sports Club with a great spell of bowling from Pat Kearney, taking eight wickets at a low run cost. Recovering from their heavy loss, Haverhill 1st XI put on their best of the season against R L Speck's XI, totalling 242 for 5 (F Rowlinson 67, A Pannell 49, J Hall 42). Then for a phase John House was in top form with the bat; in successive matches he scored 81 v Grange Park, 78 v Exning, 79 v United Banks and then, for the National Farmers Union against the Cambridge Branch, he knocked up 75, one of the best spells a Haverhill batsman had ever produced.

Two spells of inspired bowling came from F Rowlinson with 6 for 15 at Exning followed by 8 for 31 against Newmarket.

The August Bank Holiday weekend was spoilt by persistent rain but Haverhill managed to play a few over's in some matches by dodging the showers, although the games were not long and did not give a definite result. On their visit to Courtaulds, the 1st XI shone once again when they replied to the home teams 133 with 153 for 1 to win by nine wickets. The three batsmen who did the damage were J Blewett 61, J House 43 and G Fairey 38. The rest of the team who did not bat were N G Pryke, H Fairey, R C Poole, A Hinton B Haylock, R G Mills and D Poole. The main players in the 2nd XI at this time were; P Turner, S Nunn, H Farrant, E Orriss, H Willis, B Jobson, W Sephton, R Smith, W J Scrivener, J Benton and B Newman. It was the turn of Rowlinson to prove he was no mean batsman when coming to the wicket versus Camden, he promptly hit the first two deliveries for two sixes, going on to register 10 fours as he made a whirlwind 76. Following this, he hit 109 v Nomads, but with everyone else having low batting efforts, Nomads won. N Pryke, who had not been in any kind of form all season, suddenly came up with 80 for Haverhill's victory over Braintree.

On a Sunday trip to Hemel Hempstead, R C Poole's XI included the Taylor brothers who were Cambridgeshire County players. This certainly paid off when they scored 155 runs between them in the Haverhill side's 224 for 6 declared, but Haverhill could not bowl out the home side and the match ended up as a draw. The last Sunday game of the summer saw the town entertain a side called the Combined Villages who swiftly gained the 136-87 victory.

With the cricket meadow hosting more and more matches in the summer the groundsman had his wages upped to £7 for a six-day week. However soon after this was put into practice, he said he had to resign the post as he now had work that was more regular for himself and could not continue. Concern was now expressed over the ground being neglected and rats being reported in the store shed by the main pavilion. When it rained, there was also some concern over water from the shed flowing on to the public footpath. The club advertised for a new groundsman.

Cricket averages should never have too much importance attached to them with the summer game as it was at this time, only contested on a friendly basis as the Haverhill Club did. Even so, there are not many cricketers who do not love to hit a big score or rattle the wickets of opposing batsmen week after week to up their personal average. As far as the 1st XI was concerned, their 1952 performance did not compare well with the previous season, but that year was exceptional. The team nearly always provided a pleasant afternoon's sport, however, with some matches good and others mediocre to say the least.

The spotlight this season fell on Frank Rowlinson, the Withersfield farmer, who bore the brunt of the bowling as well as one or two first-class batting displays. He topped the bowling list ahead of Kearney, taking 57 wickets and while Rowlinson scored more runs than anyone else (524), he was beaten to the top batting averages by J Blewett who had an average of 33 from many fewer innings. Rowlinson had equalled the clubs record of over 500 runs and 50 wickets in a season; Bert Poole had set this in the early 1920's. Haverhill 1st XI had played 22 matches, winning 8, and losing 8. The second eleven's top batsmen were H Sephton and W Sephton, the two brothers from Sturmer, while the best bowler was H B Newman. Sunday cricket had been introduced on an organised scale for the first time, and successfully. This team never reached great heights this season and only won 4 of the 16 games played, although 5 were not given a result. The 2nd XI's averages had been topped by two of their oldest players, H Sephton for batting and H Newman for bowling. There were some promising youngsters in batting but the bowling strength was weak.

Mystery surrounded the cause of a fire that destroyed an equipment shed belonging to the Cricket Club one Wednesday night in November. The blaze was not discovered until the following morning by which time the wooden building and lean-to shed had been burnt to the ground. Equipment lost included a new Atco motor mower which had been given to the club as a present, new nets newly bought and other cricket gear. The shed was once used as the pavilion but had been in use for many years for storage. It adjoined the new pavilion, and there were signs that a wood fence that ran in front of the two buildings had caused the fire to spread towards the new pavilion. Luckily, the fire extinguished itself before reaching it.

The Annual General Meeting of 1953 saw a financial deficit once again, and the Supporters Club had to help by donating yet more. Once again the 1st XI captain said they were crying out for more young blood in the teams; for several years it had been the elder members who had held together the future of the club. To help further this, the question of professional coaching was brought up at the meeting, but some members thought they had enough decent players in the team to do a spot of home coaching for the younger members. The first item to be replaced after the fire was a new mower. Another important item on the agenda was the treasurer's suggestion that the Club's bank account be transferred from Lloyds to Barclays, to take advantage of the much higher interest rate and lower bank charges.

It wasn't a very good start to the summer game in 1953 for Haverhill when old rivals Sudbury came and conquered. Haverhill's batting seemed to completely collapse, and coupled with a weak bowling attack, led to a defeat for the 1st XI in the opening match. The highest innings was by T Ralling who managed ten runs. However, the 2nd XI brought a little pride back when they were victors over the Sudbury 2nd XI. Bill Sharples, who had a spell with Haverhill when staying in the town, was in the eleven and bowling, but only for two games. It was not much better when the Sunday XI began their fixtures as their visitors West London Indoor Cricket Club eclipsed them, although it was said the Haverhill team was under strength. Newcomers to the Sunday game were the Ralling brothers, D Freeman and L Mayes. Haverhill were also out of touch at Sawston the following week and when the home team put up 187 for 8 declared, Haverhill could only manage 83. What stood out was the club's three teams were all wearing their 'whites' for the first time.

After three losses, the 1st XI recorded their first victory of the season when the Fairey brothers helped to a win over Hoffmanns (G Fairey 58 and H Fairey 39). An excellent spell of bowling from H Farrant also gave the 2nd XI a win at Thurlow; he had figures of 5 wickets for 2 runs on a crumbling wicket that suited his style. However, this was a false dawn for Haverhill's 1st XI when they sunk lower in despair at Braintree and were all out for a paltry score of 27; the batsmen floundered, the top six batsmen failed to score any runs at all. Braintree duly won without losing even one wicket. This was followed up by RAF Stradishall inflicting defeat of the Sunday side. Another poor weekend ensued when the wet weather saw most of the games being called off.

Some pride was restored with a win over Westgate Brewery, and Haverhill players J House, N Pryke, F Rowlinson and R C Poole (who was captain) were selected for the Suffolk Club & Ground in a game at Ipswich. Other notable news during July was an easy win over Coton by the 1st XI and a hat trick by Haverhill's R G Mills versus Bury; Haverhill eventually won the game. New ground was also covered with a trip to play Ipswich Magpies which resulted in a drawn game. Along came August and a bright spot in a somewhat drab season as G Barrett chalked up 100 not out with some top quality batting as Haverhill Sunday XI beat Old Wardians, 197 for 5 declared to 168. At this stage of the season, some fresh faces were appearing for the Haverhill 1st and 2nd teams, A Charles, P Ralling, K Kitchener, E Watts, V Gurteen, M Brown and a young Dennis Levett. Two more week=ends were spent either dodging the showers or sitting in the pavilion to the sound of rain on the roof.

A prestigious match was the game between West Suffolk and the Suffolk County Club & Ground with Haverhill's D Freeman in the County side. Unfortunately, just as this game was approaching a most exciting close, the rain suddenly appeared and brought play to a sudden halt. Rain also interfered with the next week's fixtures. Frank Rowlinson then paved the way with bat and ball in a victory over Westgate Brewery. The Withersfield farmer scored fifty with the bat and then took 7 wickets for 29 runs. In contrasting fortunes the 2nd XI lost their unbeaten record to Castle Hedingham. R C Poole was given the captaincy of the Club & Ground's next fixture versus Culford School but the match ended early for him when he broke his thumb while batting. More locally the Haverhill Scouts took on Gosfield School at the cricket meadow one Wednesday and won by fifteen runs, J Poole hitting 52 for the Scouts.

Haverhill C C then ran into a bad spell of injuries following close on R C Poole's damage. Wicket-keeper Gerald Fairey received a hit in the face when behind the stumps at Braintree, resulting in a fractured jaw. Earlier in the same game, Norman Pryke stopped a rising ball, again with his face, resulting in a black eye but fortunately no broken bones.

As Sudbury had started the season off with a visit to the cricket meadow, it was Haverhill's turn to travel to Sudbury for the last game of a not too good summer performance-wise. However, the result was the same again when the 1st XI came off second best as Sudbury won by 7 wickets. In the 2nd XI's final match, Archie Pannell shone with a spell of bowling which saw him score 67 versus Horseheath whilst E Watts made a whirlwind 70 not out. The Sunday side ended their fixtures with an all-day match against A.V.D.A.L., a team from Welwyn Garden City, starting at 11am and breaking for lunch at 1-15pm, stumps being drawn at 7pm. On the same day a coach load of Haverhill British Legion members and their families spent a very enjoyable afternoon at Hepworth where they played cricket until rain stopped play, and the game was declared a draw, Hepworth BL 26 and Haverhill BL 24 for 6.

Into the Echo newspaper office one day came 89-year-old Jim Dawes of the High Street, Haverhill, in possession of an interesting memento of the cricketing 'Ashes' of 1932-33. It was a medallion inscribed with the victorious England teams names. An old cricket enthusiast, Mr Dawes still talked of the days when he earned 2s 6d a week putting up practice nets every night of the week, pitching stumps and cutting the grass for the Haverhill Cricket Club; the every day practice would have come in very handy for the some of the Haverhill 1st XI teams of 1953 after an inadequate season.

This summer it was the 2nd XI who did very much better then the 1st XI, as they only lost two games and their batsmen had much better averages than those in the 1st XI. In fact, what happened was precisely what the captain R C Poole forecast at the Annual Meeting if no younger players could be urged to become members. The main members of the sides had played very indifferently, and only half a dozen were successful through the summer. In runs scored, the Haverhill 1st XI scored fewer than their opponents, which further showed what better things could be achieved. They also won only six of their twenty-two matches while the 2nd XI were winners in eight of their seventeen games. Gerald Fairey was top of the batting and Pat Kearney the best bowler for the 1st XI while for the 2nd, newcomer Ernie Watts from Clare finished their best batsman with S Nunn close behind, making exactly three hundred runs over the summer. Roy Smith was the busiest bowler for the seconds having sent down 185 over's in total.

The **1954** Annual Meeting was switched to the Bell Hotel from the Rose &

Crown. Amongst its business was the forming of a selection committee to pick the teams each week; before this it had been done rather haphazardly by the captains and anyone else who joined in. The new groundsman for 1954 was Mr Claydon, who then decided not to take the post and an advert was placed in the Echo once again. The next appointed groundsman then took time off without sanction; he had been working under the eye of Mr Jacobs who had been the previous groundsman. This matter was to be investigated to try to solve the sudden muddle.

The 1st XI began with the usual habit of previous years with a defeat in the first game against Westgate Brewery, but quickly put this behind them with victory over Sawston. Their 2nd XI, however, put the Haverhill 2nd XI to the sword imposing on them a heavy defeat 195 to 46. The Sunday XI did better and were not beaten until the fifth game of the summer, by Hitchmans Dairies. Cambridge side Camden were once again visitors on Whit-Monday and took the honours with the victory. Veteran Henry Sephton was still going strong, producing a hat trick when bowling against Sudbury II for the Haverhill 2nd XI. Ray Shanks remembers, *"Henry was a very good bowler and always in a cap, pitched slightly to one side so as not to interfere with his bowling arm. If the batsman hit a boundary Henry would pull his hat on more firmly until it nearly covered one eye. He would always wait for the batsman to get ready before deliberately going back to his mark to turn and bowl; he was never ready first, he made the batsman do that each time."*

The usual 1st XI teams included G Fairey, P Kearney, G Barrett, N Pryke, F Rowlinson, T Ralling, J House, H Fairey, A Thake, W Sephton, R Mills and R C Poole. Amongst the seconds were E Watts, S Nunn, H Sephton, H Farrant, H B Newman, W J Scrivener, P Ralling, D Levett, R Smith, H Willis, M Brown, K Kitchener, E Chapman and D Poole. The batting, which had been not up to standard, suddenly improved but as it did so, stormy weather which caused games to be stopped or not even begun, and prevented the victories the Haverhill teams wanted. That was until the Sunday XI versus Greenford C C. This produced a record making partnership between Harry Farrant (86) and Pat Kearney (58) who put on 146 for the first wicket; this time the match was finished with a Haverhill win. This was helped along by W Sutcliffe taking 4 for 29 in his fifteen over's, of which over half were maidens.

It was back to normal the following week when rain, cricket's greatest enemy, again won its battle with the sport. The 1st XI's fixture with Bury St Edmunds at the cricket meadow started more in hope than anticipation, and at four o'clock the players had to give in and everyone went home. The 2nd XI did not even make the journey to meet Bury's second string as the ground was waterlogged. There was some high scoring in the farmers match on the Monday when the Haverhill National Farmers Union met their Saffron Walden counterparts on the hallowed turf of Fenners in Cambridge. Walden scored 148 to which Haverhill replied with 142 for 6 when stumps were drawn, missing out on a more than certain victory. Most of the N F U from Haverhill included Cricket Club players. On being invited to take part in the Newmarket Festival Cup, Haverhill was successful in the semi-final with a win over Bury St Edmunds. This was a contest = one of the very first - to be decided over twenty over's each. This ended in Haverhill's favour 96-66.

There were many cases in the past when a team waited in vain for the visiting side to turn up, but rarely had there been an occasion when two sides arrived to play the home team. Nevertheless, this actually happened at Haverhill one Saturday afternoon. This was found later to be due to a muddle in confirming fixtures. The Haverhill 1st XI journeyed to Exning and on the way they probably passed the Exning team who believed the match was at Haverhill and arrived in the town. This eventually saw three teams at Haverhill and three at Exning. However, Exning's seconds, who were due to meet St Giles at home, generously allowed Haverhill to play St Giles so Haverhill got a game after all. Meanwhile at Haverhill, the town's 2nd XI were due to play host to Thurlow, which they did. While this was to Haverhill's advantage, poor Exning did not have a game at all.

The Haverhill v St Giles game produced a dramatic finish, when Haverhill hit 152 to which their opponents wanted six runs to win in the last over. John House then bowled out the last batsman with his final delivery so Haverhill were winners by five runs. At the cricket meadow the Haverhill 2nd XI were not so fortunate, as Thurlow's E Bailey ended with figures of 7 for 12 runs as they were skittled out for 37 in reply to the village side's 111.

Haverhill's batsmen struck form over the August Bank Holiday period but sadly, no victories were recorded. F Rowlinson hit 77 as Haverhill declared at 163 for 6, but stubborn resistance from Halstead made it a draw. Then the

Haverhill 2nd XI hit out against the Halstead second team, knocking up a record 229 for 0. Their opponents were never really in the hunt and were struggling when time was called at 137 for 8. After the Sunday XI had their game cut short by the weather, on Monday the 1st XI made 160 for 4 declared, with Bill Sephton top scorer on 76. E W Pryke's XI were stuck on 97 for 6, so no wins but plenty of runs to play with. The next Thursday was the final of the Newmarket Festival Cup. Haverhill lost out in the limited over match 86 - 83 to Newmarket. This was Haverhill Cricket Club's first ever competition match, and a look at what cricket was to look like in the future.

August turned out to be one of the wettest months of the year and many cricket matches were abandoned, and some never got started at all. In the one match for Haverhill Sunday XI, the injury bug struck once again. L E Mayes tried to make a catch close to the batsman at mid-off, but as he just failed to hold the ball with his right hand, his middle finger was split. Then R C Poole again was in the same position and broke a finger making a catch. This was before the Relief Road was built, and any injured cricketer was put into a barrow and wheeled along the Meadows Walk to Mount Road, where a car was waiting to convey him to the doctors. The entrance to the ground at this time was a small gate in that corner of the ground, with a tiny pay-box just inside.

The return match with Camden saw Haverhill suffer defeat by inadequate play. They put up a medium score of 121, which the Camden side quickly passed with the loss of only one wicket. The season drifted to a close with good wins followed straight away by equally meagre defeats. Haverhill lost one of their better players when Pat Kearney decided to move back north to his hometown of Rotherham. He had come to Haverhill as the Haverhill Rovers player-coach in 1949, working at Cleales Garage, but had been playing for Cambridge United the past two seasons as well as cricket for Haverhill.

It was in August that another stalwart of Haverhill Cricket Club passed away suddenly. Alf Thake was a member of several organisations in the town and worked for twenty-seven years at Gurteen's factory. He had been a cricketer and a footballer for his hometown and worked in the background for both sports. He had begun with the Haverhill Cricket 2nd XI when leaving school and soon found himself a regular member of the 1st XI, being described as *"a stubborn batsman and a more than useful change bowler."*

The Echo newspaper carried an early headline in **1955** *"Rosier Outlook For Haverhill Cricket Club."* This was in view of a bright batch of younger players became members of the club this year, and, apart from these additions the playing strength was better than any opening of previous years. Long-serving second eleven player and sometime captain, H B Newman, had put on his pads for the last time. One of the younger players D Levett, was to be the 2nd XI captain and the Sunday XI vice-captain. It was also revealed that the cost of running the club was put at £4-7-6d for each member. Mr Jacobs agreed to be groundsman for a while assisted by Don Mead. They were provided with a new roller, which cost £135, but was able to run for eight hours on two gallons of petrol.

In spite of the new found spirit before the season began, the 1st XI went out and tasted defeat in the opening game at Bury St Edmunds by five wickets 96-74; the batting was disappointing for Haverhill. On the bright side, T Rowan, making his debut took 5 wickets for 24. He followed this by showing his batting ability with 56 versus Graveney C C. For the Sunday XI, R Chapman stood out by scooping up 7 wickets versus West London Invicta who totalled 102, Haverhill making 103 for 5 to triumph. The 2nd XI's batting was better than their seniors and they were victorious over Sudbury II, six players making double figures. Newcomers were P Allen, B Nunn and D Clements.

The batsmen of the Sunday XI continued to show their mettle winning against Northcote 176 for 7 declared to their visitors 136 for 5. D Poole followed his knock of 43 for the 2nd XI with a well-constructed 73 when going in first for the Sunday team. A tied match was fought out at Haverhill when the 1st XI scored 139, the same total as visitors Sawston. This was the nearest they got to a first win as their run of defeats began to lengthen in spite of a summer of consistently brilliant hot weather. They came close once again when the Travellers C C came to town; just a few more minutes would have produced a victory. For this match the young sons of veterans brothers Fairey contributed to the 1st XI's healthy score of 155, D Fairey with 53 and G Fairey 17. The Travellers were still twenty behind with two wickets left when time was called; a moral victory perhaps?

It was last week-end in June that saw the long awaited first win for the Haverhill 1st XI this being over a side chosen by Stoke-by-Clare farmer Julian Watson. Haverhill won by 97 runs with T Rowan the chief batsman, hitting eight boundaries in his knock of 77. Next it was the turn of F Rowlinson to top score with 73 as Haverhill were victorious in their next match versus Newmarket, this time by a smaller margin of four runs. This could not last and it was then the turn of the Haverhill bowlers to suffer at the hands of Sudbury who hit 237 for their win over the town. Veteran H Sephton proved he was still a force when taking 8 wickets for 23 for the 2nd XI, but could not stop them losing the match. F Rowlinson (90 not out) and G Fairey (65 not out) helped Haverhill to 216 for 6 against Braintree, but their opponents held out at 197 for 9 to force a draw. Rowlinson hit 9 fours and 5 sixes in his innings. The 2nd XI completed the day-double over Braintree.

F Rowlinson with 80 not out and T Rowan 70 were amongst the runs again at Bury, and N Pryke 59 and D Poole 54 the same for the Sunday XI in their win over Avdel Sports. Then another newcomer, J Woods from Sturmer, shone in a 2nd XI victory over Bury II with 74 not out. The sparks were certainly flying for a while, and it only remained for the bowlers to get into form to show what Haverhill cricketers could really do. It was becoming an enjoyable first season for T Rowan as he had scored 346 runs for the 1st XI and 380 for the Sunday XI by the time September arrived. In the middle of the month, his knock of 77 for the Sunday XI saw him reach one thousand runs for the season; this had not been achieved for a number of years. The last week in September also saw the debut of another cricketer to assist the town for some seasons to come, R Shanks knocking up 13 not out versus Halstead II. Recalling his early day Ray mused, *"You had to be proposed and seconded to join the Cricket Club. I had just left school and went straight into the 2nd XI as there was no junior side at that time."*

In a summer which was not interrupted by poor weather as in some other years, twenty-one games were played by the 1st XI, two were won and eight lost, including the first seven of the season; the remainder were chalked up a draws. It was Jack Hall who topped the bowling averages; F Rowlinson was top batsman with Rowan as runner-up in both tables. The 2nd XI were victors in five of their fifteen matches and lost seven, while new captain P Ralling was high up in the batting averages as well as the bowling. J Woods from Sturmer joined the club, and proved he was a good bat and bowler.

It was the Sunday XI that started off best in 1956 with a victory over West London Invicta, who were becoming regular visitors to the town. It was a low scoring game with Haverhill easily getting the runs with only one wicket down, 63 - 67 for 1. The team was T Rowan, N Pryke, E Chapman, R Shanks, F Rowlinson, T Ralling, H Farrant, W Sephton, D Levett, R C Poole and L E Mayes, all players who could turn a game to Haverhill's way at any given time. It looked as if Haverhill were going to have a good season, judging from the players available for all three sides. It was also hoped that they would draw more spectators to their matches as admission to was to be waived for this summer to entice more to the Cricket Meadow; a bold move. New sightscreens were also on display.

The 1st XI visited Westgate Brewery for their opening game but saw the Brewery come out on top by 9 wickets as the Haverhill team floundered. However, the 2nd XI captained by P Ralling won their first match helped by a 7 wicket haul by H Farrant. While this was going on, the Sunday team increased their winning run to three matches with some ideal weather over the Whitsun period. Haverhill 1st XI entered June still without the win they demanded, but broke their losing spell with a drawn game at home to Braintree. Two good innings from F Rowlinson, 75 versus Bury St Edmunds and 51 at Braintree, as well as T Rowan's 57 against the Travellers at Cambridge, did not bring victory, but they were now managing to fight out some drawn matches.

Sending a very weak eleven to Bury, they managed just 76 while Bury got 157. Things were beginning to look a mite better as the Haverhill fielding in this match was a credit; as they forced a draw with two 'run outs' and gave away only two byes. The 2nd XI by now had chalked up their fourth victory of the summer. As the Sunday XI went on its merry winning way, W Sephton celebrated his 50th birthday with hitting a half-century in their win over Grange Park. It showed one of the longest serving men in the team still had a keen eye for runs. Next followed a trip to Welwyn Garden City who were bowled out for 51, and Haverhill totalled 216 for 6 (N Pryke 63 D Poole 51). Then came the first reverse for the Sunday XI in the last week of July when Broomfield were the winners.

The unfortunate 1st XI finally broke their duck on 18 August to end one of the longest runs without a win. Their opponents Exning put up 94 for

Haverhill to aim for, which they proceeded to accomplish with the loss of 6 wickets. It was also the first time that Haverhill had bowled out their opponents for under one hundred. Early first-rate bowling by Chapman and Woods paved the way for this victory. In the 2nd XI's game at Exning II, P Ralling scored 93 not out in their total of 165, but after tea the home batsmen were on their way to the wicket when a sudden, prolonged rainstorm put paid to any more cricket on that day.

Three of the newer players were now beginning to show up quite well, R Rogers, T Allright and B Parker. With all three sides getting a win in the same weekend, it was frustrating when the following week all matches were called off as the rain came down once again. One of the shortest games of the season ended with Haverhill 1st XI winning their second successive match. Cambridge Travellers only managed 44 to which Haverhill swept them aside to register 45 for 2. One of the biggest innings came from G Fairey when he hit 85 against traditional rivals Sudbury as Haverhill scored 150 for 3 before declaring. However the match trickled out to another draw when Sudbury put on a 'go slow' reaching 132 for 5 when stumps were drawn.

One of the Haverhill Sunday XI's defeats came versus Harston, but it was in different conditions as a thunderstorm delayed the start, and the two teams agreed to play 25 over's each. Harston got 84 for 9 and then bowled out the Sunday team for one of their lowest totals of 64. The final weekend of the season in September found the 1st XI losing their last match against Halstead, the 2nd XI drawing at Halstead II, and surprisingly the Sunday players being defeated at Bury St Edmunds.

Of the 1st XI's eighteen games 5 were lost and 11 drawn leaving a miserly 2 games won, certainly one of the worst seasons after the high expectations when the season commenced. Unfortunately, F Rowlinson, after seven games and hitting 75, against Bury St Edmunds, had to drop out of the team due to medical advice. Head of the batting was T Rowan, the only batsman to top two hundred runs, while D Fairey was the best of the bowlers. The 2nd XI did a mite better, winning five of its 13 matches with captain P Ralling the best in batting and new youngster B Parker top bowler, his 16 wickets only costing 5.50 each, a first-class effort. As the summer ended the news came that part of the cricket ground would be needed for the new Relief Road for Haverhill, and talks about how this was to be done and how it might affect the club.

Before the **1957** season got under way a lot of work had been done on the actual ground; it had never bot in better shape for a long time. On the playing side, the club had been fortified by the acquisition of several younger players. These included Gerry Beaton, the Haverhill Rovers footballer who was stationed at Stradishal,1 said to be a good fast bowler. Two others who also played football were Ray Moore and John Wade. To offset this, E Chapman was doubtful of playing too much owing to damaging his collarbone when playing rugby. Another feature was the abandoning an entrance fee for spectators in favour of a collection box being taken around the ground. Mr R D Collie was the new General Secretary.

The Sunday XI was first out of the blocks, but in very un-cricket like, cold weather for their game against Camden, with T Ralling as their captain. Unfortunately, they lost this match by 9 wickets. The following week there were still some rain clouds about when the 1st XI started with a score of 119 for 8 versus the Camden side. Rowan and Sephton gave them a good start but the rest of the batsmen were out cheaply, and their opponents made 129 for 1 wicket. Haverhill 2nd XI started with a win over Old Ipswichians 68-67. In the Ipswich side was 66-year-old J Cobbold who was eventually run out for 9 runs. Colin Cracknell recalls another match with the Old Ipswich eleven, *"Myself and Mick Farrant put on one hundred for the first wicket which our opponents did not think much of as they got so frustrated."* The 2nd XI soon saw some young players in their midst including three debutants in the same week, D Green, G Sizer and D Taylor.

The Haverhill Sunday XI had settled down and were putting together some respectable wins. These included including a whitewash over Courtaulds who were bowled out for just 19, Harry Farrant taking 8 of their wickets at a cost of only 4 runs, in reply to Haverhill's 150 for 3 declared. Others coming into the clubs teams were S Gurney, E Bailey and C Cracknell. The latter recalls, *"With no junior side it was straight into the 2nd XI if you were good enough. I remember opening the innings with one of the best Haverhill batsmen Tom Rowan. When Walter Price who was a farmer and the wicket-keeper, had time off for his farm's harvest, I took over the gloves most of the while."* One of the most hard fought matches was against Westgate Brewery, who mostly won against Haverhill, and who had in their midst Cork, the Suffolk captain. One time after they had scored 250, Colin Cracknell and Tom Rowan went in for the Haverhill reply and started well, but when

Norman Pryke arrived with a new bat, Hargreaves of the Brewery said to him, *"Let's have a look at that bat as you will not be in long."* Nevertheless, Norman and Colin proceeded to put on over sixty runs, Colin getting 40 on his debut, and Haverhill won by 4 wickets.

By mid-June the 1st XI were still unbeaten and going well while the Sunday XI recorded a big victory over Simms C C who totalled 38 against Haverhill's 184 for 6, with Rowan 58 and D Poole 56 in fine form. It was Bury St Edmunds who inflicted the first defeat on the 1st XI (Haverhill 87 Bury 88 for 4). Whitsun was a wet weekend, and only one match even started but was abandoned at the Haverhill score of 37 for 3 in the Monday match. One of the tightest endings was the 2nd XI victory over Exning. A well-timed stroke from stand-in wicket-keeper John Green produced three runs from the last ball of the innings. In the 2nd XI victory bowler H Farrant then performed a hat-trick versus an Ipswich side. Haverhill lost out once again to Bury St Edmunds at the cricket meadow in a game that saw over 350 runs scored in the one match.

The hardest game so far for the Sunday XI came against Stowmarket when Haverhill looked like loosing several times in the match, but eventually came out on top. This was the first time for many seasons that these two Suffolk sides had met. A special match was on a Tuesday at the cricket meadow when Suffolk Young Amateurs entertained Hertfordshire Young Amateurs and a good-sized crowd assembled. In reply to Suffolk's 144, the Herts side's innings had only just begun when rain intervened and the game had to be abandoned. The question was then asked, "Are the Sunday side slipping?" as they were struggling at 47 for 8 versus St Ives who had made 121, but the Haverhill team hung on for a draw. Another youngster in the 2nd XI was D Driver who came into his own versus the Saffron Walden II. He had not really seen a place regularly in the side but he had a good knock in this fixture, his 49 runs helping Haverhill to a drawn game that looked lost when he came to the crease. After a long spell being unbeaten since the first game of the summer, the Sunday XI lost its penultimate match when the Pye works side from Cambridge won by 33 runs. Meanwhile the 1st XI was victorious in their last game over Saffron Walden.

The end of season tables of averages saw some improvement all round for the three Haverhill sides, and in the case of all three, more games were won than were lost. Perhaps most significant was the introduction of young and new players this year, which coincided with an upturn in fortune. The 1st XI scored a season's total of 2,334 runs and bowled 642 over's, of which 104 were maidens. The best bowling performance was 7 for 44 against Westgate Brewery by spinner Tom Rowan, who topped the bowling averages for Haverhill. His 32 wickets were the same as young Brian Parker who came second in the list. Gerry Fairey was best batsman for the 1st XI. Veteran H Farrant topped the batting and was second to R Shanks in the bowling table. Young David Pryke also got through 46 over's in his first season. The best record for the club for 1957 was the Sunday XI who chalked up 13 wins in their 18 matches, losing just two, Rowan and Farrant being best batsman and bowler respectively.

With some of their regular players missing for the opening match of the **1958** season, the Haverhill 1st XI visited Saffron Walden and gained a win thanks mainly to the efforts of Frank Rowlinson with the bat and Tom Rowan (5 for 25) with the ball. Walden were all out for 92 as other Haverhill bowlers took charge, seeing B Parker 2 for 9 and local school-teacher J Wigley marking his first appearance with 2 for 8. Rowlinson was also in fine form in the home game against Old Ipswichians scoring 76 not out. The 2nd XI were not such good starters and were bowled out for only 20 runs at Chatteris. However the Sunday XI were proving virtually unstoppable, being unbeaten in their first four games again.

If it was runs the spectators wanted then the Haverhill Sunday XI game against Courtaulds was the one to watch. Opening batsmen Tom Rowan and J Wigley both hit unbeaten centuries in the sides amazing 252 for 1. These two players probably broke all sorts of club records, but the visitors attack was one of the weakest seen for a while. Both Wigley and Rowan played some grand shots; the first named blasted nineteen boundaries, and one straight drive for 6 and retired at 122, while Rowan was not out for 100. Courtaulds were then sent packing for their innings total of 36, only one batsman recording double figures. Dick Poole, not usually played for his bowling, took the last four wickets without conceding any runs. Wigley was proving a fine player and followed his 100 with 85 for the Sunday XI versus Stanstead, and R Shanks made a maiden fifty for the 2nd XI against Bury St Edmunds II.

HAVERHILL SUNDAY XI.

T. Rowan not out	100
J. Wigley retired	122
R. Liston b Osbourne	1
B. Parker not out	25
Extras	4
For 1 wkt. (decld.)	252

COURTAULDS (Halstead)

P. Darkling b Shanks	1
R. Hardy c Parker b Sephton	8
D. Osbourne c Liston b Sephton	8
N. Plumb b Shanks	2
G. Hardy c Rowan b Sephton	12
E. Thompson c Ralling b Poole	2
B. Page c Driver b Liston	2
J. Tarbin c Liston b Poole	1
R. Charrington b Poole	0
C Runtle b Poole	0
L. Phillips not out	0
	36

It was in June that it was announced that a new Relief Road was to be constructed to help take away the increasing volume of traffic from the High Street and Queen Street, which were at the time part of the main road which passed through Haverhill. This new road was to run from Lordscroft Lane to Hamlet Green; this meant that the new road would slice off 3,370 square yards from the cricket enclosure. This ground encroachment by the new highway required a meeting with the County Planning Officer to set out the front of the cricket ground to the Relief Road to the best advantage. John

Boardman was appointed chartered surveyor to negotiate with the district valuer, and Mr William Morris (solicitor)was asked to provide legal advice for the club. The Cricket Club saw this as an opportunity to extend their premises to include a new indoor bowling green and larger car park. Much needed attention was given to the boiling arrangements for the ladies to provide the teas.

Before anything else could happen, the town was hit on 27 June with the biggest flooding it had experienced for over fifty years. This included the Meadows, which were always the first to be covered with water in such times, as well as the cricket ground, which resembled a large lake. The town centre was cut off from the early morning as the flooding reached from Withersfield Road to the Market Hill with the shopkeepers striving to keep their premises free from the water. Even when it subsided there was much mopping up to be done and the Cricket Club was left with a rather large bill for damage repairs which it submitted to the Flood Fund Committee.

After their enforced break from playing Haverhill 1st XI scored a last gasp victory over Braintree, who made 70 runs in a start delayed by rain. It was the last ball of the last over with both teams level, the ball went past Haverhill batsman M Ridsdall-Smith, and Brian Parker saw the opportunity and scampered home for the winning run. It was J Wigley with 89 who helped the 1st XI to a revenge win over Sawston, Haverhill's 201 for 7 declared was too big a mountain for the village side who only scored 144. In mid-July the 2nd XI were still looking for their first win but the Sunday XI marched steadily onwards. The make-up of the teams had settled down to the 1st XI; T Rowan, J Wigley, R Shanks, N Pryke, G Fairey, F Rowlinson, D Taylor, W Price, D Pryke, C Cracknell and R C Poole. The 2nd XI included R Rogers, B Haylock, H Farrant, M Mayes, K Kitchener, B Harding, W J Scrivener, D Driver, C Farrant, M Farrant, H Sephton, E Bailey, R Robinson and C Hulyer. Recalling some of his games Colin Cracknell remembered *"One Wednesday Mr Ernie Pryke brought a team to Haverhill which included Peter Smith, the Essex and England player. Another game versus Old Ipswichians Mick Farrant and myself put on 100 for the first wicket. Ted Phillips, the Ipswich Town footballer, was their fast bowler and kept getting more frustrated; he used to come down the wicket after he had bowled and glare at the batsmen. My highest score was about sixty, I never reached a hundred."*

After Haverhill's win in the last over in a previous match, the roles were reversed against Saffron Walden who obtained their victory with two balls remaining, Haverhill 90 Walden 91 for 9. In the 2nd XI fixture with Saffron Walden II, it was 14 year-old Mick Farrant who shone, first with the bat (22), then as a bowler (3-44) as the future looked respectable for the town's cricketers. Younger players were to be seen in the 2nd XI, D Green, M Ashby and P Thake. The 1st XI scored one of their best victories of the season when visiting Cambridge Travellers. With only three minutes to spare, they got 182 for 6 to overtake their opponents 179. Big scores from Rowan (61) and G Fairey (62) helped Haverhill along and after they departed, it was left to farmer Price and young Shanks to scamper the remaining runs required. There seemed to be several close endings to games this summer.

When Tom Rowan's brother J Rowan brought an eleven to Haverhill to play the Sunday XI, they had with them a celebrity in E W Clarke, the ex-England and Northants fast bowler. His son was in the Rowan's XI, and he came with the team from St Ives where he kept a public house. He was invited into the pavilion to have tea with the players and kept everyone interested with reminiscences of his playing days. To wind up the season, the 1st XI lost versus Halstead while the 2nd XI won against Halstead II in a match where youngsters Shanks (50) and D Pryke (24no) outscored their more senior team-mates.

During a quite wet summer there were fewer matches washed-out than one would expect, as the twenty matches played by the 1st XI had them winning seven and losing the same number. This was after beating Saffron Walden in their first match, then going seven more games without another victory. The 2nd XI won just two games out of the sixteen played, while the Sunday XI were the most successful and had seven victories and seven draws, losing just four. The club's best bowling performance was Brian Parker's 7 for 39 against Westgate Brewery.

For most of the 1950's the old pavilion was lit only by calor gas. After some matches, some members would sit talking and have a few drinks as it got dark. The lights would fade as the gas ran low, then it was down to one flickering light and all went home when this finally gave out. In the old pavilion was a long rail along one wall with special grooves in to hold the bats, and a metal tray underneath which held linseed oil to soak the bats. Ray

Shanks also recalls, *"At first it was only the top cricketers in Haverhill who had their own bats and the others mostly used the club's bats which were stored in the pavilion; these were good and bad. If you wanted a good bat you had to grab it early on and hide it round the back of the pavilion and bring it out when it was your turn to bat."*

Discussions continued on how the new road along the Meadows was to affect the cricket ground. There were to be five trees felled, three more marked for felling if needed and only two trees to be left. The three chestnut trees which were felled to make way for the road were replaced by six young trees, and a plastic coated chain-ling fence was to be erected at that end of the ground. It was planned to remove the ancient corrugated fence and plant a hawthorn hedge. The type of fence next to the new road created some comment with the view that it must be total enclosure, otherwise they could not charge an admission fee to attend the games. At first, it was to be a six foot wood fence, but it was finally agreed that a seven-foot oak close-boarded fence was the solution. The ramshackle old toilets were also pulled down, some saying "not before time." As well as all these alterations, the main gas pipes were laid for 180 yards under the trees near the old entrance to the cricket ground; this part of the grass verge was to be looked after by the Eastern Gas Board.

The new surrounds of the cricket meadow lapped over into **1959** and a meeting in February at the Bell Hotel mulled over several items to be redressed. These were;
(1) Erect a seven foot high board fence using old material from the Cricket Club.
(2) Leave five of the chestnut trees standing (two inside and three outside the new fence) but remove them if they became dangerous
(3) Provide a new access (subject to planning permission)
(4) Remove and re-site present buildings and plant new trees.
(5) Enclose ground before the start of 1959 season.
(6) Provide a pedestrian access to ground at Meeting Walk corner
At the same time, a cheque for £500 was handed to the Cricket Club from the Supporters Club. The Supporters Club was for both football (Rovers) and the Cricket Club; £100 was transferred from Rovers to the Haverhill Cricket Club. However, there was some gloom from the Supporters Club as they had

TOP; (16) Sunday XI 1960. Back-D Pryke, ? , M Farrant, D Poole, W Sephton, A Waters. Front- R Shanks, T Rowan, T Ralling, N Pryke, J Wigley, B Parker. Front- D Greea.
BOTTOM; (17) Pavilion destroyed by fire in 1960.

TOP; (18) Opening of the new kitchen in 1962.
BOTTOM; (19) 1961 XI (100 years old) Back- R Collie, E Chapman, E Bailey, D Pryke, T Rowan, B Parker, R Shanks, A Missen, A Waters: Front- G Fairey, T Rowan, R C Poole, J Wigley, F Rowlinson, N Pryke:

TOP & BOTTOM (20) (21) 1968 Floods cover the cricket ground

(22) Suffolk v Essex II at Haverhill 1966. B Lane of Suffolk walks off, behind him are Keith Boyce of Essex and Pritchard a Cambridge Blue

(23) Colin Rutherford the Suffolk batsman in the same match

(24) Six-a-Side Haverhill team (winners 1975)

TOP; (25) The New Pavilion 2005
BOTTOM (26) Haverhill Academy side 2008

no promoter for the weekly tickets and a new scheme was to operate from November. Fortunately, Bert Jobson volunteered to be the new promoter, and asked for 50 people to distribute twenty tickets each weekly.

It was win, lose and draw for the teams on the first weekend of the season. The Sunday XI started where they had left off from the previous campaign with a victory over annual visitors West London Invicta, while the 1st XI fought out a drawn game against Saffron Walden; the 2nd XI were the losers versus Chatteris. In helping the Sunday players to a second successive win over Graveney Cricket Club, J Wigley smashed 96 not out and R Shanks was also not out at 50 in their 182 for 2. This big innings was dwarfed when P Ralling hit 111 for the Haverhill 2nd XI versus Sawston II. Not to be outdone, a hat trick by bowler T Rowan on the Sunday helped extend the Sunday team's proficient start to the summer.

A dismal batting failure largely accounted for Haverhill's second defeat of the season at Braintree, where they were beaten by 62 runs. In reply to the home team's 136, the 1st XI could only yield 74, practically half of these came from one batsman, J Wigley (35). Young David Pryke struck three good blows for Haverhill by claiming three wickets early on but it was ultimately the batsmen who left their form behind. The Sunday players were thwarted by a last wicket stand by Cambridge Travellers who were on the brink at 102 for 9 at the close; Haverhill had posted 213 for 5 in their innings, with the two openers, Wigley and Rowan, making 153 of these between them. In addition, a stubborn tail end stopped the 1st XI from registering their first victory of the summer when the Old Ipswichians chased a total of 139. With a quarter of an hour to go, their last two batsmen came together, shut up shop and saw their team to a drawn game; they had reached 113. This side always brought their own flag with them and it was flown beside the Haverhill flag while they were in town.

After a free weekend due to stormy weather, the Sunday XI surrendered their unbeaten tag with 152 to 103 to visitors Stansted. The inability to get the visitors' opening bat Scott out was the main cause of the loss, he made 70. A blank Saturday in the fixture list was filled when Haverhill cricketers faced each other, the result being a resounding victory for R C Poole's XI over T Rowan's XI, 97 to 58. A four-wicket win over Bury St Edmunds gave Haverhill their second victory of the season on their home ground. The triumph over the star-studded Bury eleven was achieved by some good all-round play where six of the Haverhill batsmen hit double figures in reaching the Bury 147, the game ending at 148 for 6. When Bury's opening batsman E Goodenough was out for two, the comics in the crowd had a field day! This was Bury's first defeat of the season. Unfortunately the Haverhill 2nd XI could not emulate their seniors and lost to Bury St Edmunds II by 99 to 61.

The Sunday XI was severely tested when they had to hold on to their falling wickets to come out with a draw against the Ipswich & East Suffolk side. Some wet days lost the Haverhill teams chances to chalk up further victories for most of July; this included the 2nd XI versus Halstead II. The Haverhill batsmen had made 242 for 9 before declaring, Dick Poole contributing 92 of these, and Halstead were left at 46 for 3 when the heavens opened to quash any more play.

In August, the Ground Sub-Committee met at the cricket ground to decide the means of disposal of surplus fencing, to survey flood damage to the bowling green, and to determine what repairs were needed. The damaged fence had to be strengthened and Mr Fairey said he would provide the labour. Some posts were rotten but they could re-use some of the old oak posts, and the surplus fencing was sold. The club also faced the cost of repairing their machinery, had only £18 at this time, and they still owed £45 for the concrete edging to the bowling green and unpaid wages to the groundsman.

Journeying to Cambridge to meet the Travellers Cricket Club, Haverhill were on the end of their biggest defeat of the summer, losing by eight wickets. When five of their side were back in the pavilion, Haverhill looked like a low score, but a rescue stand by Norman Pryke (37) and Derek Taylor (29) pushed the score along and David Pryke kept the tail wagging with a useful 19, which included the only six hit of the match. The Travellers were always in control and reached the Haverhill target of 161 with six minutes left of the allotted time. On the same day, the 2nd XI lost by six wickets to Chatteris; not a good day's cricket for the town. It is of interest to note that in the successful Sunday side were J Woods, R Shanks, B Harding, B Parker, D Pryke and M Farrant, quite a sprinkling of youngsters who the Cricket Club was at last beginning to recognise as the future of Haverhill cricket.

Haverhill made a second visit to Cambridge to take on Camden on the

Downing College ground, and topped two hundred for the first time this year, getting the better of an eventually drawn game. Batting well down the list, they made 203 for 7 declared; Shanks with 47 was supported by five other batsmen scoring in their twenties. Camden replied with 157 for 8 in the same number of over's which represented a slower rate of scoring. Meanwhile for the Sunday side, Tom Rowan hit 100 before retiring against Cambridge Granta. This match saw A V Gurteen making an appearance for the Haverhill XI. Brian Parker also notched up his highest score of the summer for the Sunday team and included 11 fours and 3 sixes in his 86, well supported by Derek Taylor with a score of 49.

The 1959 season will not stand out as one of the successful ones of recent years. Of its twenty-two matches the 1st XI managed to win just two, although they were in commanding positions in some of the drawn encounters. Individual performances with the bat ranked high, however, with Tom Rowan and John Wigley scoring over one thousand runs for the Saturday and Sunday sides. Then there was the blossoming of Brian Parker, Ray Shanks and David Pryke, three very promising all-rounders. Veteran Frank Rowlinson continued to bat as well as ever and was a close second to Rowan in the averages. While Parker was head of the bowling table it was left-hander Eric Bailey who took on most of the bowling, sending down 264 over's. Five games were won by the 2nd XI out of eighteen played, four were drawn and the rest lost. Dennis Levett put up the best bowling figures for the whole club when he recorded 8 wickets for 7 runs against Exning. Played twenty, won fourteen, drawn five and lost one was the satisfactory record of the clubs Sunday XI who had now lost only one game in two seasons. Again Wigley, Rowan and Parker were leading the lists in scoring and taking wickets.

With the Hamlet Croft being levelled, Haverhill Rovers were playing their matches on the open Recreation Ground, and from this came a request from the football club to use the enclosed cricket field for a County Cup match in October. The Cricket Committee met this with a direct refusal. However when the Young Farmers Hockey Club requested the use of the ground, this was agreed, but not to touch the cricket square. Then the Gala Association asked to use the ground for the 1960 Gala, but this was refused as the ground might be damaged. They asked again at the next meeting but were again refused.

The Annual Meeting early in 1960 held at the Ex-Servicemen's Club, reported a 'golden summer' that is for the weather experienced, not for the town's cricketers who had had better seasons. New players had included John Woods and Eric Bailey. On the non-playing front, the cash flow was still precarious. A one-shilling match fee was proposed for all three teams. Forty-two members attended the AGM and they stood in memory of lost players, including groundsman George Coote who had been in this post for many years. The present groundsman Len Jacobs was in ill health and could not carry on.

For the first matches of the season, the Saturday side opposed Saffron Walden but could only manage 122 against their opponents' 207, while the Sunday XI scored 100 for 8 versus Camden who had totalled 197 to force a draw. The following Sunday saw West London Invicta at the cricket ground where Haverhill were the victors 200-4 against 164. J Wigley struck good form early in the season with 103 and T Rowan with 50. Early June saw the 2nd XI come out on top against Braintree II who could only manage 12 not out. This was thought to be the lowest score by any side on the cricket ground. The Haverhill bowlers to do the damage were Levett 5 for 6 runs and Derek Taylor 5 for 4 runs. Meanwhile the Sunday XI continued on their merry way and were still unbeaten this season.

One of the 2nd XI's best wins was at Bury St Edmunds 96 to 95, M Farrant getting 46 and G Barrett 32 not out. In the Sunday match versus Hoffmanns, B Parker and W Sephton put on 115 runs to win the game, Parker plundering two sixes and ten boundaries. The 1st XI unfortunately went down in one of their heaviest defeats to Sawston by nine wickets. Before the match against Exning, both teams stood in silence in memory of Mr H Gurteen, the club's president, who had passed away. He was also a life member and had been supporting the cricket club for many years.

At the final reckoning for the season, the Sunday XI upheld the good form they had produced over the past three summers and once again were unbeaten for the whole season. However, they drew more games than usual this year. Club finances were still in a sorry state, both Club and Supporters were overdrawn and some accounts were still to be paid. A sub-committee was formed to watch this. For the last two or three years the pavilion had looked a mite drab and needed painting. However, to help save money there were plenty of volunteers to do this if the paint was bought in the first place. A proposal to change the name to Haverhill Cricket & Bowls Club was not followed up.

Although Haverhill Cricket Club looked forward to one of the happiest seasons in its history, **1961** being the club's centenary year, a very gloomy shadow was cast at the Annual Meeting when the position regarding finance was discussed. The balance sheet presented by the treasurer, Mr R D D Collie, showed a closing overdraft at the bank of £91 7s 9d, compared with an opening credit balance of £5 13s. This was in spite of this year being the club's "cheapest" season and a £100 donation from their Supporters Club. *"With our expenses at over £400 we must raise a minimum of £200 plus subscriptions and fees,"* said Mr Collie. He called for greater effort all round in trying to restore the finances of the club. He said this year was one occasion that their Supporters Club did not have enough in the 'kitty' to cover their overdraft. After a long discussion a new Fund-Raising sub committee was formed.

At the opening of the meeting, the chairman Mr R C Poole had asked the company to stand in memory of Mr Horace Gurteen, their late President. "He perhaps has done more than any other individual for cricket in Haverhill" commented the chairman. What was needed, however, were fresh faces on the committee, with younger members preferred. In an all-out effort to raise funds, a jumble sale was planned plus a Derby draw (horse-racing) competition and weekly stopwatch cards, and to bring the centenary year to a close, a Grand Christmas Draw; not too exciting but necessary.

A project was put in place to install a bar in the pavilion or bar/kitchen, and to this end, £100 was received from the estate of the late Horace Gurteen via his daughter Mrs Bradford. For the kitchen extension, J Chapman and R Shanks undertook the project as soon as planning permission was granted. This kitchen was opened officially opened before the game versus Cambridge YMCA. Further to this, a new table was provided in the pavilion so both teams could sit down to tea, while a brand new flag fluttered from the flagpole. It was noticed that the boundary line next to the pavilion was unfenced so anyone could enter the ground that way, so a fence was hastily built before the season began.

The bowls section was still doing fine said the captain Mr O G Pampling, and of their seventeen games, only five were lost with J Chapman winning the singles championship and B Jobson and C H Benton the pair's champions. Nevertheless, there was some regretful news from the Bowls section when the Suffolk Association declared their bowls green unsuitable for County competitions, so they had to play tournaments away from home. The green needed to be levelled and bare patches re-sown. To see the green half levelled would cost £75 so volunteer labour was sought to attend to this, together with applying for a grant from the Playing Fields Association. Meanwhile, the Bowls Club had been given permission to use Birdbrook Green.

The centenary year celebrations included a cricketing week of nine matches starting at Whitsun when visiting teams from Suffolk, Essex and Cambridgeshire came to town to oppose Haverhill CC. A dinner and ball was also planned. The new President elected was Mrs Jane Ann Brandford the daughter of the late Mr H Gurteen. The year was greatly affected by the bad weather and some matches had taken place when the ground was hardly fit to play on. Although the team broke even, it was the bowling that needed the most strengthening. Nevertheless, there were some younger players now starting to come through. Top of the batting averages was Tom Rowan and the bowling, David Pryke. For the second eleven, Dick Poole topped the batting with Dennis Levett the best bowler. During this season, two Haverhill players were selected to play for Suffolk Club & Ground for a match at Felixstowe on Sunday 16 July.

The **1962** summer began with a bang when all three Haverhill teams won their first matches, the 1st XI putting it across old rivals Sudbury, rattling up 153 and bowling their opponents out for 89. Ray Shanks chalked up an impressive bowling performance with 9 wickets for 35 runs. Haverhill 2nd XI won against Hedingham 141 to 78, and the Sunday XI were winners over Felixstowe, the seaside team's total of 94 all out was not enough as Haverhill posted 181 for 4. For the 1st XI, a narrow defeat was then followed by three more straight wins versus College Servants, Clacton when Tom Rowan hit a chanceless 80, and Travellers (Cambridge). Haverhill Sunday were also carrying on their exceptional form of the previous few seasons.

Off the field, Norman Pryke took over as the club's secretary from T

Rowan and Mr Hubert Ince was elected as the groundsman. The Haverhill Cricket Social Club was formed with the main task of running a licensed bar; it was planned to apply for the licence at the next magistrates court. As more cars were seen at the cricket ground, it was agreed that the slice of rough ground near the bowling green be used as a temporary car park until a more permanent one was completed.

With the licensed bar up and running, it soon proved its worth when a profit of £39 was made in the first four weeks. However, a suggestion of putting in some amusement machines in the pavilion was a step too far. The Social Club also planned to hold jumble sale, a Derby draw, and to promote some stopwatch weekly tickets. The latter proved very popular and within a couple of months brought in £122-17-5d. A rotary scythe was bought for £15 for the new groundsman, and the Young Farmers Hockey Club were to play their games on the cricket field, but as far from the cricket square as possible.

All three Haverhill sides were settling down to provide the supporters with a good feeling for the season. J Wigley (87) and M Farrant (80) saw the Sunday side make 217 for 8, versus Ipswich & East Suffolk. They could not manage a fight back and were 120 for 9 at the close of play, having held out for a precarious draw. Young Mick Farrant was proving a cricket gem and proceeded to follow this up with 90 against Harston and best of all, 103 not out against Cambridge YMCA. The 2nd XI were proving much stronger than the year before and some close matches were seen at home and away. A further high inning came from Tom Rowan with 98 at Halstead, but in reply to Halstead's 235 for 8, Haverhill were 230 for six when the game ended as a draw. A rare defeat came the Sunday side's way when they were bowled out for 85 versus Hatfield Estate who overtook this total with ease, in one of just a few away games on Sundays. This shocked the Sunday XI and they then lost the next game by one of their largest margins against Sawston, going down by 115 runs. Suffolk County Young Amateurs also played a match at Haverhill versus Huntingdonshire Y A on a Monday in August. The headmaster of the Haverhill Secondary School was also given permission for a School versus Parents match, to be held on the cricket ground.

To give the Haverhill cricket teams a better look the Haverhill Urban District Council were approached to see if they would be agreeable to the town badge appearing on the club's blazers and caps; this was duly given. An approach was also made to a local gent's outfitter to supply a number of new blazers for the club. Major and Mrs Bradford handed a donation of £150 to the club, towards the proposed extension of the pavilion, New cupboards and tables were bought for the pavilion, these made by Ray Shanks. The HUDC had a few pre-fab houses for sale at reasonable prices, and the Bowling Committee was looking into buying one to use as their pavilion at the cricket ground. To enable work on the bowling green to carry on, a grant from the Playing Fields Association was being sought.

As the season drew to an end two matches were lost and two abandoned as the result of rain, an exception in an otherwise very warm summer. Tom Rowan was again top of batting and bowling for the 1st XI, Dick Poole (batting) and Dennis Levett (bowling) for the 2nd XI while the Sunday XI saw Tom Rowan (batting) and Eric Bailey (bowling) as their top of the averages. On the batting side, John Wigley scored over one thousand runs through the season. New groundsman Hubert Ince had prepared excellent wickets.

A sad occasion occurred in the middle of this season when popular Haverhill cricketer Frank Rowlinson, who farmed Church Farm in Withersfield, suddenly passed away on his 49th birthday. He had been playing his favourite sport - cricket - only the day before his death, and as usual hit a six in his last innings. The family of the late F E Rowlinson wished to donate a clock for the pavilion in his memory, and the Haverhill Gala Committee also donated £60 towards its purchase.

There was an unusually large attendance at the **1963** Annual Meeting when they started by celebrating Frank Rowlinson's twenty-five years with the club, a fine sportsman. Ray Shanks was elected captain of the first eleven and Brian Haylock the same post for the second team. Mr R C Poole had stepped down as the club captain after holding this honour since 1945, commenting that he had seen the club through tough times, but now some good young players and good times lay ahead. Two important items were concerning finance. It was noted that the Fund Raising Committee had handed over £186-3-8d to the cricket club in the past year. A letter was received from the Haverhill Urban District Council giving the club fifty per cent reduction in their rates for the next five years; two pieces of welcome news.

To bring in some extra finance the fee for hiring the cricket ground by outside organisations was set at £2-2-0d. Other items of interest were the forming of a Ladies Section of the Bowls Club and a request from the Headmaster of the Modern Secondary School for John Wigley to coach the school cricket team once a week, which he agreed to do. On the other hand, Mr E Rising complained because a member had damaged the fence of his meadow when retrieving a lost ball.

The 1963 season was marred for the first eleven by poor weather that caused a quarter of the fixtures to be cancelled without a ball being bowled. Despite the cancellations' and a feeble start in which three of the first four games were lost, the team came into form and were unbeaten for the remainder of the season. The records showed eighteen matches played, six were won, three lost and nine were drawn. However, in five of the drawn games Haverhill were close to victory, only to be thwarted by the weather or the clock, but in the other two they were struggling to avoid defeat. The losses came against Bury St Edmunds, Sawston and Braintree. The highest score for Haverhill was 195 for 8 at Sudbury.

Altogether, there were 2,514 runs scored by the first team with the highest individual score coming from Brian Parker who hit 90 against Sudbury. The best bowling performance was put up by Ray Shanks on Whit Monday when he captured 6 Camden wickets for just 28 runs. The Haverhill second eleven played thirteen matches of which they were winners of four and losers of six, the other three were drawn. The Sunday XI played only fifteen matches and of these five were won, seven drawn and three lost. The highest score was 205 for 2 versus Achilles when Mick Farrant scored a fine 117. Ray Shanks showed the first-rate figures of 8 for 46 bowling against Stowmarket. In the list of averages, T Rowan was top of batting and R Shanks bowling for the first eleven, and for the seconds Dick Poole (batting) and D Levett (bowling), the latter for the third year in succession. The Sunday team showed the same two players topping the averages as they had done for the first team.

Still with a low bank balance, the Fund Raising Committee handed over £190, and the Haverhill Cricket Club Social Club gave £40 it had raised. Mr Fred Fuller's 'Aged & Youth 'Week applied to play a celebrity cricket match on the cricket meadow during this week but the application was refused.

Meanwhile, the ground secretary had lent the mower and roller to the Rovers Football Club. The question of making the Cricket Club a limited company was discussed throughout the 1964 season, but this was not pursued at that time. Subscriptions were reviewed resulting in vice-presidents £1-10s, players £2, non-playing £1, juniors 10s. John Wigley was moving from the town so he resigned as captain and from the committee. Mr R D Collie stepped down as treasurer and the chairman presented him with a table lighter for all his hard work from 1951-64. Mr M Farrant was elected treasurer.

At the March 1965 Annual General Meeting the Fund Raising Committee and Haverhill Cricket Club Supporters Club made donations, and there was a grant from the Department of Education for £144. It was discovered that the veranda floor of the pavilion was broken and badly damaged. Mick Farrant had started to repair this and some other tradesmen were called in to help. On the ground itself, the outfield was cut and made much better, and the club continued to enlist help of the Boy Scouts to collect stones during bob-a-job week. The new Bowls Pavilion and the upgraded green were planned to be officially opened in May 1966. West Suffolk County Council gave a grant of £50 towards re-laying bowls green. The Bowls Pavilion insurance cover was increased to £2,000.The HUDC had revealed plans to lay new sewer pipes inside the cricket ground on the south side. The Cricket Club made known its views to resist to the maximum the laying of sewer pipes through the ground, and Mr W Mason was to keep an eye on developments.

A visit to long time opponents Sawston opened Haverhill's season and resulted in Haverhill holding on grimly at the end for a draw. Sawston made 185 for 5 before declaring its innings closed, while Haverhill stood at 141 for 9 when time was called. Next they lost a low scoring game at Braintree 75-71. The Sunday XI were quickly into their winning ways when they visited Stanstead to win by eight wickets (157-158 for 2), Mick Farrant hitting a magnificent 103 not out. The 2nd XI followed suit with a victory over Braintree II, D Green making 46 not out, to be the highest scorer. Abington became one of the few teams to stop the Haverhill Sunday XI winning, and had Haverhill struggling on 113 for 9 in reply to the villagers' total of 117.

The majority of games were destined to be draws as clubs began to shut up shop when they looked in danger of being defeated, Haverhill doing the same in particular matches. One match was even a tie, Haverhill 2nd XI and Braintree II both being bowled out for the low score of 68, P Cartwright being Haverhill's best bowler with 5 for 25. The 2nd XI then provided two exceptional performances with the ball, D Debenham taking two wickets for no runs and B Haylock one wicket for no runs in the game versus Exning, II; Haverhill winning of course. David Pryke also put in a fine show for the 1st XI against Broomfield when he captured 5 wickets for 19 as they won by 141 runs. M Farrant was chasing the elusive 1,000 in a season when they visited Felixstowe but he was not out on 41 when rain stopped the game.

A letter was received by the Cricket Club asking, "Would Haverhill CC be willing to make their ground available for a Suffolk County Club match versus the Essex second eleven on 22 July?." The club were pleased to say yes to this, as they realised they were getting some recognition from the officials at the top of Suffolk County Cricket. The new pavilion clock was installed on September 1965. Mr James of Saffron Walden supplied the clock, and the pavilion was used for a party celebrating Michael Farrant's 21st birthday. Once again, the Haverhill Hockey Club requested use of ground and pavilion for a 30 October match and from then onwards for their season; they were allowed as before but were asked to keep well away from the cricket square. This was agreed at £1-1-0 per match.

With two more important innings of 55 not out and 78 in the final game of the summer, Mick Farrant wound up his exceptional season by topping one thousand runs. These had been made in the Haverhill 1st XI and the Sunday XI, often playing two games each weekend. No surprise that he was top of the batting averages with an average of 40 each match. Dennis Levett was top of the 2nd XI batting.

During **1966,** the Fund Raising Committee had lapsed considerably. The club had to look into this as this committee organised the main fund raising activities. The bar takings had also dropped alarmingly, with only £70 profit made. On top of this, a break in at the ground had seen a further £14 being spirited away. On the back of seeing the youngest teams being put out this year, a Colts XI was formed with Mick Farrant in control of this new venture. On 4 May, the Bowls Section opened their new ground . Some work on the sewers next to the ground was ongoing but this was nearly finished before the matches started for the summer and did not disturb the cricket matches.

For this season, David Pryke was appointed first eleven captain with Mick Farrant his second in command; Bill Easey was second team captain and Dennis Levett vice-captain. Ray Shanks and Colin Cracknell filled the posts for the Sunday team. Other positions included Norman Pryke as General Secretary and Brian Parker the Match Secretary. On the other side, the club saw the retirement of the stalwart Tim Ralling as a playing member.

Statistically the Haverhill first eleven did not come out too well in the 1966 season, winning only, three of their nineteen matches. On the other hand, only six were lost, nine ended as drawn games and one was abandoned. Highest total was 188 for 7 versus Braintree. R Shanks finished top of the batting with an average of 23.5. The second eleven's record was just as poor as their seniors and saw only two games won out of the sixteen played, nine being lost and two ending as draws. In addition, one match was tied and two abandoned. Bill Easy topped the batting and P Gilbert the bowling. The Sunday eleven fared just a badly being the victors in one solitary match against Abington, but on the other hand they only lost two games. Nine were drawn and one abandoned because of bad weather. M Farrant topped the averages with his batting rattling up 369 runs, and a top score of 91 not out versus Hoffmans. In bowling, Eric Bailey was the best.

For the bulk of the season the 1st XI consisted of D Pryke, M Farrant, C Hulyer, D Debenham, B Parker, D Poole, E Bailey, C Hill, R Davidson, P Ralling and R Shanks; a fair sprinkling of youth and experience. The 2nd XI included W Easey, D Levett, B Haylock, P Gilbert, N Ward, I Porter, R Lamb, J Blythe, T Stokes, P Scott and R Beavis.

It was not a very good summer as all three Haverhill teams won a meagre six matches among them out of the forty-eight played. If this were not enough, after the playing season had ended, vandals damaged the shed where the mower and other equipment was stored, but had not been able to get inside; it was another expense however. The Suffolk Club & Ground XI were given the go ahead to stage a match versus Norfolk in the near future, and to this end, more trees were planted around the cricket ground. The club had now built a small building for Ladies and Gents toilets.

Eager to start **1967** after some satisfactory sessions in the nets, Haverhill went out and gained a victory in their first match at home to Ipswich St Pauls. After scoring a modest 117, Haverhill skittled their opponents out for 54. They quickly followed this on Whit Monday with another win 86-77 over Camden. During June one game was lost and the others won. The 2nd XI performance was not so good as they settled into a pattern of winning one week and then losing the next, but at least they were not finishing second best in all their games. It was proving a summer of lower scores than usual until the game against Stowmarket, which saw Haverhill total 234 for 6 declared. Towards this score P Ralling got 80. Stowmarket could only manage 166 in reply.

One week-end in July all three Haverhill sides lost, the 1st XI to Cambridge Grasshoppers, the 2nd XI to Poslingford and even the Sunday XI going down to Ipswich & East Suffolk. However, they did record victories over long-time rivals Sudbury and Halstead. The return game against Grasshoppers was delayed by rain, but in a shorter match, Haverhill won 157-120. Brian Parker's 95 versus Camden was not enough to force a win as their opponents hung on to draw the contest. It was a late end to the season as on 28 September both sides met Halstead. The 1st XI won their match 140 to 135, and the 2nd XI were beaten 120 to 103.

After some anxiety once more on the financial side of the Cricket Club and over a plan to make sure all members paid their way, the **1968** season started badly when Haverhill lost to Bury St Edmunds by 8 wickets. Haverhill's total of 157 was passed by Bury with just two wickets down. When Haverhill made 201 for 9 against Westgate Brewery and things were looking up, the rain stopped their opponents from taking their part at the wicket. The match versus Littleport saw R Shanks cheated out of a possible century when the rain caused the game to be abandoned when he stood at 96 not out.

Came the well documented 'Haverhill Floods' of 1968 and the cricket pitch and the bowls green were completely covered with water. It couldn't get away on the bowling rinks as these were in a shallow dip, so Halliburton's brought one of their pumps (it was also a test for these new large pumps) and although they could not get right into the ground as the gateway was too small, they pumped the bowls green free of water. It was sent flowing speedily down the new road (Relief Road) and Hamlet Road. To help get the water off the cricket pitch a trench was dug to the west of the ground to help it drain away by itself.

SUFFOLK COUNTY CRICKET CLUB

Telephone: FELIXSTOWE 2588   15 PRIORY ROAD
                                                                          FELIXSTOWE

DEAR Farrant

You have been selected to represent ~~The County~~ The Club & Ground in the match versus Norfolk Club & Ground at Bury on June 3rd 1969 start 11:30

Will you please let me know <u>by return</u> if you are available.

Yours faithfully,

J.P. *[signature]*

Hon. Team Secretary

P.S. Transport Cars / Bus

Hotel accommodation

Mick Farrant was selected to play for Suffolk Club & Ground in 1968

While the first match of 1969 against Littleport was a success, it did not provide a victory; as chasing Haverhill's 111 for 9 declared, Littleport ended the game struggling at 61 for 9. The following encounter at Saxmundham was unusual in that it was played as a 12-a-side match. It resulted in the home team getting 105 for 11, winning against the Haverhill score of 81 for 11, a quite abnormal score. More defeats came from Sawston, Braintree and Stanstead as Haverhill struggled this summer. The 2nd XI went down the same path and started with a string of losses as well. Suddenly one week both sides only lost by one run; were things improving? Two more drawn matches saw the 1st XI near to winning, and they recorded their top score of 190 for 5 (Brian Parker 56, Peter Ralling 50) versus Old Ipswichians, only for the visitors to hold out to 139 for 8.

The young Haverhill Colts side finally showed the way to victory when beating Braintree Colts by 110 for 0 against 45 all out. Even a typical Clarence Hulyer innings against Copdock of 72 could not bring a first win of the season to the 1st XI. Haverhill 2nd XI at last broke their duck at Exning when a low-scoring game went their way 53 to 49, and they followed up with a victory over Thurlow 116 to 70. P Ralling made 57 runs in forty-two minutes versus Halstead, again with no result in the match. On the same day, the 2nd XI beat Halstead II away by rattling up 135 for 8 in reply to the home team's 134 for a welcome win. N Ward opened the Haverhill innings and was still there at the end to hit the winning runs in his 77 not out.

Even when registering 201 for 6 against village side Poslingford, the 2nd XI were beaten at the end by one run, as the opposition eclipsed a high score from Haverhill. The season went well into September again this year and it was at the beginning of this month that the Sunday XI were on the winning side against Barrington, 197 for 8 against 179, C Hulyer hitting 91. However, the season flittered out on a low note with the 1st XI not winning any of their seventeen games although some were draws. The 2nd XI did slightly better with four victories while the Sunday side had a bad summer with just two wins; not the side of previous years. For the Sunday XI, C Hulyer was top of the batting averages and bowling, while for the 2nd XI, N Ward topped the batting and D Lazaro the bowling.

The bad news of 1969 was the death of young sportsman Stephen Parker, who played for the town at both football and cricket. He was in a car crash at Little Wratting, which claimed his life. The upside was the grand effort of the Fund Raising Committee who handed over £370 to the Cricket Club. Next season it was hoped that the club would be competing in a cricket league for the first time.

At the beginning of **1970** there was encouraging news regarding the formation of a cricket league in Haverhill, this coming from a meeting held at the Youth Centre in the town. This had been called at the request of the Youth

Centre who were interested in entering a cricket eleven into such a league, but as usual, time passed and the idea slipped out of the news until the Haverhill Echo carried an interesting article entitled 'Is Haverhill ready to start a local cricket league'. This was in the middle of April, and time was certainly against a league operating for the current season. The article suggested a limited over game; certainly there were sufficient pitches available in the town, including Motts Field, the school grounds, Haverhill Meat Products and the Haverhill Cricket Club's ground, if they entered a side. Some local factories including Pye, Addis and Halliburton's were already playing friendly games so half the teams required were already in place.

The Haverhill Cricket Club made history when they entered the new Suffolk Cricket League, as secretary Norman Pryke declared that the games this season were more than just a *"jolly old afternoon game."* However, it remained to be seen if this would add that little bit extra interest to the game, as the number of over's would call for a more positive and subtle approach to cricket. The fixtures saw sixteen league matches in addition to friendly encounters, while the seconds and the Sunday XI were operating the same as usual. Hard work behind the scenes left the cricket club and the bowls section looking better than for numerous years. This was also true on the financial side, and after last season's overdraft of £31, the club were now in the position of £56 on the right side. The club's budget for the whole of the previous year was £856.

As for the town club, they were due to make a start on their season, weather and ground conditions permitting, with a friendly home game versus Copdock. Their entry in the newly formed Suffolk County League saw their first match in this competition the following weekend when Westgate Brewery visited Haverhill. The new league was based on a 40-over game and was to provide spectators with some exciting cricket well worth watching. As it was, the league match was a disappointment for Haverhill who crashed to a defeat against old adversaries Westgate Brewery, who won by 52 runs, despite Brian Parker top scoring with 79 not out for the losers. Haverhill made 124 for 9 against the Brewery's 176 for 8, but the winners only gained two points instead of four as they did not bowl Haverhill out. It was the Haverhill 2nd XI who gained a victory over the Pimpernel Club thanks to David Farrant's excellent bowling figures of 6 wickets for 10 runs, the home team being out for 40 to lose by 63 runs. On Sunday, the visitors were

Camden who toppled the Sunday XI by 74 runs with Harry Mills (65 runs) being the only Haverhill batsman to get amongst the runs.

Haverhill, who failed to register a victory last season, were still trying to find a winning formula this summer and lost their second County League game by seven wickets to visitors Hadleigh. Haverhill's inning closed at 138 of which Parker again was their best batsman with 66; Hadleigh soon passed that with 143 for 3. Haverhill 2nd XI managed to hold out for a draw in their match at Hartest, ending at 104 for 8 to their opponent's 169.

Finally, a meeting took place and the Haverhill Cricket League was formed to run on a knockout basis and to operate as a proper league system next season. There were to be two sections, with the top in each playing off for the Echo Cup in the final. This was a league playing the 20-over system and the bowlers having a maximum of five overs. 26 May was the closing date for entries and the secretary was Mr John Disley of Mansols. The games were to be played each Wednesday on the grounds of the Town Club, Sainsbury (HMP), Helions Bumpstead and possibly the pitches at Motts Field and the school grounds.

A third defeat on the trot was Haverhill's fate when losing by five wickets at Sudbury, where they also hit their worst batting form by being bowled out for 94. This was soon beaten with five wickets to spare by the home club. After failing to reach three figures, Haverhill sat firmly at the bottom of the league table with no points from their opening matches. The 2nd XI again provided some respite, however, with a draw in their first home fixture versus Sudbury II. For Haverhill, P Senior took an impressive 7 wickets for 39 runs but could not swing the game in Haverhill's direction.

Haverhill were on the brink of victory, then near to defeat in their match at Sawston, which was eventually drawn. Haverhill were poised at 157 for 9 against the home team's 159 for 7 when stumps were drawn; so near and yet so far. Keith Ayrton was the best Haverhill bowler, capturing five wickets. The team lined up H Mills, D Bradley, W Easey, B Parker, R Shanks, J Senior, C Hulyer, D Pryke, E Bailey, P Senior and K Ayrton. Disaster turned into triumph for the 2nd XI who recorded a win over Sawson II, 181 to 180. At one time, the Haverhill side had lost 4 wickets for only 13 runs, but 58 from P Ralling, 43 from B Wakeley and 42 from C Dyche provided them with the victory. Disaster, however, came on Sunday when Haverhill were wrecked by county bowler Bloomfield of Saxmundham 86-84.

Haverhill then came the closest yet to a victory when they scrambled for a win in the last over at home to Braintree, but the game was eventually drawn. The visitors were definitely on top and finished 161 for 6, with only five runs needed for a win. The 2nd XI also had their opponents tottering at 126 for 9, while Haverhill had hit 162. The Sunday XI got their best score of the season but still lost out to Stansted. A week later it was back to league action but another loss this time at Felixstowe, as Haverhill began to find the standard of the new Suffolk League a bit too hot. They were bowled out for a low score of 55, which Felixstowe soon overtook for the loss of only one wicket. On Sunday, the Travellers came to Haverhill and conquered 173 to 93.

The 2nd XI lost their unbeaten record versus Exning but it had been an encouraging run from the beginning of the season, and was thought to be a good omen for the future of cricket in the town as several youngsters were in that eleven. The Colts also lost their first match of the season but quickly got back on the winning trail seven days later. Still looking for their first league points, the 1st XI went down at Exning, then were defeated at Bury St Edmunds 155-154, but were reported as looking a lot better. They had played five games and lost every one and were still bottom of the table.

It arrived at last, a dazzling 80 not out from Brian Parker on Sunday against the County League's strongest side, Ipswich & East Suffolk, which gave Haverhill their first win and four points. Chasing the Ipswich 114, Haverhill lost their first five wickets for just twenty-one runs; Parker's innings paved the way for a five-wicket victory. Haverhill 2nd XI found their opposition too good for them again when they visited Bury Railway, and were eclipsed by nine wickets after only managing to put up a measly 53 in their innings. The 1st XI made it two wins in two weeks versus Braintree, but this was a friendly encounter in which Rogers provided some bowling zip to take six Braintree wickets; Haverhill won 72 to 75 for 8. Braintree II had the last laugh, however, as they won the battle of the seconds by six wickets. The Sunday XI trounced Stowmarket with seven batsmen in double figures in their 201 for 6 declared; Stowmarket were all out for 52.

One Saturday and Sunday saw two County League fixtures as Haverhill dropped the points at home to Felixstowe. The next day they journeyed to Chantry Park and brought off an exciting league double over Ipswich & East Suffolk with their batting hero Ray Shanks 89 not out. He followed this with 73 against Cambridge Railways for Haverhill 2nd XI. Haverhill's bowling attack was weak, however, and the Railwaymen gained the victory. Bowler Steve Rogers was amongst the wickets again when he grabbed 9-36 against Exning but could not stop Exning taking the game 87 to 35. The 2nd XI extracted some revenge by being victorious versus Exning II (B Easey 80 not out and D Bradley 71 not out) and pasted the opponent's bowling. The Haverhill Colts, who were having some outings this summer, were strong and going well in the Haverhill League, their latest win being 76 for 3 to 75 against Helions Bumpstead.

Haverhill Sunday XI made a disastrous start to their innings in reply to Hatfield's score of 170, and stood at 7 for 3 wickets at one time. They staged a recovery to overtake this total scoring 172 for 7, N Ward and J Senior being the batting heroes. The 2nd XI win over Poslingford was greeted by the headline *"So Easey for Haverhill,"* Bill Easey being top scorer with 80. With a record of winning two of their twelve County league games, the Haverhill side were in the rock bottom position. Chasing 186, Haverhill saw a bright second wicket stand bring them near, but they were 30 runs short at the end. A side of West Indian cricketers paid a visit to Haverhill to oppose the Sunday XI and a fine knock by John Wigley of 94 helped Haverhill to an exciting victory. The third County League win came for Haverhill against Hadleigh, and a visit to old adversaries Sudbury provided Haverhill with victory number four due to a seven-wicket margin. A friendly match at Halstead saw Haverhill splutter to defeat by nine wickets.

The Colts eleven were the most successful Haverhill side when they topped their section of the Haverhill League and saw off their opponents Pye to take the Echo Cricket Shield at HMP. In all, the Colts scored the grand total of 972 runs in their matches, a worthy effort, and things looked bright for the future of the Haverhill Cricket Club. In the tables of averages, B Parker was best batsman and K Ayrton the top bowler. In the new Suffolk County League, Haverhill ended the season sixth out of nine teams, the two wins near the end of the season helping them to rise to this position after a very poor beginning to league cricket. Another interesting position was discovered at the end of the season, the actual cricket ground was much higher than the meadows and land around it, a fact revealed by the floods of two years previous.

Good news greeted the members at the Annual General Meeting in March 1971 when it was announced that a benefactor, who wished to remain anonymous, had come forward to back the scheme to build an indoor bowls green on the Cricket Club complex at Manor Road. £3,000 was promised; this, plus a grant of £5,000 from the Eastern Regional Sports Council which had been applied for, could have seen the building ready for use the following winter. Unfortunately, the grant had not yet materialized and the scheme was put on hold for the time being. In the Town and Country Planning Act 1971, there was another attempt to move the public footpath that had been in contention over the years. However, it was still within the cricket ground and not many people knew for certain where it actually was. Plans were also put forward for a Haverhill Cricket League for youths under twenty years of age.

The prospect of League cricket for the second year gave the summer game the impetus needed to make both players and spectators sit up, and to bring in more supporters for the Haverhill club. The new captain was Eric Bailey, who commented, *"In my experience it is a much better game to play as it brings out the right type of player; someone who gets on with the game."* The club was now well equipped with players like Clarence Hulyer, who could change the course of the game in a couple of over's, while Brian Parker had proved himself as good a batsman as there was around West Suffolk. Most of the previous season's players were still at the club, and there were some good quality players in the Haverhill area who could flourish in competitive cricket. The nets were busy in pre-season and there were to be three senior teams and a colt's side for the coming season.

Haverhill made a flying start to the summer with four league points from a three-wicket win over Westgate Brewery. Chasing the Brewery total of 121, it looked at one time that victory would be easy, but at the end, it proved a tight finish with two over's left. The 2nd XI went down by 93 runs, however, against Pimpernel at Barrow. The Sunday XI also had to fight in their first outing and forced a draw versus Camden. The 1st XI came back to earth with a jolt in their second league game when they were beaten at home by Hadleigh who posted a score of 113 for 9. A win looked well in the hands of

Haverhill, but after being 43 for the loss of 7 wickets at one time, the total of just 70 was not good enough to match the run rate of the visitors.

The Haverhill Cricket League had two sections, the A group being Halliburton, Haverhill Colts, Helions Bumpstead, Pye and Hempstead. The B group comprised HMP, Mansols, Addis, Koch-Light and Gurteen's. The two group winners were to meet for the Echo Shield at HMP at the end of the season. This meant that there would be a game at Motts Field nearly every Wednesday, although some teams had promised the use of their grounds. The first games started on Wednesday 19 May.

The Sunday XI were on peak form in winning against Littleport, opening batsmen J Wigley and D Bradley both scoring forties. They followed this with a draw with the Pilgrims C C. The first away league game for Haverhill was at Sudbury whom they put to the sword in winning by eight wickets. Haverhill had the batting power to follow their bowlers who took out Sudbury for 109. Three wickets in two over's by P Senior started the rout of the home team, and when Haverhill batted, only four batsmen were used to take all four points with 113 for 2. This success put Haverhill's morale on a high level and meant they had taken eight points out of a possible twelve, no mean feat in such a high standard league. The youngsters were gradually coming to the fore; two of them, Paul Senior and David Farrant, were the best bowlers in the Sudbury match, David following in his father Harry's footsteps as an all-rounder for the town. The 2nd XI faltered at home to the Sudbury II at 121 to 118.

Friendly games were included in the fixture list for the Haverhill 1st XI. Sawston were the first of these, and the eleven for this match were E Bailey, B Parker, J Wigley, S Rogers, D Pryke, J Senior, D Farrant, R Shanks, P Senior, P Suffling and W Easey. The club's official scorer was J Porter. Wigley and Shanks put on over one hundred for the first wicket in this game but were denied a win by the stubborn Sawston side. The 2nd XI, however, got their first win of the summer at home to Sawston II, with captain N Ward leading the way with a top knock of 34 and bowling figures of 3 for 24. The Colts side were starting well in the Haverhill League and certainly benefited from practice in the nets.

Another special match was an all-day affair versus Bapchild, a Kent side touring Suffolk. However, Haverhill were on the end of a heavy defeat, and although it was programmed as an all-day match, it produced fewer runs than an ordinary afternoon game. The home team were let down by their batting as they crawled to 85. Wigley and Bradley who opened the innings took forty-five minutes to score fourteen runs, and only two of the last six batsmen scored any runs. Bapchild were in no rush to wipe off the runs and the game finished early. Haverhill seconds were also the losers in their match against Bury Railway, this by the considerable 114 runs.

Unpredictable as they were, Haverhill 1st X put on a much better show the next week against a star-studded Felixstowe side at the seaside. Facing 165 for 7, Haverhill soon lost two wickets, but this brought Pryke and Parker together who set about their task with discipline and some aggression. They both finished not out, Parker on 56 and Pryke with 79, to earn two league points and victory. The 2nd XI also perked up against Cambridge Railways, and opener Phillip Seccombe hit 93 in their drawn game. The Sunday XI was interrupted by rain but their opponents gave them a hiding, the Travellers XI being successful by nine wickets. In mid-week, the Colts kept up their good work with a win over Helions Bumpstead.

Following this good win, Haverhill then put on an all-round display to come out on top against Ipswich & East Suffolk at Chantry Park, and looked to have boosted their chances to bid for the league title. Their opponents were contained to 107 for 7 in their allotted overs, with their top player dismissed for one run thanks to a brilliant catch by wicket-keeper John Senior. Haverhill's Parker then entertained with a boundary strewn innings of 40 assisted by Wigley and Pryke, saw Haverhill to victory. A four-point win over Exning put Haverhill on top of the league in a match where fast bowler Steve Rogers onslaught of 6 for 34 helped the cause. Pryke was hit by a bouncer but returned later to the crease and hit the winning run. However, in the return with the same side, Haverhill went down by 34 runs despite John Wigley's 79 not out.

The stiffest test came for Haverhill when visiting the Victory Ground to play Bury St Edmunds, but they did not produce their best and slid to a 112-run defeat. The home side galloped to 203 for 3 to which Haverhill had no real answer, and Haverhill slipped down to third in the table. On the same day, the 2nd XI also lost by 118 runs to Leiston; not a very good day all round.

On Sunday, facing Ipswich & East Suffolk at Haverhill, the home side left it late and won the match with just one over to spare. A top-drawer fielding display gave Haverhill an exciting two-run victory at Orwell Works although the match was a low-scoring one, 85-83. The weather continued to play a part in the 2nd XI games and just when a win looked likely against Poslingford, the heavens opened to cause an end to proceedings.

Haverhill Sunday XI produced one of their best batting shows versus Copdock in a friendly, with David Pryke coming into his own with a top innings of 97 not out, figuring in a stand of 163 in 74 minutes with Bill Easey (67 not out). Copdock held out for a draw at 196 for 8 when time was called. Meanwhile in the League, Haverhill needed just five more runs to win versus Hadleigh but suffered a late collapse and surrendered the points. It is fair to point out that both Clarence Hulyer and Eric Bailey were dazed for a time after they collided when both going for a catch off a no-ball. It was a non-Haverhill C C game that produced a one-off display by Albert Waters for HMP when he took five wickets in consecutive deliveries versus Stowlangtoft. He was on a double hat-trick but the last ball of his over did not quite make it.

Clarence Hulyer had a profitable weekend when he hit a run-a-minute 67 against St Margarets at Bourne Park, then 77 versus Stowmarket the next day at Manor Road. Westgate Brewery then avenged their one defeat all season by Haverhill by winning the return fixture. Hulyer's runs could have been needed the next week when Haverhill finished their season on a dark note at Halstead. They were all out for 100 versus Halstead who proceeded to pass this total with only one wicket down as they showed Haverhill the way home. The Haverhill batsmen, except David Debenham, who managed a fine 42 not out, seemed not good enough to tame the home teams attack.

Something could always happen when the hard-hitting Hulyer walked to the wicket, and a match against Braintree at Manor Road provided some fireworks. Clarence played an innings to be remembered when it took him just eighteen minutes to reach fifty, and a few more minutes to score 61. In one over, he took 22 runs off the Braintree slow bowler including 3 sixes. It was quite dangerous on the A604 as the balls kept popping over the fence. After three balls were lost, some Haverhill colleagues positioned themselves outside the ground to keep a tag on the balls. They also had to warn the road traffic. Brian Parker also contributed a not out innings of 58 with some fine strokes, including one final six which cost the club the match ball.

'ECHO' FINAL SCORES

HAVERHILL COLTS

P Suffling run out	1
D Bradley b Driver	13
P Senior b Driver	64
G Poole lbw b Corbett	40
R Beavis c Driver b O'Farrell	2
P Jobson c O'Farrell b Smith	22
D Farrant c Nunn b Smith	4
T Smith not out	3
R Willett not out	2
Extras	4
Total (30 overs) for 7 wkts	165

MANSOL

V Robinson b Willett	2
J Gowers run out	1
B Chuck b Willett	6
K Corbett c Bradley b Senior	16
F O'Farrell st Bradley b Willett	2
F Smith c Suffling b Radford	52
M Nunn b Farrant	22
P Bruty b Farrant	0
M Robinson c Senior b Beavis	11
A Rogers c Bradley b Radford	1
D Driver not out	0
Extras	2
Total (27 overs) all out	115

The season ended in scorching weather for a change and the Colts side, after a tie in their last game (113 for 6 against Hempstead 113 for 7), topped their section of the Haverhill Cricket League and faced Mansol in the play-off for the Shield. The works side made the Colts fight hard but they eventually tasted victory by fifty runs. P Senior was the Colts leading batsman with 64, while F Smith top scored for Mansol with 52. To wind things up, the Colts were matched against a strong side dubbed 'The Rest', mostly Haverhill's first eleven, for whom Ray Shanks knocked up 74 not out; the Colts going down gallantly 187 to 133.

The 1972 summer began slightly differently when a full-scale trial match was arranged between two sides of all the club's players, in an effort to see the strongest eleven selected each week when the season proper started. This took place one Sunday at the end of April after some practice had continued during the winter in the nets at Haverhill Sports Centre. The weather also played fair; there was not a cloud in the sky when Haverhill played their first match of the County League, against one of their bogy sides, Westgate Brewery. Unfortunately only J Wigley and E Bailey made substantial runs as Haverhill crashed to the Brewery by eight wicket's; Haverhill making 126 for 9 which was then passed by the Brewery with 131 for 2. The 2nd XI also caught the same bug, and it was also their batting which let them down against Poslingford, 116 - 115.

A friendly versus Littleport on Sunday saw Haverhill run out of time in an effort to win the game. The Sunday XI made 148 for 8 and had restricted their opponents to 93 for 7 when time was called and it remained a draw. Next up were Sudbury; this time the tail-enders let the opening batsmen Wigley (46) and Pryke (30) down after they had given the team a good start amongst the runs, and the second league game was lost. To make things worse, the 2nd XI also lost to Sudbury II on the same day. One of the clubs young players took 5 wickets for just 1 run when playing for Halliburton in the Midweek League. The Colts XI started well in this league and won their first two games with some ease.

It seemed that Haverhill had reached rock bottom when they could only manage to take eight players to their match in Sawston to fulfil their fixture in Cambridgeshire. Although the players took Haverhill's innings into three figures, Sawston with their full complement were winners. It was strange, however, that the 2nd XI put out a full line-up at home to Sawston II. Even on Sunday, Haverhill went down to Saxmundham. A defeat versus Copdock was tempered with a fine innings of 46 from 16-year-old Graeme Poole who was looking good for the future. Haverhill did it again for the second away fixture in a row when they travelled to Felixstowe with only nine players, and they lost the league points to a strong home side. Haverhill 2nd XI entertained Felixstowe II, but after the visitor's innings had been worth 83, Haverhill had only reached 13 without loss; when a sudden thunderstorm forced the game to be abandoned.

To try to stop the rot, some youngsters, including R Beavis, G Poole, D Debenham and D Farrant, were drafted into the two sides for the home game against Exning. This did not really help matters as Haverhill were left struggling at 79 for 9, chasing Exning's 160 for 7. Appalling batting was reported as the club's downfall, but by not being bowled out, they collected their first league point of the season. A bright light appeared on the horizon when unexpected Haverhill took the scalp of Bury St Edmunds to register their first victory and some precious league points. Versus the same opponents the following week, Haverhill were going great guns with their score at 126 with seven wickets in hand, but the chance of a quick double victory evaporated when they suffered a major batting collapse and finished sixteen runs short. Haverhill's top scorers were J Wigley (64) and W Easey (54). Wigley carried his batting into the Sunday fixture against St Neots and hit a fine 92. T Webb added 6 fours in a quick spell and David Pryke made some entertaining shots including 5 fours and 3 sixes in his run making; Haverhill scored 202 for 4 declared. The match, however, ended as a draw as St Neots stuck on 164 for 6, but with the Sunday XI on top.

In top batting form, Pryke went on to lash a century in his next game versus Abington, ending on 101 not out. This was just what the Sunday side wanted but with the village side hanging on, the match was also drawn. Two fixtures on one weekend were the chance to pick up some points but both games were lost. With only one win, Haverhill 1st XI were rooted to the bottom of the Suffolk County League table. After a disastrous start to their innings against Deben Valley, Haverhill made a spectacular recovery but thanks to a brilliant knock from Clarence Hulyer of 71 in 36 minutes, but they fell short at the end by just three runs. The target was 201 and Haverhill stood at 29 for 6 when Hulyer made his entrance. The 1st XI were also close to a victory the next day at Ipswich & East Suffolk, making 141 for 9 against 143 for 7; nearly! This was followed by a 10 wicket hammering by the Grasshoppers, while the 2nd XI forced a draw versus a strong Cambridge Railway side.

A Surrey team known as the Oval Nondescripts included a sprinkling of former Surrey and second XI players on their visit to Haverhill one Sunday. This provided Haverhill with a rare taste of victory in a 25-overs match which ended with the visiting team 42 runs behind with only one wicket left; opener Terry Webb (49) and Dave Bradley (25) led the Haverhill scoring. Making runs was catching and an opening stand of 132 between John Wigley and Tony Smith paved the way for a rare league win at Deben Valley the following Sunday; Wigley made 81 and Smith 55, further runs came from Nigel Ward with 36 not out.

It was back to the poor form of early season when from the brink of victory, Haverhill slid to defeat by one wicket at Exning. Haverhill made only 74 all out but had their opponents on the rack at 58 for 9, however the Exning last pair put on 20 more runs and the game was won. Haverhill bowlers D Pryke and P Senior were the pair amongst the wickets. With just two victories from their 18 games, Haverhill finished bottom of the County League, and they ended the season with two losses in two friendly matches. It was the Colts who brought some fame when they took the Echo Shield for the third time, beating Mansol in the final.

In all, this was a dismal summer for Haverhill Cricket Club and successes were rare. In fact, they came out winners in only three games compared with eighteen defeats and a couple of draws. Bill Easey who was top of the batting averages with J Wigley running him a close second, and C Hulyer being the best at bowling. For the 2nd XI, newcomer L Snell was top of the batting averages after playing just eight matches, and W Massey was the best bowler. John Wigley was the Sunday XI batting success and the top Sunday bowler was D Pryke. The Colts good season saw N Ward top the batting averages, while the bowling was headed by D Farrant.

Haverhill started the **1973** season with two defeats in the Suffolk Cricket League, the first by 8 wickets at Deben Valley, then to Ransomes by 75 runs. The 2nd XI opened with a friendly game playing John Holm's XI, resulting in an entertaining draw. Ray Shanks was the early batsman to score 50 in the 2nd XI's victory over Cambridge Railway (96 - 152 for 7) A weekend of games versus Bury St Edmunds resulted in two low-scoring encounters. The 1st XI could only manage 95, which was overtaken by their opponents who lost just one wicket in doing so. The 2nd XI were slightly better when they restricted Bury II to 59 all out and replied with 60 for 4. On Sunday, Haverhill was on top of Oval Nondescripts when time was called. Bradley with 66 saw the

Sunday XI reach 186 for 6 and their opponents struggling at 83 for 8.

The 1st XI were losing regularly and looking to string a few wins together, but the 2nd XI took revenge on Felixstowe II with a victory 121 to 107; the 1st XI having been beaten on the same day when the two 1st XI's met. Once again, the 1st XI lost against Exning, but in the two 2nd XI's match Haverhill came out on top, scoring 187 for 7 then bowling out Exning for a paltry 19. Two more victories came their way versus Horseheath, 207 for 8 to 203, Haverhill's Suffling top scoring with 68. This was followed by a win at Halstead II 127 - 113. Then came a rash of drawn games as Haverhill struggled to score runs.

Again, the 2nd XI won in a low-scoring match versus Cambridge Rail,. Haverhill 73 for 4 against Railway's 69 all out. However, the 1st XI lost a match that at one time looked to have lifted the gloom, eventually going down to Westgate Brewery, 90 to 94 for 1. The Sunday XI at least registered a victory over St Margaret's (130 all out) as John Wigley completed a half century in their 141 for 9, a narrow win but much welcomed. Deep into September came a victory for the Sunday XI who showed fine batting form in a 238 for 8 against 214 for 9 win over Barrington. John Wigley once again showed the way with a well constructed 67.

However, before the season ended the 1st XI did taste victory over long-time rivals Halstead. The Essex side chalked up 142 for 5 to which Haverhill reached 205 for 8. The 2nd XI who were the winners in the two seconds match 83 to 82 once again equalled a narrow loss to Sudbury 148 - 134 all out. A very inadequate summer was brought to a close with yet another defeat for Haverhill by Sawston. Altogether a season to forget.

It was not very much like cricketing weather when the **1974** season opened. It was bitterly cold when the 2nd XI played its first match versus Hartest and were victorious by 93 runs, the Haverhill side treating this as a warm-up game and including a sprinkling of first and second players. The village side struggled with the bat, but Ray Shanks top-scored for Haverhill with 59 runs. The next week brought a friendly for the first XI against Camden, and despite 152 for 9, Haverhill lost by 8 wickets. The first match in the Suffolk County League was against Westgate Brewery, which was lost by 15 runs. All but one of the Haverhill batsmen were clean bowled while new pace bowler Tom Almond looked very capable. At one time this first match looked to be going in Haverhill's favour but it turned into a dismal defeat.

The first league points came with a win over Hadleigh by 2 wickets as Pryke and Shanks both scored half-centuries. On the same weekend both the 2nd XI and the Sunday XI won their games, and things looked brighter for the coming summer. The Sunday team soon became unstuck when they failed in their quest to reach the Pilgrims' score of 188 for 4. The Sudbury versus Haverhill fixture went Haverhill's way by just one run; Sudbury wanted two runs off the last ball of the day but scrambled just a single. The Colts started their season with a win.

Came June and the 2nd XI were shunted to one side by Bury Rail by one hundred runs, but the 1st XI made it three league wins in a row. The Sunday side were proving unpredictable as they crashed to Stanstead, while the Colts record stood at two losses in three matches. The Cricket Club put on an informal evening with three West Indian test players, including captain Clive Lloyd, who were at Cambridge for a match against the University. Haverhill cricketers took advantage to put some questions to the West Indian's. The 1st XI saw their opening run of victories brought to an abrupt end by Broomfield who scuttled Haverhill out for a paltry 59, but it was a friendly. Nevertheless, it was a different tale in the league as they took another scalp in Exning by 8 wickets. The 2nd XI made it a double by beating Exning II as well. Bury St Edmunds inflicted a first league defeat on Haverhill 205 to 139, G Poole getting 57. A well-constructed 130 from Brian Parker helped to pep up the seconds as they won by 161 runs over Bury II.

Bury II soon had their revenge as the two teams met the following week when they won by 7 wickets, while on Sunday the Haverhill XI lost out to March. Another league game was pointless as Ipswich & East Suffolk beat them, but only by one run at the end. Ransomes then inflicted another defeat on Haverhill by 101 runs in a match when the batting failed again. The match versus Deben Valley saw a great bowling performance by T Almond when he took 8 wickets for 24 runs in the Haverhill victory. This was a feat which was thought would get him amongst the awards at the end of the season. This was followed by a dreadful weekend when all three teams lost their matches, and it looked as if the Deben Valley victory was just a flash in the pan. A rain-lashed fixture saw the Sunday XI lose out to the Grasshoppers in a match that was noted by low scores all around. The Haverhill league team seemed to have entered a spell when they were let down by some very shabby batting, and another week-end was marked by no victory by any town side.

On the August Bank Holiday week-end, a Minor Counties fixture between Suffolk and Lincolnshire on the Haverhill ground honoured the club. It was a two-day match for which the groundsman was working overtime to have the pitch in perfect condition. Play was advertised at 11-30 to 7pm on Sunday and 11 to 6pm on the Monday. Unfortunately, there were no Haverhill players in the Suffolk line-up. When the time arrived for the start of this match there was an embarrassing moment when it was found there were no balls for the game, the Suffolk captain having left the ball bag at home in Ipswich. Nearly an hour was lost as the players stood around, until a supply was brought from Bury St Edmunds. The wicket had also received a soaking from an early morning rainstorm, but the match went on; better late than never!

To wind up the season Haverhill thrashed Hadleigh, then the batsmen fell short as they went down to Westgate Brewery for the second time this summer. C Hulyer hit a quick 84 for the 2nd XI in a tame draw and the Sunday XI easily beat St Margaret's. Now called the Haverhill Cricket & Bowls Club, the season ended with the grand opening of the brand new indoor bowls green; over fifty bowlers from all over Suffolk were there to try the new conditions out.

It seemed that Westgate Brewery were always the opening fixture for Haverhill in the County League, and so it was for the beginning of **1975**. When Haverhill were all out for 67, the game was lost; only two batsmen managed to reach double figures as the Bury club were successful by 81 runs. A report said, *"The batting of Haverhill was a shambles."* It was nearly as bad for the Sunday XI as they managed to hang on with little to spare to gain a draw versus Littleport. The 1st XI then came within a whisker in their friendly encounter with Sawston, Haverhill posting 144 and their opponents 60 for 9 when stumps were drawn. It was the same for the 2nd XI versus Sawston II when the bowlers put on a good show to give them a victory chance, but Sawston eventually won. With the batting too slow, Haverhill lost their next league game to Bury Rail by 6 wickets.

Entering June, Haverhill had no points against their name in the County League, and when the next two games were lost, they were stranded at the foot of the league. While the bowling was nearly up to standard, the batting performances left the former too much to do in most of the matches. In the Mid-week League, the Colts were not as successful as in previous years, standing bottom of Section B. With J Wigley (69) and G Poole (63) reaching form at last, this time some poor work in the field saw the town lose again to Bury St Edmunds, by 7 wickets. Success was getting nearer when Mildenhall only managed to win against Haverhill in the last over.

At last it happened, the first league victory when Bury St Edmunds were faced for the second week running; this time Haverhill were victors 179 to 134. The 2nd XI made it a double as they were also winners against Bury II. Following another loss, Haverhill gained another league win, this time against Deben Valley by 107 runs. It looked as if the tide had turned. A home fixture versus Felixstowe provided Haverhill with some more league points but they had to be content with a drawn game

After a win over Halstead in a game of high scores, Haverhill then thrashed Sanderstead on Sunday, the visiting Surrey side being all out for just 69. The top Haverhill scorer was D Bradley with 67. Then came the first 6-a-side competition on the Cricket Ground. This attracted several local teams, villages and works elevens and proved a feast of cricket, Horseheath beating Haverhill Hockey Club in the grand final. The next two matches saw quite a few missed catches by the Haverhill fielders, resulting in a draw versus Grasshoppers and a last ball defeat against Ransomes at Ipswich. This was quite a cliffhanger when one run from the last ball of the day gave Ransomes the victory. League points were becoming scarce for Haverhill when a run of games were lost as the town club's 1st XI struggled. They ended the season in the lower reaches of the County League.

With the Haverhill Cricket League's final arranged for the Cricket Ground, the club secretary Nigel Ward made an appalling discovery when he checked the ground at 8-30am on the Sunday morning. Hooligans had struck overnight and daubed ''Free George Davis' on the scoreboard. (Davis became well known after a campaign to release him from prison after a wrongful conviction for robbery in 1974). In addition, more paint was splashed on the actual wicket. Black paint and an aerosol paint had been used to splatter the pavilion, but the worst was that the pitch had been dug up and holes left full of oil. A month before, the Leeds pitch where England were playing Australia had received the same treatment as had that at Hadleigh, in Suffolk, the day after Haverhill had played there. As it transpired it had been a wet night and the League final had to be put off anyway as it was too wet.

Cricket in the area of Haverhill and its district was looking up in **1976** with an increase of teams in the local midweek league, which now had three divisions, the Cricket Club's Midweek XI being in Division One. Amongst the newcomers were Haverhill Police in the town and Great Yeldham from further afield. There was, however, some trouble when children were seen riding their bicycles over the cricket pitches on the Council's Chalkstone and Castle playing fields.

The Sunday XI were the first in action this summer when they played out a drawn match with Littleport. The 1st XI got underway with a visit from a Dutch touring side, VRA Amsterdam, which was also drawn. Their first Suffolk Cricket League fixture was against St Edmundsbury which they lost by 19 runs, followed by another defeat by Hadleigh by 97 runs. Overall the Haverhill fielding was good, even though the Hadleigh top scorer was dropped three times in his match winning innings. The Midweek side were the only club side to start with a win over Suffolk Punch. The first century of the season came early on when Peter Southgate hit 105 when Haverhill conquered Sudbury by 95 runs. The 1st XI were mainly represented by J Brownbridge, P Southgate, J Wigley, P Suffling, T Webb, N Ackerman, J Thompson, K Ayrton, D Debenham, E Bailey, J Almond, with the umpire A Osborne and the scorer P Farrant. In the 2nd XI were D Joyce, D Pryke, R Shanks, W Easey, A Bailey, D Farrant, C Hulyer, S Read, N Ward, J Poole, D Bradley, and C Dobell acting as umpire and the scorer S Miller. Newcomer Peter Southgate was proving a talented addition to the club.

After a promising opening to their Suffolk League campaign, the Haverhill 1st XI took a step back as they crumbled to defeat at Felixstowe. Then came a dramatic batting collapse after a solid start when they lost out to Exning by four wickets; this was their opponent's first win of the season. From 124 for 2 Haverhill managed only twenty more runs as terrible strokes cost them dear. Exning kept up the run-rate and they overtook the Haverhill total with some ease. A rain shower interrupted the match versus Bury St Edmunds which was won by Bury. The short spell of rain was welcome by many people as this summer was beginning to turn out some blistering heat, and went on to be a record-breaking summer weather-wise.

A victorious weekend provided Haverhill with six league points with wins over the league leaders Ransomes and then Ipswich & East Suffolk, putting Haverhill in the top group of teams each with a record of six won, four lost and one no-result. Set to score a run every ball, Haverhill stuck to the task and tasted victory over Ransomes. The man to help bring this off was Graeme Poole, home from Bristol College for his first match of the season; he hit 88 in fine style. Phil Suffling and Poole put on 116 for the first wicket to guide Haverhill to their second victory of the weekend over Ipswich & East Suffolk, who were all out for 89. In this game the first three Haverhill batsmen, Poole, Southgate and Suffling, all scored over sixty runs each. The 2nd XI were in winning mode as they romped to a win over Bury St Edmunds II by 8 wickets; a good batting display was followed by good work in the field.

Gathering momentum Haverhill joined the race to win the league with two more wins in one week-end. Journeying to the east Suffolk, they were successful over Ransomes on Saturday; camped out on the works club ground on Saturday night, then went to nearby Woodbridge for Sunday's game versus Deben Valley that they also won. Against Ransomes, G Poole registered a magnificent 80, which included nine fours and two sixes. Haverhill came back to town with twenty-six league points in the bag. A string of Haverhill victories lifted them to second spot behind Ransomes, a strong position from which to press on for the championship. Graeme Poole was quite a run-machine and continued his purple patch of batting with another impressive innings of 94. A swashbuckling century from Clarence Hulyer saw Haverhill, still unbeaten, win a splendid four-wicket victory at Bury Railways. He ended on 105 not out. On top of all this, the Haverhill 2nd XI were unbeaten by the time August had arrived, and giving admirable support to the 1st XI. David Debenham took four wickets, taking his tally to nine over the weekend.

With seven games left to play, Haverhill were soon in level position at the top of the league and faced a breathtaking race to the top. However, after seven consecutive wins Exning halted Haverhill's progress. Veteran Eric

Bailey posted a high-quality bowling performance for the 2nd XI as he took 8 wickets for just 19 runs in the victory over Exning II, partly making up for the 1st XI defeat. A special meeting was hastily convened when the Haverhill Club's chairman resigned; Mr Ray Dagg had been in that position for three years, and said his action was taken on personal reasons, but added that there had been some upsets in the club which had proved hard to rectify.

From this point, Haverhill suddenly hit a bad run in the league and two defeats came quickly. First Hadleigh were victorious by 101 runs and next was another loss to Bury Railway, this time by two wickets; two heavy reverses. Then in early September, St Edmundsbury inflicted a third consecutive loss on Haverhill to leave them struggling to keep on the leader's tails. When Sudbury beat Haverhill in the final game of the season, the challenge for the title was over for Haverhill; they finished third as Bury Rail were the champions. The 2nd XI had a very good summer and lost just once, while the Sunday XI had many drawn games in their record and the Mid-week side were high up in their section of the Haverhill League.

Before the 1977 season could get under way, a problem arose with the Haverhill Midweek League when Horseheath were told they were too good for this competition, and the league asked them to play slightly weaker teams in the league. Horseheath were one of the top clubs in Cambridgeshire and had quite a few players on their books. The Haverhill Club said the village used the league as a training ground for their Colts. A meeting voted 12-2 in favour of strong clubs playing only three top players in their eleven's for the next season.

Following their near challenge for the County League championship, the Haverhill 1st XI were feeling there was a chance they would be up with the top clubs again this season. It was only on the run-in that they fell back, and they would be striving to be more consistent in their performances this time. Other league sides still looked on Haverhill as one of the 'also-ran' teams after some years around the basement of the league. There was also a new captain in David Pryke who said "*I am hoping that we can improve on the third place we ended in last year.*" It looked as if the Bury St Edmunds club would be the one to beat as they had amalgamated with the St Edmundsbury club. Haverhill, on the other hand, had lost wicket-keeper John Bainbridge and opening bat John Wigley. Haverhill also started out minus lead bowler Tom Almond who was on the injured list. Newcomer was G Swinfield who had played for Nottingham University; he replaced Bainbridge as wicket-keeper.

Of the opening games, Sudbury were victorious over Haverhill who came unstuck for the second season in succession, while the Sunday XI sustained a big loss by 9 wickets to St Giles. The Midweek XI started with a defeat followed by a victory as they began life in the top division of the league. Fireworks were seen when Clarence Hulyer hit a very fast century in the Haverhill eleven against Haverhill Furniture in the Echo Jubilee Competition. He clobbered the bowling all over the field in his 136 not out. By June, Haverhill were languishing at the bottom of the Suffolk County League having not won a match yet.

Middlesex Cricket Club paid a visit to Haverhill, but not to oppose the local club. They were in town at a special evening to raise the profile and also cash for their captain Clive Radley, whose benefit year it was. This event was in the Haverhill clubroom and also included a talk on the England tours of India and Australia. The evening, which was very well attended ended with a grand draw for a cricket bat signed by the whole of the England Test Team.

The 1st XI found their feet at last, but this was in a friendly match versus a touring team from Kent. Haverhill scored 183 for 8 and their opponents managed to hold out for a drawn match. When the Sunday XI crashed to defeat against March by 115 runs, it was said to be down to 'very poor batting'. It was the Midweek side that upheld some pride when P Suffling (62) and Debenham (6 wickets for 16 runs) drove them to a win over HMP. The 1st XI ended June with yet another loss, this time to Mildenhall by 7 wickets. The annual six-a-side tournament attracted sixteen teams this year, the third time it had been held, and the Rose & Crown Cup for the winners went to Kedington who beat Stambourne in the final.

Haverhill then pulled themselves out of their deep rut to conquer visitors Ipswich & East Suffolk by six wickets in a run-feast match. This was their second win of the summer, and the man they had to thank was opener Peter Southgate who weighed in with a fine knock of 87. Together with J Thompson (44), he saw his side past the Ipswich total with a few over's to go.

The 2nd XI drew with Bury Rail who scored 200 as Haverhill managed 154 for 6. The previous Saturday Haverhill were the losing side in the league game versus Ransomes. Haverhill then came face to face with league leaders Lakenheath. Haverhill struggled and were no match for their visitors, but went down fighting after Lakenheath put up 199 for 7, Haverhill coming up with 150 for 8. Haverhill then took a hammering from Deben Valley on the Sunday and could only score 54 to Deben's 197. The town batting was a total disaster with only three batsmen in double figures. It was Julian Poole who with bat and then ball helped the 2nd XI to victory over Culford. Newcomers to the Haverhill sides were G King, I Matthews and N Hurrell. Haverhill seemed to be the bogy side for Ipswich & East Suffolk as they completed the double over the Ipswich team, this time by 62 runs. Looking to boost their record, Haverhill took on a friendly match versus Sanderstead from Surrey, but they lost again under wet conditions.

The brothers Poole were the stars of the 2nd XI victory over Bury Rail, J Poole took 6 wickets for 21 runs while his brother G Poole held the batting together to secure the win. Batting was still the main reason for the Haverhill club's inadequate showing during 1977. There were some bright lights on the horizon as when Haverhill delighted everyone by a 55 run win over Exning with some fine individual performances. Clarence Hulyer made 60 including 2 sixes and 8 fours while David Debenham captured 6 wickets for 57 runs. Haverhill made 225 which Exning were always striving to match.

The poor showings also affected the usually competent Sunday XI who were on the brink of a defeat versus Linton when Hulyer and J Poole saved the day; with Haverhill at 49 for 7 they added the 67 runs needed for a win. The 2nd XI wound up their fixtures with a good display at Halstead where they bowled their opponents out for a meagre 30 runs and knocked off the runs off wanted for victory in a very short time. The team for this match was R Shanks, S Bishop, N Ward, W Easey, G Swinfield, P Lee, M Wilkins, D Farrant, J Holm, E Bailey and C Bailey. Haverhill ended their Suffolk League programme in the best possible manner, beating Sudbury by 19 runs. Skipper David Pryke played a big part in this satisfying win over long term rivals. With a record of winning 5 and losing 10 of their league games, Haverhill ended up in eighth position out of eleven clubs.

Cricket seemed to be booming in Haverhill and its immediate area when in **1978** new teams entered the Haverhill Midweek league making a total of eighteen competing, still including the Haverhill Cricket Club's Midweek XI. For the Saturday and League eleven David Debenham took over as captain, and they opened the season with a visit to Broomfield for a friendly encounter in very cold conditions. This game produced a draw as in reply to the Haverhill score of 148, of which David Pryke contributed 67, Broomfield managed to struggle to 101 for 8. The first County League match was the following week when Haverhill collected fifteen points for their victory at Bury St Edmunds. It was the lower order of batsmen who won the game for the visitors after they slipped to 86 for 8 against the Bury total of 106 for 9, but they reached their target with three over's to spare.

Another win came when Sudbury travelled to Haverhill and lost by 77 runs, but the Haverhill Sunday XI slumped to a defeat to St Giles. Playing two league fixtures in the same weekend did not really suit Haverhill as they went down to Bury Rail but managed to turn things around against Tuddenham on the Sunday, with Debenham taking 8 wickets for 38 runs to seal an easy win by 8 wickets. Showing their old form, Haverhill then crashed heavily to defeat versus Lakenheath, who won by 9 wickets. The 2nd XI however, had begun the summer with two successive victories. The Sunday side then won a dramatic match against Stansfield when the village team's last two batsmen were run out trying for a last minute win. For the 2nd XI Bill Easey battled hard for his century against Cambridge Railway, and fully deserved the ovation he received from his team-mates. He was eventually out attempting a last big hit and was caught right on the boundary line.

A narrow defeat was Haverhill's fate at Felixstowe, the third in a row. They lost a member when D Pryke was side-lined with a broken shoulder, leaving Haverhill to play out the match with ten players. Bowler John Coleman was in great form for the 2nd XI against Abington, taking 5 for 18 as Haverhill thrashed their opponents by a 7 wicket margin. It was then the batsmen's turn as Nigel Akerman made a excellent century in Haverhill's win over Exning 230 to 90. His 100 runs came up in just eighty-six minutes, and seventy of his runs came from boundary hits. Unfortunately this display was not seen by any Haverhill batsmen the following week when some 'disastrous strokes' led to a defeat by Bury St Edmunds.

The Midweek XI were going great guns, and after winning their first six matches they stood at the top of their division. The next three 1st XI games saw them lose all three through the batting not being up to standard, but they did break the losing sequence against a touring team from Kent on a Wednesday, the opponent's last two batsmen managing to play for a drawn match. August came and with it a welcome victory for Haverhill over Exning, but the batting was still noted as shaky. The 1st XI's hopes of success in the West Suffolk Newspapers Competition was abruptly ended at the first hurdle This was tempered a bit by the Midweek side gaining promotion from their division to reach the top teams next summer. The County league fixtures could not end quickly enough for Haverhill and they finished in mid-table, with more net practice needed for the batting side of the team. A visit to Tuddenham gave Haverhill another win at last but their final league match was lost to Sudbury.

The season ended with three friendly matches; versus Brentwood was lost by 8 wickets and another lost to Halstead. They did, however, win their last game of a difficult summer, with a last gasp effort over Hoddesdon with L Gooding hitting 75, one of the highest scores by a Haverhill batsman in this season.

For the **1979** season, the Suffolk Cricket League had a new cash boost when a Sudbury Engineering company entered into a sponsorship deal worth £1,000, and the competition became known as the Willingale League. The previous season position of seventh for Haverhill was commented on by captain David Debenham *"Hopefully we will be able to improve our batting this season and I would like to think we could aim for a top four place. We need a good start and to carry on throughout the season, as we are quite well off for bowling."* An increase in practice sessions was hoped to help the new summer ambitions, although a trial match between the Possibles and the Probable's had to be called off because the ground was still too wet.

The three teams selected for the first week-end of matches were- 1st XI, D Debenham, P Suffling, L Gooding, N Ackerman, H Shinn, C Hulyer, J Poole, D Pryke, J Coleman, G Swinfield, K Ayrton. The umpire was E Bailey and the scorer P Webb. The 2nd XI was J Holm (captain), P Lee, W Easey, D Kenrick, S Bishop, C Bailey, N Hurrell, P Lucas, M Pope, K Camplin, D

Farrant. umpire A Bishop and the scorer M Wilkins. The Sunday side lined up with C Hulyer, E Bailey, M Wilkins, J Poole, I Matthews, S Copson, L Gooding, D Joyce, P Suffling, G King and H Shinn. All three sides were playing away, at Bury St Edmunds, Long Melford and Broomfield.

What a start! Haverhill 1st XI started off in style with a superb win over Bury St Edmunds by 40 runs. Despite losing an early wicket Haverhill's Easey and Suffling steadied the boat and made 182. Bury opener J Wigley, the former Haverhill player, was the top scorer at 64 but they could only total 142 for 5. This was certainly a boost to the morale of the town club. The 2nd XI drew their opening game, and the Sunday XI just missed a victory, scoring 119 and restricting Broomfield to a precarious 80 for 8 when stumps were drawn. In the next Sunday fixture some superb bowling by J Coleman destroyed the British Sugar side, setting figures of 7 wickets for 19 runs in a Haverhill victory. It was then left to skipper Debenham to score the winning run against Hadleigh at the cricket meadow, which was a difficult pitch for the batsmen. Hadleigh 55 were all out and Haverhill 56 for 9.

The Haverhill 2nd XI were contesting the League for 2nd teams and beat Sudbury II for their first points of the season. However, the 1st XI lost against the Sudbury I, but were in third place after just three games, winning two and losing one. Came June and a slump for Haverhill when everything went wrong versus Lakenheath, and Haverhill were all out for 108, a total which their opponents soon overtook. Peter Suffling starred in the 2nd XI victory over Thorley, scoring 117 out of their score of 173 while the 1st XI lost again at Saffron Walden. The misery continued when Felixstowe inflicted a 9 wicket defeat on Haverhill.

It was a story of two David's when Haverhill destroyed Exning by six wickets. David Debenham took 6 wickets for 31 and Dave Kendrick produced an unbeaten 59 on his league debut, hitting an almighty six for the winning runs. to steer the club to victory; Exning only managed 97 which proved inadequate as Haverhill wrapped up the league points. To complete a good day, the 2nd XI also won their game with Exning II as youngsters Simon Bishop and Nigel Hurrell were the principal run-getters. Paul Lucas also took on the tiring Exning attack to help Haverhill to a 60 run victory. A comfortable win versus Bury St Edmunds 174 -101 took the 2nd XI to the top of their section of the County League. Another fine bowling performance by

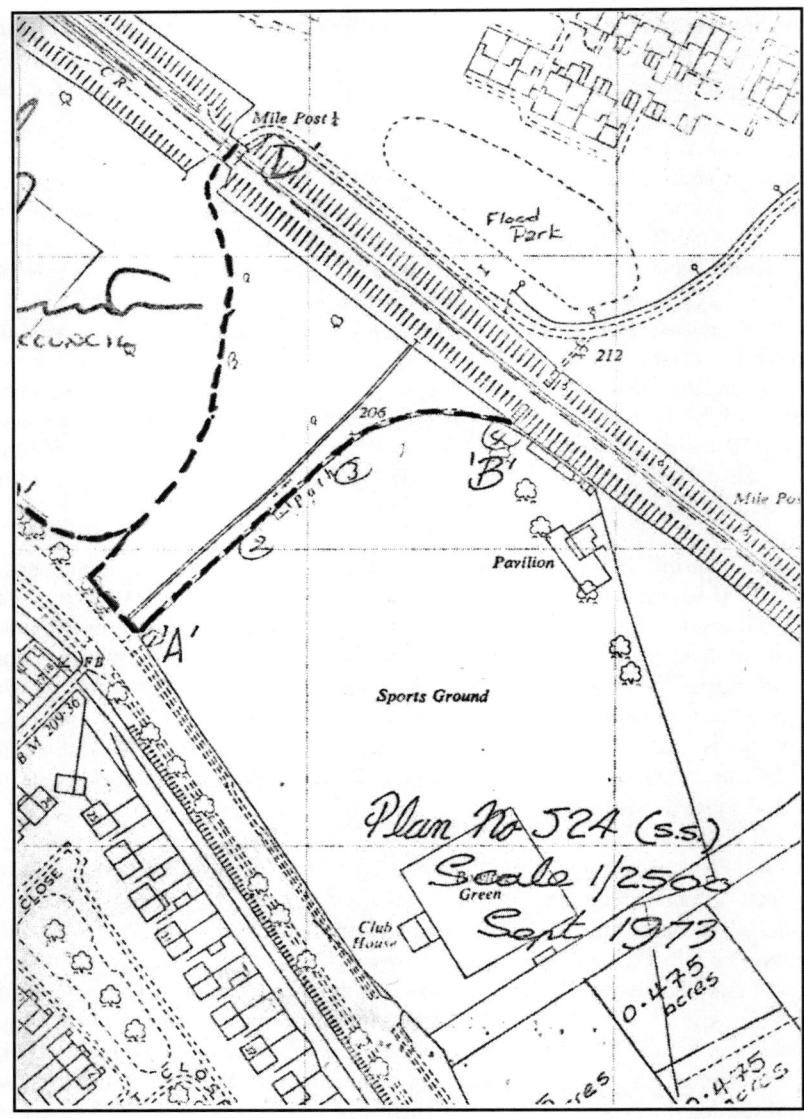

After many years the offending footpath was diverted away from the cricket meadow 1973

captain Debenham then helped Haverhill to a league double over Bury St Edmunds. Bury were all out for 98, Debenham taking 5 for 37 and H Shinn 4 for 46. Without a run on the board, Haverhill lost an early wicket and then Kendrick went for a 'duck' before the batsmen took control and totalled 101 for 6.

The newest Haverhill batsman David Kendrick, who joined the town club from Ipswich, handed a warning to the opposition bowlers with two fine innings in friendlies in one week-end. On the Saturday he made 92 against Baldock, and the following day he did even better, scoring 100 not out against March. He commented on the next match which was versus his former team, "*I am certainly hoping to score some runs against them for sure.*" Of interest was the fact that before he had scored any runs in his two high scoring displays, he was dropped by the opposing fielders, this proving expensive for the opponents. Despite hitting some penetrating scores, Haverhill could not put together a run of victories; they lost two league games in the same week-end and dropped to three places from the bottom.

Unpredictable Haverhill took revenge on Ipswich & East Suffolk but straightaway went down badly versus Felixstowe. The 2nd XI, however, were going along splendidly, and were unbeaten, topping their division and were unbeaten. Kendrick posted another skilled innings of 86 and N Ackerman hit 85 for the 2nd XI as they won at Hadleigh. A victory over Bury Rail put the 2nd XI in a position to become champions of their league, and this was the result when the season came to an end. A draw with Mildenhall and victory over Sudbury rounded off the 1st XI's summer, this not being so successful as had been hoped for.

****

A DOWNWARD TREND

As with several seasons the form of Haverhill's cricketers was not very consistent in **1980** with the Sunday XI upholding the spirit of the club A century maker was Steve Bishop who posted 104 not out for the 2nd XI. It was not far into the season that a bottom of the league table match was seen between Haverhill and Deben Valley, with Haverhill squeezing a victory 124 to 100. The return match did little to breed confidence as it was lost, as was the next game against Lakenheath by 99-97. The 2nd XI then hit a bit of form with Julian Poole scoring 106 not out at Lakenheath II and M Pope top bowler with 7 for 13 in the same match. The Haverhill Mid-week XI was looked to as the side to restore the club's reputation but they were vulnerable and lost games they were thought to win easily, including to the Teachers eleven from Haverhill, who totalled 77 for 3 to Haverhill's 75 for 7. They also bowed out of the RA Cup semi-final to Abington. Both Saturday sides were in the County League now known as the Willingdale League. The 1st XI were shown as two places from the bottom of their division and the 2nd XI third in Division Two.

The annual six-a-side tournament organised by the cricket club attracted sixteen teams with most village clubs entering, together with one-off elevens Farmers XI, Birdbrook Plough and Stambourne Red Lion. Neither sides of the Haverhill Club managed to string together a run of victories of any sort although they both produced some enjoyable wins, often in friendly games. W Easey hit 89 in the friendly victory at Poslingford, and the 1st XI caused a dent in the league title aspirations of Bury Rail when they beat them by two runs. Bury scored 173 for 9 and Haverhill were 21 for 3 when J Poole came to the wicket to steady the boat, seeing them through to victory with a determined knock of 53, Haverhill ending at 175 for 9.

In August there came a disaster when a fire gutted the seventy-year-old pavilion on the cricket ground. The Fire Service were called to the scene in mid-afternoon on Saturday and found flames coming from every opening of the building as it was well alight. When the fire was brought under control the pavilion was just a shell. It had been more or less disused for about six years and an investigation was to be made to find the cause, although it was not thought to be arson. As the remains of the structure were looked upon as being dangerous, it was pulled down completely.

1981 began under a new captain when John Holm took over the post, but two players were not with the club, David Debenham and Nigel Ackerman. The first two week-ends produced some very wet weather and all cricket matches were cancelled. Against Littleport in their first match, Haverhill struggled on a drying wicket and totalled 106 to which their opponents reached 89 for 6 to force a draw. Next game saw the batsmen let the side down as they scored a mere 91 and Bury Rail overtook this to take the victory. One bright spot was a cultured 44 from young Graeme Poole. Two more disastrous matches and Haverhill had lost five of their opening seven games; they touched rock-bottom when they lost by 10 wickets to Bury St Edmunds. The 2nd XI were not much better and were struggling in most of their County League matches. They even had to travel to Baldock for a friendly with only nine players.

Up against a strong Felixstowe side, Martin Wilkins hit a defiant 63 but this was not enough to turn the match in Haverhill's way. When the bottom two clubs met, Haverhill crashed to defeat to Exning with only two batsmen in double figures. Even two league games in one week ended in losses for the 1st XI, but in the last week of July there was a celebration when they tasted victory with a 5 wicket win over Lakenheath. It was bowler Phil Suffling who took the honours with figures of 7 for 32 in just 12 over's. The 1st XI then came back to earth with a bump as they descended to their poor ways and lost their next two matches followed by a simple draw.

August brought the top score of the summer for a Haverhill batsman when swashbuckling Lou Goodey scored 110 not out in the game against Sawston, who hung on at 105 for 8 for a drawn match. Julian Poole was also out on his own with his 58 in Haverhill's answer of 153 to Bury Rail's 200. To confuse everyone, the 2nd XI were said to have 'played like champions' in beating Sudbury II by 152 - 150. With D Debenham returning to the fold and taking 5 wickets for 50 against Sudbury, one more match was won before closing the season with two more defeats. Haverhill Sunday XI wound up their fixtures by winning against Wimbish; Kevin Cracknell and Ken Campkin were top scorers with both in the forties.

Haverhill began the **1982** season with high ambitions, hoping to run a first eleven, a second eleven, a Sunday team and a side in the Haverhill Mid-week

League. In the latter were teams from Delta RA, Addis, Teachers, Woolpack, Clements, Castle Manor School, the Fire Service and the Rugby Club, so it seems that there were quite a few cricketers in Haverhill and district. The first side to take the field were the Sunday XI, and helped by a score of 74 from J Senior, they forced a draw with Cambridge YMCA. A well struck 56 by Senior then saw Haverhill play out a tie of 162 each with Lakenheath. The Mid-week XI then lost their opening match to Weston Colville.

More sponsors were beginning to come forward and the Haverhill 1st XI were supported by Barclays Bank, Gurtex and Greene King to name but a few. A victory for the Mid-week side versus Abington was a false dawn however and they promptly lost the next group of games, and they stood bottom of the league and losing five of their first six matches. A positive approach enabled the 1st XI to gain a welcomed win over St Giles 151 for 4 against 150, but on the same day the 2nd XI were well beaten in a game when both teams struggled to reach the seventies.

Haverhill in the league on Saturday were unlucky as after they had managed just 110 for 8 against Bury Rail, rain forced a stoppage at 20 for 1 in Bury's reply. Play did resume with batting tricky on a well-soaked wicket but some dropped catches by the Haverhill fielders saw the game end in the Railmen's favour. The next Saturday it was just as sunny as it had been rainy the previous week and the 2nd XI crushed Newnham Croft by 99 runs. In their total of 204 for 4, Richard Wilkins contributed 87 and Arvind Matkar 62, while John Coles bowled excellently to take 5 for 27. The summer had not settled to any kind of pattern and there was not one week where all Haverhill sides won their matches. Usually a good display of batting was let down by the poor bowling that followed and some times the other way around,; not many games saw both options come together. In the victory over Broomfield it was the steady accurate bowling by Clarence Hulyer, Julian Poole and Martin Wilkins that swung the match.

Back in the local Mid-week League the Teachers side were unfortunately forced to withdraw from the league, having been the most consistent sides for over seven years; lack of players was the suggested cause. It was the lowest score of the season when Haverhill met Bury St Edmunds, Haverhill being all out for 67 and Bury won in a canter. To be fair, the conditions were not very good for this match and gradually got worse as the game went on. A whole programme of mid-week games were also lost as a rainy few days set in over the district.

Entering July, Haverhill were close to victory versus Ipswich & East Suffolk. In reply to an Ipswich total of just 83, Haverhill stood at 63 for 3, but then came a collapse amongst the batting and they were soon bowled out for 71. The 2nd XI brought a victory for the town, however, when they were successful over Bury Rail 158-154. Although Haverhill won one and lost one over the next week-end, they were one from bottom in the County League having won just one of their seven games so far. The 2nd XI were also one place off the bottom spot in their division. Another whirlwind innings from C Hulyer of 63 (5 fours and 3 sixes) plus J Senior with 44 could not force a Haverhill victory over Deben Valley who triumphed by 17 runs.

The 1st XI then batted disastrously and collapsed to 88 all out versus Felixstowe, but a sparkling century from Lou Gooding on Sunday saw the Sunday side romp to a win over Ipswich & East Suffolk; he notched 103 not out in Haverhill's total of 169 for 3. The following week saw both elevens victorious over Exning I and II. This was not continued as four run out disasters lost the game against Mildenhall in the league. Hulyer was the one who brought the game alive against Sawston with his quick 44 but it then petered out as a dull draw.

The first week in September saw the precocious talent of teenager Kevin Cracknell help the Mid-week XI to a win over Horseheath in the final of the Delta RA Cup. He was named the man of the match. However, the very mediocre run by the 1st XI continued as they lost to Sudbury by 9 wickets in a low scoring match 63 to 64 for 1 wicket. The Sunday team, who were having a really up and down summer, had a decent victory versus Wimbish with Graham Sadd top scorer on 50, his first half century for the club. The league fixtures were wound up with a gripping win at Tuddenham which kept Haverhill from the bottom position, and they finished with a friendly with Burrough Green, winning 209-46, Julian Poole 63 and D Kendrick 51 hitting the highest scores.

A new competition started in **1983** when the local newspaper sponsored the West Suffolk Newspapers Jubilee Cricket Cup; this involved most of the local villages as well as those around Bury St Edmunds. Meanwhile the Haverhill C C started their new season with the following team: J Poole (captain), D Kendrick, P Suffling, K Cracknell, G Sadd, A Dellar, J Mallett, J Coleman, C Hulyer, R Haylock, C Blyth. This was the selected eleven but the weather took a hand and the first week-end of the season was blocked out with some stormy weather. The Sunday XI were the first in action with a dull draw with Sawston. In the senior section of the West Suffolk Cup, Haverhill went out at the first hurdle when Hadleigh hit the winning runs in the last over of a rain affected match.

Facing long term rivals Sudbury, a marvellous spell of bowling by Howard Shinn (7 for 36) could not force a victory for Haverhill as they were left on 91 for 9 in reply to Sudbury's 145. There was an equally tight finish to the 2nd XI match, Haverhill claiming a one run win in the last over, 46-45. The 2nd XI consisted of E Bailey, S Rex, J Holm, R Chapman, C Burley, S Sergeant, D Joyce, N Talbot, S Sadler, T Pinkney and N Haylock. A victory slipped from Haverhill's grasp versus Lakenheath who finished on top 140 to 112, then they lost their next match against Bury Rail. The opening bad spell for Haverhill continued when they were beaten into submission by a very strong Felixstowe batting side 184 to 115. They picked themselves up and broke their duck with a victory over Exning. For Haverhill the innings was dominated by McFarlane with a score of 73.

An improvement was seen when Haverhill showed tremendous spirit when chasing a daunting target of 225 to gain a victory over Deben Valley on Sunday. Every one of the Deben fielders ringed the boundary as Steve Sargeant faced the last ball. He needed a four to tie the game and a six to win for Haverhill. However, he and J Coleman could only scamper two runs and the game was lost by two runs. The close endings to several games continued into the next game when a poor start by Haverhill saw them being defeated at Bury St Edmunds 137 - 135. The Mid-week XI were also having a dreadful start to their season and after seven games they had lost every one. For the 2nd XI Colin Bailey, the seam bowler, had a tremendous week-end, taking all but one of the Bury Rail wickets and following this up with six wickets versus Ipswich & East Suffolk.

Recognition came Haverhill's way when Howard Shinn represented Suffolk Club & Ground against Suffolk Senior Schools, while Kevin

Cracknell turned out for Suffolk Schools Under 19's versus Middlesex Under 19's. As well as this, two schoolboys, Graham Sizer and Tom Barton, were in the West Suffolk Under 14 squad for an encounter versus Essex Under 14's.

Breaking up the league games, Haverhill played a friendly against Bishops Stortford Ramblers when a top score of 67 from M Wilkins helped them to an 8 wicket victory. This was followed by P Jones with 82 not out in a 2nd XI win over Bury Rail II. After showing an assured performance to beat Lakenheath the 1st XI came under the Felixstowe hammer once again whose score of 237 was way beyond the capability of Haverhill. Shinn and Wilkins were among the wickets again for the 2nd XI versus Exning when they tore the opponents batting apart. The pattern of this season was one of surprising wins being outdone by equally poor defeats. The season ended on a high however as Sudbury were beaten in a hard fought game, by seven runs, and the 2nd XI also gained a victory over the Sudbury II to give them the runners-up position in their league.

1984 opened with the Haverhill Sunday XI entertaining the Cambridge West Indian XI, the town losing by 3 wickets in a well contested game. New signing Garry Roper announced his arrival with a good quality 80 runs, Lou Gooding backed him up with 70. The scores at the end being Haverhill 189 and Cambridge W I 190 for 7. The 2nd XI started with an impressive win over Lakenheath II, scoring 203 for 7, of which John Mallett got 76. However the 1st XI went out of the Nat West Suffolk Cup at the first hurdle, beaten by Tuddenham. They did force a d raw against old rivals Sudbury, Haverhill ending on top but just could not bowl their opponents out.

The 1st XI then went on a proficient run of victories, this included a fine win over one of their bogy sides Felixstowe, 125-121; Haverhill were gradually moving up the table. One of the best bowling figures was put up in June when Julian Poole took 6 wickets for only 34 runs against Broomfield for the Sunday side. Two more victories put the 1st XI in second place while the 2nd XI were standing on top of their division. Another new name cropped up as Charlie Blyth hit 63 for the 1st XI in a victory over Exning; 181-180. Another youngster Steve Rex made his 1st team debut making a rapid 29 versus Stowmarket. This was followed up with fifteen-year-old Bill Moran hitting 36 in his first game for the club. The young cricketers in Haverhill were attracting attention, and Richard Wilkins was selected in the Suffolk County squad to play four representative matches.

The Mid-week XI, mainly the Colts, were sitting comfortably in mid-table of the Haverhill League. Meanwhile, eight wins in the last ten matches saw Haverhill making a determined bid for the championship, with S Rex scoring an impressive 87 in the latest victory. A friendly fixture versus Stowmarket was lost by the 1st XI, M Churchill ending on 97 not out when he ran out of partners. Lucky it wasn't the league game! Then another fine bowling spell from P Suffling (6 for 30 in 10 over's) gave Haverhill another league win.

The annual six-a-side tournament had to be postponed until the following week owing to wet weather, but the Woolpack side took the honours for the second year in succession, beating Stambourne in the final. Their team consisted of M Wilkins, C Blyth, J Poole, R Wilkins, P Webb, D Ince and M Churchill. The 1st XI's long run of success continued as they beat Bury St Edmunds who were the league leaders, the Haverhill side hitting the heights and feeling confident of doing well for the remainder of the summer. However, two defeats for the side by Bury Rail and Mildenhall effectively ended their chances for the league title and they had to be satisfied with runners-up position. A well hit 101 not out by M Churchill was the top score in Haverhill's win over Sudbury to end the season on a high note.

The **1985** season started well for 2nd XI batsman Richard Last when he hit a century in the first week versus St Neots II. With Bill Easey contributing 63, the Haverhill score of 178 for 4 declared was too much for their opponents who only amassed 137 for 7. The Sunday XI also recorded a victory in a friendly against HMP by 91 runs; N Haylock took 4 wickets for just 7 runs. Unfortunately, the 1st XI lost their first outing to Sawston by 7 wickets. When the serious business of league fixtures began, hard hitting Sudbury were too good for the 1st XI, 258 to 137, but the 2nd XI won against the Sudbury II by 6 wickets.

Two more defeats over a weekend underlined the need for improvement in all departments for Haverhill. Then the Achilles Cricket Club inflicted a massive defeat on Haverhill by 10 wickets, their opening batsmen easily hitting the 167 runs for victory. Moving into flaming June did not help matters as two more losses to Bury St Edmunds and Lakenheath firmly rooted the 1st XI to the bottom of the league table. The 2nd XI were doing slightly better and beat Ipswich & East Suffolk but then the next day tasted defeat again.

Right-unexpected Haverhill pulled off a win over Stowmarket in a final ball thriller chasing 149; Haverhill made 150 for 8. Then two more matches were won, as the 1st XI seemed to improve overnight with virtually the same team. When Ipswich & East Suffolk came to Haverhill for the return match, they had as their captain Don Freeman who had moved to Ipswich from Haverhill. He had once ran a shop in Haverhill and had been playing cricket for around fifty years. Haverhill scraped home in this encounter by 2 wickets, with C Hulyer (4-49) and K Ayrton (5-62), doing all the bowling, showing great stamina. Another last ball win against Lakenheath saw the 1st XI move slowly up the Willingale League table; Haverhill were 50 for 5 at one time in this game. The 2nd XI were sitting in mid-table as they were having a chequered summer so far.

In the semi-final of the Nat West Plate, Haverhill put up a brave fight - A Dellar scored 71 - but went out of the competition losing to Sudbury. At this point Sudbury headed the league and Haverhill were four places off the bottom. The 2nd XI stood three from last place in the Reserve League, out of eleven teams. Meanwhile the Mid-week XI won their Delta R A Cup against the Woolpack. Away from club cricket, Phillip Shanks made a good contribution to the Suffolk Schools Under 15 side versus their Essex counterparts.

Continuing their bright run, Haverhill then scorched to their most emphatic victory over Ipswich by 10 wickets. An excellent spell of bowling from Richard Wilkins, who finished with 5 wickets for only 3 runs, and a sparkling 85 not out by Dave Ettridge sealed the win. It was a good all-round performance on a very damp wicket. Ipswich made 112 which the 1st XI passed by not losing a wicket. The 2nd XI all-rounder Robert Chapman hit 57, then took 7 wickets for 71 runs in their latest victory. The annual six-a-side competition was played out in drizzling rain and in the final, Helions Bumpstead beat Thurlow to take the trophy.

After six successive wins, the 1st XI's winning streak ended when they lost by 94 runs to Mildenhall. Stowmarket, followed by Bury St Edmunds, then put paid to Haverhill's chances of finishing in the top half of the table. Steady rain also saw another game abandoned. An improved showing meant a narrow 1st XI loss to Bury Rail, and the 2nd XI lost another match when they could not hold on to their catches; fielding practice was badly needed. The following two matches saw Haverhill put out a very weakened eleven and lose both games to wind up a season which was described by captain John Coleman as a *"holding season"* as they struggled with depleted sides in some games. It had been a promising season for three of the younger members, Phillip Shanks, Stephen Sadler and Stephen Rinaldi. J Poole was top of the averages for batting, and R Wilkins top bowler.

The Haverhill Sunday XI were first out of the blocks in **1987** and in a friendly beat HMP by 11 runs, 110 to 99. The 1st XI for their opening match against Southwold were, S Price, A Bailey, M Jolland, J Poole, B Moran, S Taylor, S Rinaldi, R Chapman, R Ellicott, P Goff and M Rinaldi. This was a very low-scoring game which Haverhill won by one wicket, 63-64. It was a rain affected wicket which was probably why runs were hard to come by. On the bowling side, M Jolland had a good match and had figures of 8 for 27. The following week rain was still the order of the day, and the Haverhill game versus Deben Valley was abandoned with a young Haverhill team on 26 for 2 in reply to their opponent's 207.

At this time Haverhill put out an appeal for more players to join the club, as the future of the 2nd XI was under threat, due to the problem of fielding two sides each week. The club had lost six players from last year's 1st XI and were now very much down in numbers. They were in a sound financial position and had facilities which compared favourably with most Suffolk cricket clubs. Their appeal read *"Anyone interested in keeping senior cricket in Haverhill please contact the club, or come along to the Manor Ground on Monday or Friday evenings, or when games are being played."* The Haverhill 2nd XI lined up C Hulyer, D Joyce, D Ince, A Abdulali, C Thompson, P Bryant, M Thomer, A Harling, R Haylock, C Chapman and J McKenzie. Others who came into the Sunday side included A Dellar, S Rex and P Goff.

A friendly versus Sawston produced a drawn match with honours shared. Then two Dairytime Suffolk League matches were lost by Haverhill, to Lakenheath and Bury Rail, when hard work in the field was let down by some disastrous batting. Haverhill then managed to claim a draw versus Worlington. A week of effort in the nets made an improvement as a more mature Haverhill grabbed league points with a victory over Exning. Torrential rain had soaked the wicket before this match and prompted the comment *"Anything over ten runs will be difficult to beat."* Exning totalled 102, and Haverhill replied with 103 for 7. The 2nd XI made it a rare double on the day when they beat Exning II by 8 wickets, 41- 44 for 2,. B Easey, P Jones and J Holm hitting off the runs required. This was the first victory for the 2nd XI.

While the Sunday XI were not doing as well as they had in previous seasons, a high turnover of players was pointed out as a possible cause. However, the Mid-week XI was top of Division Two after six games had been played. Losses for both Saturday sides in their league games, the 1st by 97 runs and the 2nd XI by 10 wickets, showed up the weaknesses in the sides. Another disastrous weekend in searing heat was next with defeats for both the 1st and 2nd XI's. Ipswich piled up 255 runs as Haverhill tried seven different bowlers to try and contain them, to no avail. Haverhill could not match the strength of the Ipswich batsmen and also put down several catches. Other defeats saw a regular spectator observe, *"I see the ancient and arthritic players are out today."* The poor displays continued throughout August. Just when it was thought that another victory would never come, Bury St Edmunds came to town and Haverhill finally stopped their dreadful run with a 28 run win. On the same day the 2nd XI produced a good display to end victorious over Southwold II by 5 wickets.

Unfortunately this was just a bright spark in a dull and dismal season, and the league games were completed with three more Haverhill defeats. The misery carried on, and although the bowling was quite decent, the batting form let the side down and they never really looked like winning any of their lost games. However, the Mid-week side ended their season top of their league, to give a little hope for the future, as they had included some of the younger players of the club.

After the previous season's disappointing results, the Haverhill club was to rely even more on proven players such as Julian Poole, Bill Moran, Phil Jones, Alan Bailey and Stephen Rinaldi. Young players coming along were Russell Ellicott, Ian Jacobs and David Green amongst others. The Sunday XI were the first into action with the team of C Hulyer, C Blythe, P Shanks, C Thompson, D Green, S Rinaldi, M Rinaldi, L Jacobs, M Jolland, G Carroll and D Ince. A friendly against Sawston was lost by Haverhill, and unfortunately, this set the pattern for the summer ahead. Haverhill 2nd XI surprised everyone with a victory in their opening fixture by eight wickets over Halstead II. This was an extremely low-scoring match, the scores being 33 against 35 for 2.

Starting their Dairytime League Division One matches, the 1st XI lost to Southwold by 23 runs. Their opponents totalled 103 to which Haverhill replied with 80; this looked impossible at one time when they stood at 40 for 8 wickets. P Shanks was tops with the ball taking 5 for 21, but to no avail. A second defeat followed quickly to make it a desperate start for Haverhill. Tuddenham were next to put it across both the Haverhill Saturday sides, followed by Lakenheath and Bury St Edmunds. A friendly with Sawston gave the Sunday XI a draw with C Hulyer smashing his way to 96. The Sunday side actually won a game winning by 21 runs over local side HMP, the Saturday sides still suffering two more losses.

In came June and at last a win for the 2nd XI, by 37 runs over Worlington II. Then a bright light appeared above the clouds when they won their second game in a row with a impressive victory over Bury St Edmunds II, thanks to a century from Bill Moran (123 not out) and a solid 57 by P Shanks. A draw from a friendly with Ipswich & East Suffolk only came after the opponents had reached 107 for 6 when rain saw the game abandoned. After a wet period that affected all matches, Lakenheath were the next to do the double over the Saturday sides, winning both 1st and 2nd XI matches against Haverhill. The Mid-week XI were not as successful as the season before; after seven games they had lost five of these and were low down in their league table. Gloom continued to spread as another loss came versus Worlington, despite some good fielding by the Haverhill side and having three run outs. Worlington did not make a large score but when Haverhill took the bat it was a dismal procession of walks back to the pavilion; Haverhill only provided a ten-man side as well. For several of the games the Haverhill sides failed to reach three figures.

A ray of sunshine in this depressing season came when the Haverhill Colts team took the honours at the club's annual 6-a-side tournament, beating Helions Bumpstead in the semi-finals before winning the final against Carver Barracks. This was better, and the afternoon was full of glorious summer sun for a change. Bill Moran ended the final with a mighty six to take the trophy. A September friendly game versus Halstead saw a rare Haverhill victory by 50 runs. However, only two batsmen reached double figures, one being P Shanks (52), and S Rinaldi was amongst the wickets, taking 6 for 34. While the 2nd XI gained a second win over Tuddenham II, the 1st XI arranged another friendly and won this by 5 wickets over Helions Bumpstead. In the defeat of Tuddenham II, C Hulyer took 6 wickets for 38 runs; bowling was not really his forte but this was most welcome.

Despite four Haverhill batsmen getting well into the thirties they still lost to Deben Valley as the season ended with the 1st XI losing their place in the top division of the Dairytime League. It was left to the 2nd XI to gain a victory over Worlington II to wind up the season, which was certainly one of the worst in Haverhill's history. R Ellicott chose this final game to score his highest score of the season, making 93 to end his own summer with a flourish.

To begin the **1989** season, a Haverhill XI played a friendly game versus HMP, one of the best works teams in the area, and so they proved when the match was drawn. In reply to HMP's 171, of which M Wilkins scored 102, Haverhill were 143 for 5 when time was called, R Ellicott making 96. Haverhill's 1st XI were in the Suffolk Dairytime League Division Two and the first match saw them beat Lakenheath II by 145 runs, a startling win. All the batsmen played well and Ellicott was top scorer again with 69 to his name. On the same week-end they also won against Little Clacton by 34 runs, as everything looked to be good for the campaign.

The next week-end brought the first league defeat too early when Tuddenham ended victorious 118 to Haverhill's modest 95. They did, however, beat Ipswich & East Suffolk by 45 runs. Over this week-end Steve Rinaldi had a haul of 11 wickets for 91 runs. Of the victory over Bury St Edmunds, captain C Hulyer said "*It was an excellent result, I can't remember the last time we won against Bury at Manor Road.*" Last man in for Haverhill was seventeen-year-old M Rinaldi who rattled up 60 runs in quick time. The usual eleven included C Hulyer, D Joyce, C Thompson, R Chapman, S Rinaldi, M Rinaldi, D Green, J Holm, G Carroll and R Ellicott, with the umpire I Moss. A century by S Rinaldi (100 not out) was not quite good enough for Haverhill when Bury Railway were the opposition. The total of 187 for 5 was passed by Bury for five wickets down.

A high scoring game was next as Exning were the winners 211 for 5 over Haverhill 210 for 9. But the town gained a decisive success over Worlington by 7 wickets, with opening batsman Ellicott still in fine form with 90 runs. Next was a poor week-end with no victories by any town side. The Mid-week eleven had the worst record so far after playing ten games, winning just one. A last wicket stand foiled Haverhill against Lakenheath who won by two runs. It was becoming an up and down summer and it was made much worse when the 1st XI had to forfeit the league points to Southwold as they could not raise enough players to make the long journey. Despite withdrawing from the Premier section and playing in the second division, Haverhill were still having trouble in getting a side together most of the summer. They had also failed to draw better support to the home matches which were very often witnessed by only a sprinkling of spectators.

The club's misfortunes took a back seat, however, when they achieved the most astonishing and brilliant victory. Only eight players turned up for Haverhill against a full strength Mildenhall side. But the eight players played above themselves having just three bowlers, a wicket-keeper and a scattering of fielders, on a cloudy and damp afternoon. They managed to restrict Mildenhall to 169 for 6. Starting their batting at 5-45pm, they hit out to grab victory at 171 for 3, R Ellicott 81, C Thompson 47 and D Green 31 being top scorers in a most unlikely win against the odds. Three more points came Haverhill's way when Ipswich could not get a side together to visit Haverhill, eventually calling the match off at the late hour of 1-30pm.

A home loss to Southwold and a drawn match versus Sawston ended the season which went well into September, the Rovers having already played four football matches by the time cricket finally ended for the 1989 season

The summer of **1990** greeted the cricket season with a mid-week game for the Haverhill Club when they gained a four wicket victory over Abington. This was a limited over match of twenty over's each side, and the scores were 58-54. Pacey bowler Neil Williams was the Haverhill hero with 5 for 18. The following eleven represented Haverhill in the opening Saturday fixture versus Great Cornard; C Hulyer, S Rinaldi, M Rinaldi, N Williams, R Blackmore, G Lane, B Chesnaye, R Chapman, D Joyce, G Hulyer and J Holm. They beat Cornard by 97 runs; M Rinaldi was not out 77 in the total of 160 for 4, and Holm was the best bowler with a match record of 6 over's, 3 maidens and 6 wickets for 6 runs. Meanwhile on Sunday, Haverhill were again the winners over visitors Lakenheath with the team of. P Nealon, P Jones, C Blythe, C Hulyer, P Goff, S Price, M Rinaldi, I Jacobs, R Chapman, L Basire and M Roper.

In the return match against Lakenheath, the victors were Haverhill once again. They had a very bad opening to their innings when they lost three wickets down for 23 runs but hit back to pass the Lakenheath total with three wickets to spare. Then Haverhill lost for the first time in the Suffolk Dairytime League when Tuddenham beat them by five wickets, S Rinaldi hitting a top score for the town side with 61. The Mid-week XI then spoilt Kedington's unbeaten run when they were the victors on the cricket meadow.

Haverhill hit the heights on Sunday when they recorded their highest score so far against Southwold, P Shanks smashing 94 and narrowly missing out on a century. Young D Green had a good spell, taking one wicket for a paltry 6 runs, as Haverhill won by 137 runs. Sponsors were coming into the game of cricket much more now, and Glasswells were the sponsors of the cricket ball for the match versus Bury St Edmunds. Meanwhile the Mid-week team were on the losing side when HMP, who were doing very well, were winners by 8 wickets. Helions Bumpstead, another strong village side, then knocked Haverhill Mid-week XI out of the RA Cup. The Haverhill XI were standing halfway in the league table so far with half a dozen games completed. They were stated to have been deducted two points for some reason which was not reported anywhere.

The Haverhill Sunday XI took on the village of Withersfield one weekend; the village team put up a respectable show before suffering a defeat. A special match was held to celebrate the forty years of Mid-week League cricket in Suffolk. The Provincial League (Haverhill) met the Mick McNeill League at HMP, with P Shanks representing the Haverhill side in the Provincial team which won the match. Haverhill were doing quite well in the league this season and showed their best style when beating Linton away. It was not so for the 1st XI when they could not find their peak form and sank to Bury St Edmunds. However, they were just as good as they were bad the next week when they showed some solid batting at Mildenhall in the Dairytime League. Most of the batsmen scored twenty or thirty in their total of 172 for 9, the home team could not score as many, especially from Haverhill's S Rinaldi who took 7 for 28.

On a very sunny week-end in July, the Haverhill Saturday team were at Great Cornard. Russell Ellicott (95) and John Holm (37) put on 103 for the first wicket for Haverhill who built up a first-class tally of 201 for 7. They were denied a victory as Cornard were stuck on 124 for 7 when they ran out of time. Then a friendly game on Sunday against Bury Rail was won by Haverhill by 18 runs. In the Midweek League, the leaders Wimbish played Haverhill and showed why they were top of the league by winning against the town side. amongst the younger cricketers of Haverhill, Parkway Middle School had a very successful season and won the Under 13 West Suffolk Schools Trophy. Haverhill Midweek XI finished their season quite early as the league was not very large, and they ended up fourth out of eight teams. Their record read 14 games played, of which 8 were won and 6 lost.

Travelling to distant Southwold, Haverhill 1st XI produced a real demolition job to dismiss the opposition for just 48, then took complete control to overtake this total in only nine over's. The bowlers who did the damage were G King 6-33 and M Rinaldi 4-13. Haverhill lost their final friendly to Sawston by 19 runs, but signed off in style in the Suffolk League with a victory over the strong Ipswich & East Suffolk XI by 17 runs, 101 to 84.

May **1991** brought the decision that many expected but hoped they would never hear, when it was announced that there would be no week-end cricket at Haverhill's Manor Road ground for the coming summer. This was due almost entirely to not having enough players to put a side out each week, for the first time in 120 years. There had been a five or six year slide to this point, and no new or younger players were joining the club to improve the state of affairs. The surrounding village clubs were very strong, and better town players had moved to other teams in the wider area, rather than play their cricket in Haverhill. Strange as it may seem, the club's youth policy resulted in Haverhill Cricket Club consisting of the older players, some over 40 years of age, and a small bunch of very young cricketers. The club was hoping to fit in two or three friendlies but most cricket would be in the Midweek League. The club was not about to fold as it was the Haverhill Cricket and Sports Club and included the successful Bowls Club section. A bright light on the horizon was the news that two schoolboys of the town, Scott Webb and Ben Mansfield, who attended Castle Manor, had played cricket for the Suffolk Schoolboys eleven.

After last summer when the Haverhill Club were allowed to run just a second XI in the Suffolk League on Saturdays, the decision was made not to do the same this year. That the Haverhill Cricket Club was held in some high esteem by the officials of the Suffolk League was visible when they were 'flabbergasted' by the announcement of Haverhill's withdrawal at the Annual League Meeting. The Haverhill team in the Midweek League was led by Phil Shanks, who was planning to play his week-end cricket with Braintree. The few other players who had been ready to play for Haverhill in the Suffolk League had to search for another club, and those who were playing for the mid-week eleven were not expected to pay any subscriptions this year.

So the sad season began with Haverhill Midweek XI competing in Division One of the League. By June they were in a mid-table position having played four matches, winning one and losing two, and one game which was listed as no result. Their next match against Abington saw them get off to a good start after their opponents made 140 for 2. Haverhill stood at 127 for 1, then lost quick wickets as they went for the runs to give them victory, but ended six runs short. They also went down by thirty runs to Horseheath, reckoned by many to be one of the best village sides. In a lower division were Withersfield who were flying high in their section while Helions Bumpstead were also one of the stronger sides from the 'sticks'.

The Wenden versus Haverhill fixture brought a tie. Wenden totalled 80 for 7; Haverhill had matched that score with nine wickets down and the last ball of the match to be bowled, but they lost that wicket and had to be content to share the spoils. It was in another game that Dave Tunnell of Lowery Engineering made everyone sit up during a fantastic short spell of bowling against Kedington White Horse. He was put on to bowl, and twelve deliveries later he had taken seven wickets for only one run, a feat it would be hard to surpass. The only century scored in the League this season was from Richard Wilkins who also played football with Cambridge United; he hit one hundred not out for HMP versus Wenden.

Haverhill lost once again to Horseheath by scoring 105 for 4; this was passed with 107 for 6 and a half an hour to spare. Then Haverhill began to improve and by August were up to third place in the League. A proficient win was secured over Wenden, Phillip Shanks making 66 in Haverhill's total of 158 for 5, to which their opponents put up 118 for 6 by the close of play. This was a strong late burst by the town side but Linton were crowned champions of Division One.

Haverhill Midweek XI had their reward by reaching the final of the R A Cup in which they played Abington at Linton. The conditions were excellent when they met but Abington took the honours by twenty-five runs. The Haverhill team lined up C Thompson, P Shanks, N Williams, P Jones, S Taylor, S Price, S Rose, G King, L Basire, G Hulyer and N Brunning. After making 79 for 9, Haverhill reduced Abington to 2 wickets down for 9 runs before the village side recovered to 102 for 6 and took the trophy presented by that year's Miss Echo. Haverhill eventually finished in third place in the League, and N Williams was given the best bowlers award.

Early headlines in **1992** did not exactly help matters, *"Little hope now for Cricket Club with no team."* The outlook was indeed very bleak as the next season loomed, as more efforts to save the club had failed. At the Annual Meeting in January, held earlier to see if anything could be done to get going once again at week-ends,. A decision was made to keep the flag flying with just a midweek team captained by Michael Rinaldi. There was also a move to run the cricket club separately from the Bowls Club, but this was soon talked down as the title had been the Haverhill Cricket and Bowls Club for many years.

As the season began former Haverhill players were settled into their new clubs, leaving just a few older and experienced players to help the town's youngsters in the nets. There was some hope of arranging one or two friendly encounters on Saturdays during the summer. Unfortunately this never materialised as most teams, who themselves had trouble in finding players to represent them, could not fit a game in with Haverhill.

After performing so well the previous season, the Haverhill Midweek XI had moved up into the first division of the league, and after a few weeks were settling down to a position in mid-table. The first four matches resulted in two victories, one drawn game and one loss. Scores were also up and down with a loss to Abington 71 for 6 against 72 for 5, followed by winning against HMP 104 to 103, the Little Wratting side being one of the better teams in the district. After a second defeat to Horseheath, Haverhill then humbled the league leaders Wenden by 4 wickets, with N Sheldrake making 80 not out. Good knocks from N Williams 42 not out and G King 34 not out then brought another victory for the town side over Helions Bumpstead, a strong team at this period.

In contrast to the fortunes of the cricket club, the game was flourishing in other parts of Haverhill including the schools. Parkway Middle School took part in a West Suffolk School Tournament, and after beating three other schools in their group matches, they eventually went out in the quarterfinals; a good showing by the young boys. They were hopefully the future of Haverhill cricket, as the seniors of cricket in the town club were working hard to encourage this sort of junior player to become members of Haverhill Cricket Club. The season drifted to a close, but the main thing was that a team representing the town were still in place, just waiting for the slumbering giant to awake once more.

1993 and another season in the virtual wilderness, with no Haverhill eleven on the traditional week-end. The Midweek XI thought they had started off well against Abington in their first match, but after scoring 111 for 7, the village side passed this with 114 for 6. Meanwhile the Castle Manor cricket team also began with a defeat versus Thurston School; there were some young players coming along in the Haverhill school team but they were not quite old enough to step up to the town side. In a high-scoring game against Horseheath, G Gooday hit 75 not out for Haverhill as they posted a victory

139 for 2 - 138 for 2.

This win did not set the season alight for the Haverhill XI as they promptly lost the next six fixtures, which included a heavy reverses versus Linton by eight wickets and a 79-77 defeat in the R A Cup against Stradishall. At this moment they were low in the league table, playing six and lost five of; then they were defeated twice more and slipped to the very bottom. As the summer rolled on they could not rise from the last place, although they did gain one more win. The winner of Division One of the Provincial Midweek League was Newmarket Foods who won their last two matches to take the title.

Youngsters of the town got the chance to get some professional coaching from a sporting star from down-under. Cheton Patel of the New Zealand Under 21 side took some time out to visit Haverhill and teach some of the basic skills to local youngsters. He had been having a few games for Halstead and came to Samuel Ward School in Haverhill to run courses from 23-26 August from noon to 2-30pm; each session costing £10.

Wratting Lions, Castle Manor, Fire Service, Newmarket Foods, Withersfield, Helions Bumpstead, Horseheath, Withersfield, Ashdon, Kedington and the Queens Head all put out cricket teams each week in **1994**. It was no secret that any of the village clubs would be successful against Haverhill's Midweek eleven. In fact Helions were strong enough to have matches three days of the week throughout the 1994 season, and ended up playing thirty games. Haverhill's week-end team, in contract, had been non-existent for some years, the ground was substandard; the pavilion was an eyesore, having been virtually destroyed by fire, and the pitch had been worsening over the years. The other sport at the cricket meadow was doing well however. The Bowls Club A team topped the Steeple Bumpstead & District League, and the Ex Servicemen's Club were top of the second division of the same Bowls League

The start of the 1994 season found the club at possibly its lowest ebb. With many of the better players having left to play for other clubs, there was only a nucleus of half a dozen members, most of whom struggled to commit due to work commitments. The young captain and grounds man, Michael Rinaldi, had been struggling on with this situation for several years, since the demise of weekend cricket, and could only see it getting worse. Haverhill were managing to fulfil fixtures as Rinaldi was asking players from Braintree, where he had gone to play weekend cricket, to come and help out. Even so, they were often fielding less than the allotted quota of eleven men, and subsequently sank to some heavy defeats.

After another home defeat that season, and having been unable to gain access to the pavilion to shelter from a cloud burst due to a bowls club dinner taking place, Rinaldi returned home with thoughts of calling time on the club. This would mean no more cricket at Manor Road. After having a long discussion with his father and local businessman David Rinaldi, the pair agreed that this could not be allowed to happen. They would do all they could to rectify the situation and make Haverhill Cricket Club one of the premier Suffolk sides once more.

Speaking several years later Michael Rinaldi said, "*In a funny way, the club being at such a low was probably one of the best things that could have happened. It meant that we were starting with a completely blank sheet of paper and could build the club we wanted. The aim back then was the same as it is now, in that we wanted to build a club and facilities of which the town can be proud.*" It was agreed that in order for the club to set about its transformation it required a pavilion of its own. Since the building of the indoor bowls club in 1974, both cricket and bowls sections had shared facilities, but his had never really worked. David Rinaldi then called upon local architect Peter Philbin to draw up some plans for the building, whilst with the help of newcomer Kieron Bailey, Micjael Rinaldi drew up plans for the marketing of the new club and how to get them back to top flight cricket.

Expert help was being sought to improve the pitch, but many other things had to be in place before the club could say it was up and running successfully once again. The saving group admitted that it would take two or three years to achieve what they wanted, two elevens each week, a midweek side and a junior eleven to bring the players through the system, in short a team to cover all levels. Meanwhile the team would still only operate in the Midweek League as the time had expired for applying to take part in any week-end games. The main aims were to achieve Suffolk Premier League status and to upgrade the Manor Road ground. To this end, next season's sponsors for the team had been obtained, Linton Place Stores in Haverhill. It was a start.

In the middle of March **1995** plans were coming along well and the cricket club announced £65,000 improvements to the ground and buildings. The brand new pavilion would be on two tiers, a clubhouse on the ground floor plus changing rooms and showers, and a veranda above. A seating area for spectators was to be provided along the clubhouse wall. There then came the announcement that the UK were to launch a National Lottery, with funds being granted to these kind of projects. The timing could not have been better as the club were ready to begin their application immediately. After a huge amount of work from David Rinaldi the finance was in place, the building was designed and permission in place, and so work began. Construction was hoped to start in the following September. Club member Neil Williams, who was a teacher at Samuel Ward Upper School, was to became youth coach; it was said by him that every lunch break between twenty and thirty boys converged on the nets at the school. It was thought this talent could be to the towns club's advantage.

Unfortunately, cricket for the Haverhill Club was still restricted to one team playing in the Midweek League as the management committee worked for the clubs survival. The captain Mick Rinaldi hoped to arrange a few friendlies for week-ends to test the water, to see if Haverhill wanted a cricket club or not. The summer of '95 was probably one to forget as the team struggled on, The club winning and losing the same number of games and the week-ends still not seeing any worthwhile cricket.

****

A RISE FROM THE ASHES

The **1996** season was earmarked as the most important one in the Cricket Club's history. The club announced that they were feeling confident of a grant from the National Lottery to improve its profile. When the nets were opened, there was, however, only a very small group who took advantage to prepare for the season in the Provincial Midweek League. The next step was the amalgamation of the Haverhill C C and the Fire Service C C to be known as Haverhill I and Haverhill II. More friendly games were hoped to be played at some weekends with a view to operating in a league the following year.

Work was done on the playing square with advice from the groundsman of the Bury St Edmunds Victory Ground, while a number of events were held, a casino night, a quiz night and a big band evening with the 42nd Street Band providing the music. Sponsorship was obtained from AXA Equity and Legal for an inter-company tournament and fun day in July.

The first fixture was in May, a friendly versus Thurlow which was won by Haverhill by 45 runs. The town eleven paraded N Williams, S Price, D Poole, N Proctor, M Rinaldi, P Nealon, K Bailey, L Basire, M Cook, D Goodwin and R Jones. They then began the midweek matches by beating Lowery Engineering by seven wickets. They continued this opening form with wins over Hundon and Thurlow. It was in the match between Kedington and Newmarket Foods that two centuries were hit in one game, M Giles 105 for Kedington and 109 by Richard Last for their opponents. In the RA Cup the Haverhill II side were victorious against Mill Green II while Helions Bumpstead came to the cricket meadow to upset Haverhill by 64 runs.

Halfway through the season and Haverhill I stood midway in the Midweek League table, but Haverhill II were bottom as they had lost all the nine games played so far. With a town such as Haverhill struggling to keep the club alive, the village teams in the district were flourishing with Withersfield, Kedington, Ashdon, Horseheath, Steeple Bumpstead, Hundon, Thurlow and Wratting joining Helions Bumpstead in putting strong teams of local cricketers in the field each week. The July tournament, however, brought some factory teams together, if only for this event. It was a total success and the cup and shield went to Newmarket Foods who defeated Project in the final which was played in very sunny weather. The prize for the best turned-out eleven went to Gurteens Factory who looked very smart in their matching blue and white kit. On the cash side, however, it was not quite the success they wished as numerous other events were on the same day. The season ended with two losses for Haverhill I, but the Haverhill II only chalked up their first win in the penultimate game against Thurlow by four runs, and ended bottom of the heap. Haverhill I were stuck in the middle regions of the Midweek League which could be said to be a fairly good summer

---

Just before the **1997** cricket season got underway a surprise announcement came from Newmarket Foods that they were withdrawing from the Midweek

League as they had not enough players to raise a team each week. They had been one of the top clubs the last few years, and their comment was that there were not enough cricketers in Haverhill to keep the game alive in the town. This prompted a reply from Castle Manor School who also had an eleven operating in the midweek league, saying that the game was alive and well at that school, with most years having a team.

The new Haverhill Club had been accepted in the Mick McNeill League, but they had been placed in Division Five as all fresh clubs had to start at the bottom tier. A friendly match was played versus Hundon which gave several players a chance to stretch their legs; the best of the young bowlers was Simon King who took 4 wickets for 24 runs. The following Saturday saw the first competitive game played by Haverhill for six years. They were up against Ampton & Culford, when they proceeded to beat handsomely, helped by a top score of 67 from M Rinaldi. A feature of the game was that Haverhill proved they could hang on to their catches which probably gave them the edge. The eleven who represented Haverhill were D Poole, S Price, S King, D Miller, N Proctor, L Basire, N Green, N Basire, M Page, G Hulyer and M Rinaldi. Only two bowlers were used in this opening match, Rinaldi and Miller bowling successfully throughout the innings.

The Midweek XI also began on a high note by beating Hundon, scoring 161 for 6, with the great innings of 114 blasted by L Scarfe. Pitting themselves against one of the best village clubs found Haverhill wanting, however, as they went down to a defeat 264-3 - 89 to Helions Bumpstead. The next weekend and a second victory for Haverhill in the league, scoring 228 - 5 (S Price 108) versus Needham's 45. After four matches Haverhill stood top of the league. The Midweek side also recorded another victory against Thurlow. The club were now looking at plans that had been drawn up for the new pavilion; backing was coming from several local businesses with the main sponsor being Nat West Bank.

It just needed a jolt to remind the new Haverhill that things were not going to be easy. This came when they lost their unbeaten record by being second best to Bushey CC, tumbling to defeat by seven wickets. The captain remarked, "*We won the toss but it was the wrong decision to bat first on second thoughts.*" It was back to winning ways the next game, a low scoring affair versus Rougham. Halfway through the season and Haverhill were near the top, and the Midweek XI halfway up their league table. The six-a-side tournament was unfortunate with the weather which caused it to be postponed until later in the summer.

Haverhill then pulled off its best win yet when playing the team running them close to win the league. Ampton & Culford were defeated by four wickets, to see Haverhill climb back to the top of the league once again. For the first time for many years, a touring side played at the cricket meadow, Haverhill entertaining the Olicarnions from Yorkshire. This match saw S Jones hitting 7 sixes and 7 fours in his outstanding innings of 93, Haverhill demolishing the opposition. The new Haverhill were going great guns and demolish Risby in their next outing, presenting their opponents with a score of 315 for 4 to win the game; Risby made 89 in reply. For the winners, C Thompson 93 and M Cowell with a very quick 50 from just nineteen deliveries were the top batsmen. Funds were also looking up with £250 banked from a casino evening put on by the club. Haverhill ended the summer highest of Division Five, losing just one match in their march to the top, and making a fine comeback to Saturday cricket. The Midweek XI settled for a place halfway in their league. There was already talk of having a weekend 2nd XI for the weekend next season.

In preparation for the **1998** season, the whole of the cricket square was re-laid at a cost of £2,000 to go with the brand-new lottery funded pavilion. Along with this, the team had gained promotion in the Mick McNeill Suffolk League and was now in Division Four. Also, for the first time in several years, a second eleven was to operate in Division Five. The club were looking to Simon Price and Dan Wilkins to score readily again, and the main wicket-takers were hoped to be Mick Rinaldi and Steve Jones. The services of a full-time groundsman had been obtained in Tony Roberts, who was hoping the weather improved to start the season, as rain had pushed back some work on the wicket.

Without five regulars for their first match, the 1st XI entertained Brockley II who included ex-professional Neil Williams, but even he could not prevent a Haverhill victory. Haverhill had started out disastrously when two wickets went down with no score on the board, but aided by a 69 from P O'Hare who also took 4 wickets for 13 runs, they outscored the village side 169-80. The

2nd XI also won away at Rougham. Woolpit were then beaten, with scores of 78 from M Rinaldi and 72 by S Taylor being the highlights. On the other hand, Taylor was out first ball in his next match. A Wednesday evening match saw the Colts team playing against a slightly more mature side. A side were also competing in the local Midweek League.

Facing Brandon, who were a league higher than Haverhill, the town side came out on top to reach the last eight in the League Cup, the margin being 110 runs. When Haverhill won against Brockley II by 124 runs the town stood unbeaten after the first four matches, as were the 2nd XI. Castle Manor School was playing in the Midweek League. Samuel Ward School received a visit and a coaching session by Quinton De Brun, the six feet tall South African cricketer who was on a tour of Suffolk Schools. The town's 1st XI could probably have done with his services when they had a very poor week-end, lost their unbeaten tag and went down by six wickets to Stansfield, their opening bat hitting 93 not out. The 2nd XI suffered the same fate and lost to Lavenham by twenty-six runs.

Haverhill Cricket Club's annual six-a-side tournament attracted a lot of support on August Bank Holiday Monday as seven teams entered. These included the Australian Arms, Haverhill Colts, Gurteens, Teachers and Grampian Foods, the latter ending up the winners. The Club president Mr C Gurteen commented, *"It's good to see so many people here enjoying themselves, that's what it's all about."* The Haverhill sides were also back to winning form the next week when putting up a score of 227 versus Bushey who could only manage 82. The seconds were not so lucky and lost to Hadleigh by 98 runs, as did the Midweek eleven losing to Mill Green. A week-end off came along when it was stormy all over the country.

Haverhill faced a team thirty-one places above them in the league in the Knock-Out Cup, but turned in a fine display to progress to the semi-finals with the victory over Newton. It was in bright sunshine that M Rinaldi hit 69. He had started in the right frame with a straight drive for six and continued to slap the ball to all areas of the ground in a highly entertaining calypso-style innings. This latest win prompted the Haverhill Club to announce that it had prepared an application to enter the Two Counties League the next season. They had the players and facilities up to standard with a good youth set-up, and the new pavilion and dressing rooms were also widely envied. A lottery grant was applied for to provide better sight-screens and nets.

Even with a very depleted side the 1st XI journeyed to Stowupland and the replacements stood up well to record a win The mid-week side now consisted of N Williams, R Jones, S King, L Garner, J Smith, B Salter, M Shepstone, V Doran, P Abbott and K Bailey. The first injury of the year came when Kieron Bailey was taken to hospital with a serious looking hand injury. He had been the best bowler with 7 for 24 as Haverhill easily beat British Sugar to reach the League Cup final; three Haverhill batsmen also reached their half centuries in this game. A milestone came in the game between Haverhill and Risby when Steve Jones hit what was probably the highest score so far by a town batsman. His innings of 196, including 7 sixes and 26 fours, saw Haverhill reach 339 for 4 wickets.

One Wednesday the cricketers of Haverhill were seen playing a day's golf, this was leading to the first mini-tour that the club had entered for many years Basing themselves at Otley in Yorkshire, they first met and for their first match versus Pool Town, a very good side. Their paid Australian and his opening partner hit 100 and 101 each in the total of 210 for 1 wicket, while Haverhill managed 152 all out. The second match against the Olicanions CC saw them face a side with three such Australians in the team, and Haverhill lost again. Meanwhile back at home, the seconds were getting the better of Elmswell by 13 runs; Bill Moran was amongst the runs with 114, nearly half the team's total. During the next league match against Ampton, the first eleven got back to winning ways. In the game Steve Jones was knocked out when the ball slipped from the opposing bowler's fingers and caught him in the temple. He recovered to resume his innings, and together with a M Rinaldi 95 and P Brazier's 61 not out, took the victory.

After all the skill and excitement of reaching the league knock-out final, it was certainly an anti-climax when Cavendish took the honours in the final played at Walsham-le-Willows. It was a story of dropped catches that lost Haverhill the game; the Cavendish top scorer was given at least four lives as he went on to make 95 and with only three wickets down, the village side quickly passed Haverhill's total. Following this the Sudbury Police won their match versus Haverhill I to take the promotion place from the town. Haverhill 1st XI ended the season in third spot, but things were looking up as Haverhill Cricket Club worked to re-establish itself in the regional cricket world.

The disappointment of missing their climb to the next division in the league was soon forgotten, as before the end of the year the Club heard that its application to join the APS Two Counties League had been successful. The club responded, saying *"A big step up in standard and quality, and new players are needed to consolidate our position in the new league."* New sight-screens and nets were the first things to change, and a Junior XI was formed. To this end, two teachers offered to coach the younger members of the club in the evenings, while the 2nd XI would still be in the Mick McNeill League Division Four.

Before the business of playing cricket began, a bright day in March saw a group from the Haverhill Cricket Club enjoy a taste of summer one Sunday as they raised £500 from a sponsored walk. The cash was put towards the new, up-to-date sightscreens. More financial help was brought in as the result of a casino night in April. The team's sponsor, Nat West Bank, also gave the club a boost, handing over a cheque for £250.

The **1999** season was the dawn for a new era of the cricket club as they looked forward to taking part in the Jaygate Two Counties League for the first time. This marked the return to the top level of cricket for the town. Before their first competitive match, a friendly was played with Helions Bumpstead which saw a narrow victory by 103-101. There was disappointment all around when the opening fixture versus Debenham was rained off. *"Just when we were all keyed up and ready to go,."* commented Mick Rinaldi. The Haverhill side in the AXA Midweek League started their season with two defeats, to Thurlow and then Stansfield.

The 1st XI were now in a league eight divisions higher than the previous year, but showed no signs of being outclassed when they set off with an easy victory over Long Melford, 133 to 135 for 6. When the first league table was published it showed Haverhill on top, but this was after a win in their only game, and could not be seen as too exciting. This was proved in the next match when Haverhill's two top bowlers were unavailable and they went down by 3 wickets at Boxford. Despite an immaculate 50 by Julian Poole, the 2nd XI lost a friendly to Woolpit, then won their first league match beating Stowupland by 6 wickets. When a complete batting collapse resulted in Haverhill 1st XI going down by 95 runs to Eye, they had quickly tumbled down the league table and were fourth from bottom.

The 1st XI achieved their second win, versus Little Bardfield as the Haverhill batsmen began to earn their places; P O'Hare knocked up 96 before being bowled; another top scorer was B Moran 62 as Haverhill totalled 270 for 6. Unfortunately the following week Felixstowe, with the help of a century maker, beat Haverhill by 164 runs. It was certainly a new experience in the higher league, as Haverhill showed their inconsistent form with two victories over a week-end. The win at Achilles was interesting as the home team were well on the way to a victory, so much so that their number eleven player decided to go home early, thinking he would not be wanted. When Achilles collapsed and they needed two runs to win, the missing playing could not be contacted to return and Haverhill took the league points.

The 2nd XI had a poor week-end, being knocked out of the League Cup on Saturday and losing a league fixture to Elmswell the following day. A trip to league leaders Boxford saw why they were riding high and Haverhill were in the lower reaches, Boxford winning 290 to 151. A wet weekend allowed just one match to be played and the 1st XI again tasted victory followed by a second win over Earls Colne. The Rinaldi's starred in the match versus third place Kelveden in searing heat, Steve scoring 52 and Mick taking 6 wickets for 37. Despite the heat, both teams had to run for cover for a short time, as a sudden downpour turned up in the second innings. The up-and-down season ended in Haverhill occupying a respectable tenth place in their initial season in a much higher league.

Just a few years before the Haverhill Cricket Club had virtually collapsed with just one midweek side in action, the pavilion burnt down and the cricket square looking like an allotment. The local villages with small populations boasted decent cricket teams, and it seemed that over one hundred years of cricket in the town was finished. The club's chairman Dave Rinaldi supposed, *"It was obvious that if something wasn't done quickly the club would very hastily fold, and the National Lottery Grant enabled us to build a brand new pavilion together with help from St Edmundsbury and the Bowls Club. This was all done in conjunction with our architect and organiser Peter Philbin."* The clubs captain also commented *"The players are coming through now from the youngsters upwards and as we progress through the leagues upwards more people will join up with us."* The club's progress was certainly fantastic for the town as a whole and the entire strategy to rebuild the club came together to the highest degree.

****

NEW CENTURY, NEW HOPE

2000, the start of a new century and high hopes for Haverhill Cricket Club. As well as fielding four weekend sides - with players to spare - the club boasted a midweek side, a newly laid square and a £140,000 pavilion including a bar, a balcony and superb changing facilities. They were now competing in Division 4 of the Jaygate Two-Counties League. The 2nd XI was in the Mick McNeill League Division 3, after two successive promotions. There were two midweek sides, the first of these in Division 2 and the other, known as the Jolly Boys, in Division 3. In his third year with Haverhill, Dan Wilkins was the new captain of the 1st XI. Apart from this, a new Colts XI (under 12) would be playing some friendlies over the summer, coached by Neil Mitchell. This was to be a platform for the future. As more sponsors were being attracted to the club, new advertising boards were appearing around the ground. Plans were also in place to renovate the whole ground in the near future, and create an outdoor nets area.

Before embarking on the league fixtures, the 1st XI arranged a friendly with a top village club, Helions Bumpstead. However, incessant rain made it impossible to play any cricket. First opponents in the league were East Bergholt whom Haverhill beat by one wicket, on a spongy ground but in glorious weather. This win came in spite of Haverhill losing three wickets in the first two over's. Sudbury then knocked Haverhill out of the Senior Cup with a victory by 6 wickets. Haverhill replied the following week with a win over Kelvedon by 5 wickets. It was a gritty performance for their first home game, 167 - 168 for 5. The groundsman had put in some hard work to get the pitch looking great and the whole pattern an absolute picture.

In the match at Long Melford, Simon Youngs stroked his way to 122 not out as Haverhill sustained their unbeaten run in the league. Youngs commented, *"I owe the club some runs and it's nice to be able to pay them back with their confidence in me."* Stand-in captain Steve Jones won the toss and elected to field, showing every confidence in the team's bowlers. After four matches, Haverhill stood top of the league; the next week saw them take a day off as heavy rain stopped all cricket. In the McNeill League, the 2nd XI

TOP (27) Joe Woodley in action
BOTTOM (28) Wicket Keeper Dan Wilkins

TOP (29) Neil Winter strikes a pose
BOTTOM (30) A determined Mike Rinaldi

TOP (31) Nural Hoque after his bowling feat of 7 for 11
BOTTOM; (32) Talking tactics, Adam Dellar & D Poole

TOP. (33) Haverhill 2nd XI record scoreboard 345 for 2.
BOTTOM (34) Sam Powell batting on one knee.

(36) Chairman Stephen Woodley

(35) Ray Shanks, one of the coaches.

(37) 2011 Haverhill Youth Side winning the League Cup

(38) Haverhill players doing what they like best, celebrating the fall of opponents wicket (2010)

(39) One of the latest Haverhill line-ups

were in third position having won their latest game by 8 wickets, with B Salter hitting 56.

The first defeat for the 1st XI came against Elmstead, Haverhill's fielding which had been good was awful. A town supporter concluded "*Haverhill are not as good as they thought they were.*" Little Bardfield were next for a top of the table clash and were victorious by one wicket. For the 1st XI, N Proctor hit a six to reach his half century. Wicket-keeper Steve Rinaldi, had two stumpings and a run out turned down by the umpire, and tempers began to flare but settled down quickly. Then, when Ross Nickerson caught a Bardfield batsman brilliantly, somehow the umpire (the batsman's father) gave him not out to the disbelief of everyone on the field. Once again, the game threatened to boil over. When the match finished there were some hard looks between the two sides.

Fourteen-year-old Ben Hickes came good in his first season in the Haverhill Midweek XI with 55 not out against Wratting Lion. Following their winning run, Haverhill were now on a losing streak and dropped down the league table very quickly. Even the 2nd XI were not doing very well; and the worst defeat was a mauling from Thurlow. Subsequently the town's cricketers put their bad spell behind them and were still in with a chance of topping the table. They dominated the game against Dunmow and won 100 for 3 against the Dunmow's 99 all out, showing what a full strength Haverhill side could achieve. However, a defeat against East Bergholt, when their batting let them down, left Haverhill with too much ground to make up on the teams above them.

The cricket ground had come in for some attention during the summer and hard work by members had provided a new seating area at the ground. Some of the grass area had been shingled over and public benches put there. This was made possible with a grant from St Edmundsbury Council. This was part of a three-year plan, to do a bit at a time as the cash became available. The teams also got some new kit, thanks to their president Mr Christopher Gurteen.

The 1st XI were back to winning ways the next week. Then in the return match versus Long Melford, Simon Youngs once again went to town against their bowlers, this time amassing 128 of Haverhill's successful reply to

Melford's 211, Haverhill taking the league points. They now stood in second place behind Coggeshall, but having played more fixtures than the other teams, their title push was really over. After another victory over Debenham, the captain said, "*It was an amazing game because everything changed. Simon got wickets when he normally gets runs, and Smithy got runs when he usually got wickets.*" There was some high class fielding by the Haverhill teams as well.

The midweek sides and the 2nd XI were meeting with varying success so far. The Colts saw an excellent performance by their bowlers in a win over Ashdon, when their opponents were bowled out very cheaply. Joe Woodley took 5 wickets for 2 runs, and Dan Poole 1 wicket for 4 runs. A weekend of very heavy rain washed out nearly all the cricket matches in the neighbourhood, but fine weather the subsequent Saturday saw a magnificent century by Bill Moran helping the 1st XI to a 4-wicket victory over Coggeshall. This proved the last win of the season when the final game ended in an exciting draw. The facilities at Manor Road were noted as one of the finest in the area and Manor Road was chosen as the venue for the League Cup final between Elveden and Thurston.

First team regular Dan Wilkins summed up the summer, "*It has been a much better season than we could have hoped for, but it could have been even better, one more victory and we would most probably been promoted.*"

For the third year in a row, Haverhill faced Helions Bumpstead in their opening friendly fixture. This was late in April **2001** and the appalling weather looked like causing a postponement, but they managed to get the match played. New opener, Scott Webb, who batted superbly for his 52 not out, helped Haverhill to victory. In the Two Counties League, he also put up 74 but could not stop Dunmow winning against Haverhill. Newcomer Neil Winter announced his arrival when playing for the 2nd XI against Capel St Mary; hitting 114 not out as the Haverhill side won by 100 runs. K Bailey took 4 wickets for 14 runs.

The first home league game brought Hadleigh to the town, with Haverhill winning by 9 wickets. A scorching hot day saw the visitors bowled out for 89, which the 1st XI passed with little effort. It was proving a batsman's season when S Jones made 91 and N Winter 80in another victory versus Abberton. The bowlers then performed in what was an emphatic win over Abberton. Ross Nickerson had figures of 4 wickets for no runs in four over's, and Scott Webb 2 wickets for 3 runs in just four over's. Winter continued his great form, and was out just three runs short of a century against Thurlow. Also in this game B Delderfield took 6 Thurlow wickets for 37. Despite their wins Inconsistency was showing its face again this year with up-and-down performances by Haverhill. After one match versus East Bergholt, stand-in skipper Rinaldi remarked, *"I must have gone through every emotion out there, but I am just so proud of the boys. It shows how far we have come."*

The 1st XI lost their first game of the season versus, and then promptly won the following week. When Kelveldon were beaten, it was the sixth win in a row. N Winter (117) and S Webb (66) starred in the victory over Achilles in the return fixture. This meant Haverhill went to the top of the league, if only for a short while, as they had played more fixtures than most other clubs,. and the formally unbeaten Bardfield surprisingly lost a game. After nine matches Haverhill 1st XI were riding high. Following this spell, the cricketers were left frustrated when two week-ends were lost to the bad weather.

The July game against Needham Market produced something special for the Haverhill side when Neil Winter registered a record-breaking score of 208 not out, his second hundred coming from just thirty-one deliveries. This was the highest individual score put up by a town batsman since the club was founded, and Haverhill won the game 285 to 136. The 2nd XI were back in action after a three-week lay off and a couple of back-to-back defeats. A upset befell the 1st XI, however, when they were unexpectedly beaten by 8 wickets by bottom of the table Abberton

Haverhill quickly put this loss behind them and went back to what they did best, winning their next three games. A 'ton in the sun' by S Webb (139) saw Bergholt beaten by 165 runs. S Youngs carried on the scoring with 69 in the win over Long Melford, and the captain reported, *"There was some impressive fielding. The boys were flinging themselves around stopping boundaries, and Ron on his own stopped seven or eight fours."* When they were victors over Kelveden, the 1st XI were all geared up for promotion, which was confirmed the following week.

With storms threatening to stop the cricket, Haverhill made sure of being the champions as well by gaining a victory over Achilles in a low-scoring game. This meant they were to play in Division 3 of the Two Counties League the next year. The 2nd XI finished in the middle of their McNeill League, winning four and losing six of their ten matches. The Haverhill captain summed up the season, *"We want to go on from this, but we need to strengthen our team with two possible new players, as things will be tougher next season."*

Long Melford visited Manor Road for a friendly match to start the 2002 season. The visitors staged a go-slow in their innings after Haverhill put up quite a big score, and the match was drawn. It was still a good work out to prepare the team for the new season in a higher division. Hopes were high for another successful year with two sides in the AXA Haverhill Midweek League and the formation of another colts team. This was the Under 11's, and Julian Poole and Neil Mitchell were coaching the young boys' two teams. For the 1st XI, the captain was Steve Jones and the vice-captain Simon Youngs. The 2nd XI were also hoping to progress further this season. A second warm up game had to be called off due to rain, but the Midweek XI began with a victory over Castle Manor.

For their opening league fixture, Haverhill made the long trek to Harwich. This proved a long day of suffering for the Haverhill side as they were promptly put in their place as newcomers. In cloudy and breezy conditions Harwich scored 168 for 4, to which Haverhill were skittled out for only 53. The main difference between the two teams was that Haverhill dropped at least sixteen catches in the field. The 1st XI got this out of their system and won the next match against Brightlingsea by 71 runs with a much better batting performance. Unfortunately, Steve Jones injured his ankle while warming up and was virtually a passenger throughout the game. A second win came over Dunmow, by 61 runs.

In the McNeill League, Haverhill 2nd XI started with a defeat by Brockley by 7 wickets. The team then made a much better start when they completed a victory over Meadowlands by 10 wickets, with openers J Poole and P Jones hitting off the runs needed for the win all by themselves. Two more 1st XI wins then gave way to losses at Frinton and Woolpit; in the latter game N

Winter hit a fine 97. Haverhill captain, Steve Jones stated the obvious when he said, "*I think this season we will win a few matches, and also lose a few.*" A thrilling game with Boxford ended in a win for Haverhill when S Fletcher hit a mighty six off the final ball of the innings.

St Margarets proved the weakest team so far and Haverhill again tasted victory by 10 wickets. St Margarets scored 234 and N Winter (128no) and S Webb (109no) saw the 1st XI home at 258 for no wickers lost. This opening partnership was a record-beating stand for the club, the opponent's fielders seeming to give up after the 150 was passed. The win put Haverhill securely on the promotion trail again. The 1st XI promptly suffered a batting collapse on a damp wicket, losing to top team Harwich for the second time this summer. Harwich were helped by the inclusion of Indian leg-spinner Sergey Dhosh who saw off the greater part of the Haverhill batsmen. The comment was made "*Players get paid elsewhere and this is a problem in attracting new players. First of all we have to look after the players we have now got.*"

The Midweek teams both stood at mid-table and were both proving their worth to the club as a whole. The 2nd XI were winning and losing on consecutive weeks, but at least they were not the worst team in their league. The players were doing what was needed, and when called into the 1st XI, they did not let the side down. Entering August, St Margarets were beaten once again as N Winter and S Webb both hit half-centuries. Haverhill now stood third, and two league games in the next weekend settled the fate for the season. Boxford were beaten, then Copford. Haverhill then looked to Copford to help them by winning their game against Harwich, which they did not. Although the Haverhill 1st XI won versus Woolpit, they ended in third place and could not clinch promotion for the second season on the trot.

For the **2004** season, Haverhill had a different look as Scott Webb and Neil Winter were not playing. These two top players had been the club's opening batsmen for the past three years. On speaking with them, captain Simon Youngs said that they both wanted a break from the game. In the opening matches, others were missing, including Dan Wilkins, Paul Abbott and Dave Goodwin, who were still playing football when the cricket season began in late April. However, Greg Street was back with the club after not playing for seven years. The loss of players and other changes created a great hole in the side and made the summer of 2004 a very different season.

A friendly at Histon was the first fixture, which Haverhill won by 3 wickets, scoring 189 for 7 in reply to Histon's 188 all out. Haverhill's Australian bowler Rob Sullivan took 3 wickets in his first 3 over's with some genuine pace, finishing with figures of 3 for 31. Thunderstorms caused the first league match to be postponed, and the opening Marshall Hatchick Two Counties League Division Two game versus Woodbridge the following week, was a close affair which Woodbridge won by 3 wickets. P Jones with 62 was the 1st XI's top run-maker in a game which Haverhill let slip away. The season's first victory then arrived by way of a one run win over Maldon. Helped by B Moran (62) and S Youngs (69), Haverhill made 227 for 7, and Maldon stood at 226 for 8 with one ball left, their batsman being run out to leave the 1st XI winners.

The Haverhill 2nd XI began their season with a defeat against Halstead II by 53 runs, the batting letting them down after a good start to the game. Their first victory came versus Brockley II by 8 runs. Meanwhile the 1st XI posted a fine win over Lakenheath by 9 wickets. This was even more satisfactory as Haverhill could field only ten players. Julian Poole with 91 and Joe Woodley 43 not out steered Haverhill to victory, the latter fast becoming a good all-rounder. Meanwhile, the Midweek XI went down to Castle Manor in their initial game of the summer.

June blossomed with one of the best displays by the 1st XI when they swept away the early unbeaten league leaders Ipswich II by 131 runs (195 to 64). This was despite a very poor start to their innings as Moran was out first ball and Jones quickly fell for a duck. This victory was a massive lift for the club. The good feeling did not last very long as the 1st XI lost the following week at Thurston, on what was described as a difficult pitch. Haverhill 2nd XI were competing in the Harpers Sports Suffolk League and were also proving to be up-and-down side.

Early in July, an Under 13 side from Kampong in the Netherlands. made a mini-tour of the Haverhill area Former Haverhill player Mick Farrant who lives in the Netherlands, was helped by Ray Shanks from the home end to arrange the tour. The four games played were against Hundon, Weston Coville, Parkway Scholl and finally Haverhill Cricket Club Colts. Kampong's tour became an annual fixture for the Colts. Youngsters were thought to be the way forward for Haverhill. A bright performance from 14-year-old Dan Poole, who slammed his first ball for a boundary, was the highlight. of a generally woeful display when the 1st XI lost to Dunmow. An all round display from captain S Young, who was amongst the runs and the wickets, saw Haverhill gain another win over Harwich. Sullivan was also in top form with his fast bowling; his first delivery knocked back an opponent's wicket. Inconsistency raised it head once again as the 1st XI promptly lost to Woolpit with some mediocre displays with bat and ball. Sullivan tried hard to turn the game Haverhill's way with a fiery spell of bowling that saw the opponent's batsmen ducking and diving, one batsman having to retire after being hit by one express delivery. The 2nd XI then had a convincing victory over Maldon II.

The Cricket Club proceeded to close off their ground at Manor Road to the public after thefts of the boundary ropes. Youngsters often played or sat on the outfield when there were no matches in progress. The club were sorry for those who used the cricket ground correctly, but a few had ruined it for the rest. The club captain Simon Youngs said, "*It is a shame that this has happened. Last year we had break-ins, and this year things are being stolen from the ground. The problem here is there are so many ways of getting on to the ground.*" It was also announced that anyone found on the ground without the proper permission would be deemed to be trespassing, and notices were put up to that effect. After being approached about mending the fences that circled the ground, St Edmundsbury quickly replied that they were not responsible for these, the fences being the property of the cricket club. Some gaps in the hedges were also patched up.

With fourteen league games played the 1st XI had won 5 and lost 8, but more alarming was the slide down the table towards the bottom two who would be relegated at the end of the season. They were well beaten at Halstead, being bowled out for the lowest score of the season (119), and although B Moran hammered an admirable 94 in a victory over Thurston, the fight for survival went on. The Midweek XI were sitting in 2nd place in their league and had few troubles all season as the younger members of the club were anxious to prove their worth. A crucial match versus Brockley was then washed out as their opponent's pitch was under water. The calculators were out for the last game of the summer, the captain remarking, "*We are in the best position of the three clubs fighting to stay up, and it is in our own hands in what we do. We also have M Rinaldi back for the last match after being absent for most of the season.*" However, the last group of matches were washed out as the bad weather struck again, and the 1st XI were safe, as were the 2nd XI who also hovered near the bottom of the table for most of the summer. Haverhill's best bowler was Simon Youngs, who also scored the most runs all season (380), but he had to admit second place in the batting averages who boasted an average of 47.4to Bill Moran.

For the 2005 season there were a few changes, one most welcome was the return of Scott Webb who had taken a year out. Also joining Haverhill was Martin Wilkins who had been playing with Thurston. He was to be the new coach for the club along with his brother Dan, as they had been teammates for the Midweek side. Also making the move from Thurston to Haverhill was Neil Wallis, who had been their captain and wicket-keeper. On the other hand two players not available on Saturdays were Bill Moran and Roy Jones. For their opening fixture, a friendly versus Histon, the 1st XI lined up S Young, G Street, N Wallis, S Webb, M Wilkins, R Sullivan, J Woodley, M Rinaldi, S Taylor, S Nowles, A Smith, E Bailey and J Watkin. In spite of a knock of 102 by S Webb, Histon were the winners.

Beginning their league matches a week before the 1st XI, Haverhill's 2nd XI won their first game in the Harper Sport League against Brockley II by 3 wickets. A victory by 9 wickets at home to Woolpit got the 1st XI off to a good start. S Webb again top-scored with 68no, while bowlers Rod Sullivan and Joe Woodley caused many problems for the opposing batsmen. The following week-end saw both teams recording victories; Worlington were the second victims of the 1st XI while the 2nd XI beat Horringer by 6 wicket's; P Jones 79no. Haverhill made it three wins in a row when 33 runs dispatched Mildenhall. This pleasurable opening run was brought to a sudden end when they slipped up at Copford, but only by 11 runs, in a match when the batsmen did not come up to scratch. Haverhill were not helped when M Rinaldi injured his calf muscle and retired from the match, only to come back to try to make the runs for victory.

Flaming June announced its arrival with some real cricketing weather. Over four hundred runs were scored in a single day at Elveden, Haverhill edging it in reply to their opponent's 215 for 8 with 216 for 5. With four wins from their first five matches, Haverhill were standing in second position in the league table. Unfortunately, it was the batsmen once again who lost their form against Brockley in the next match, and Haverhill recorded their second defeat. A ten-wicket victory came the way of the 2nd XI versus BSSSA, the opening batsmen, P Jones 76 and J Poole 64 carrying them home.

The hot summer continued and the 2nd XI were the most consistent of the town's sides. The 1st XI had some very good wins, but surrendered their unbeaten home record when Dunmow took the points away from Manor Road. Haverhill then batted back to form against Hadleigh as Greg Street made a brilliant 134 out of Haverhill's 181. A catalogue of losses then saw Haverhill setting up headlines *"Gloom increases as Haverhill lose again."* The captain also remarked, *"We got ourselves in good positions and this always happens. I can't put my finger on the problem; our team-work should be a strong part of our game."*

The 1st XI stumbled again on the short journey to Mildenhall and after being in second position in the league table, they had slipped quickly down the placings. The 2nd XI had contracting fortunes and won their encounter with Mildenhall II. Unexpected Haverhill then showed just what they were capable of with a grand win over Copford by ten wickets. There were different headlines now, *"Hooray! Haverhill wins."* Facing a target of 226, the 1st XI went to work and took the victory, with N Winter 123 and S Youngs 106 both not out topping the batting' Winter went to his century in style, clipping the ball into the road for a mighty six. Youngs was more subdued but showed his delight as he put the recent bad run to rest. He won the game with yet another six hit. This set a club record partnership of 232.

It was the 2nd XI who then caught the losing bug and versus Brockley II; they were all out for 55, being 29 for 8 at one time. The 1st XI match against Ipswich looked to be going Haverhill's way when Ipswich scored 155 for 7 and Haverhill had reached 104, but rain caused the game to be abandoned. The Midweek side were the most successful of the town's teams, ending in fourth place in their league. Tributes were also going to the Haverhill Colts Under 11 side who beat Hundon in their cup final. and also won their league. The spectre of relegation then haunted Haverhill when the league officials were thinking of four teams going down. However, this did not happen, if only for the present year.

Cricket club activity started early in April **2006** when the pavilion was given a complete facelift, mainly through financial help from Delstar Engineering who was sponsoring the club this summer. When the playing season got underway, the first game was a visit to Copford. This produced a record that would go into club history. With Haverhill's bowling and fielding in excellent form, Copford were all out for just 35,. Joe Woodley taking 3 wickets for 11 runs and Rob Sullivan 7 for 12. Haverhill were scoring slowly in reply until their opponents put on a spin-bowler. Winter promptly smashed his first ball for six, then proceeded to send the ball all over the ground to bring a simple victory to Haverhill.

The next match was a home game versus Ipswich, and this was made into a special day. Townsfolk were invited to take advantage of free admission, to bring along the family and enjoy a day in the sun. There was plenty of space for the children to run about and partake of a picnic meal around the boundary. The week-end saw victory in drizzling rain crowning a good day. Facing a Haverhill total of 234 for 5, Ipswich failed by 23 runs. Dan Poole had an old head on young shoulders when he blasted the last ball of the Haverhill innings into the trees for a six. The club now seemed to be going from strength to strength and gained another new sponsor, Travis Perkins Building Supplies. Aussie Rob Sullivan spoke of this game, "*I was amazed at Ipswich carrying on their innings to get a result; they were given the opportunity to accept a draw because of the wet conditions. It probably would not occur in Australia.*"

The return match with Copford also went the 1st XI's way by 34 runs, a star knock from M Wilkins with 95 not out paving the way. Another match in the rain again another victory, Sullivan taking 6 wickets versus Kelveden. The game was broken into two halves when the heavens opened before Haverhill could take their turn on a then sodden wicket. After a month of watching the weather ruin their cricket, the 2nd XI got into the winning habit by 150 runs against Stansfield. Both Haverhill and their opponents Stansfield were missing players; While Haverhill made up their side with two 1st team players who were not playing that week, Stansfield played the game with just nine men. Two batsmen on form were Martyn Farrant 108 and A Dellar 65, helping Haverhill to an unbeatable 288 for 5. Captain Nurul Hoque remarked, "*Finally we had a game and I am looking forward to more commitment as the season continues.*" However, a home defeat inflicted by Sudbury stopped Haverhill in their tracks with their opening bat scoring 200 as they won by 160 runs.

The 1st XI were now sitting proudly on top of their league and celebrated with a 10-wicket win over Wivenhoe, the Haverhill fielding being the strongest for many summers. Strength throughout the club was the policy aimed for, and in the local Junior League, the Haverhill Under 11's had two teams, called A and B. The Midweek XI were standing third in their league as well. Entering July both the 1st and the 2nd XI's carried on with their winning streak, with some tight bowling and a never-give-up attitude in the field bringing them some exciting wins. The first defeat of the season against Copdock, this after the previous week's demolishing of Ipswich by 9 wickets and a great 126 not out by N Winter. By this time Haverhill were closing in on promotion. Newcomer Sam Powell then saved Haverhill from their second loss when he hit a superb 112 against Boxford. This was better than it seemed, as the score was 30 for 4 wickets when he came out to bat.

Not all smaller clubs' grounds were up to the standard of the Haverhill ground, as the 2nd XI found out when they won against Stansfield by 8 wickets on a wicket described as interesting! Once the bogy side for the 1st XI, Felixstowe were again beaten at Manor Road, this time by 103 runs. Haverhill had blasted a big 322 for five, of which N Winter hit 183 not out. This proved too much for the visitors who were all out for 220, for a total of nearly 550 runs to entertain the spectators. At the other end of the club's ladder, the Colts Under 11 side were champions of their league, as were the Under 13 side, who also won their cup final.

Walsham-le-Willows, who had yet to win a game, were next up and saw the 2nd XI victors, bowler D Webb taking 6 wickets for 44 runs. Then a tight match went to Brockley by one run. The Haverhill side at this time was J Poole, D Poole, M Farrant, A Nicholls, T Pinkney, P Jones, J Watkin, N Mitchell, R Davis, K Bailey and N Hoque. Haverhill entertained the top side Woolpit who showed their class, winning by 60 runs. D Poole chose this match to put up his highest score of the season with 82. The season closed with a victory over Eye. The Haverhill 2nd XI enjoyed an excellent summer, winning ten out of ten games.

The final game of the season for the 1st XI was versus St Margarets who gave Haverhill a target of 164. But a sudden tropical downpour as Haverhill began their innings at 32 for 1, saw the game abandoned. Nevertheless, this did not stop Haverhill being crowned champions and gaining a quick return to Division III. The other matches on the last week-end went Haverhill's way and the summer ended with them top of the heap.

In **2007** the Cricket Club were concerned about the new car park for the cinema complex being built just over the fence from the cricket ground.. It was argued over which side of the cricket fence a new higher fence was to be built, to stop balls damaging cars in the new car park. If the new fence were erected on the cricket ground side of the old boundary marker, it would make maintaining the fence the club's expense; on the other hand, the council would be responsible.

One of the early matches in Division 3 was a visit to Ipswich where the wicket looked decidedly green. The home team took advantage of the conditions and scored 138 for a flying start. Wickets then began to topple, and they ended their allotted overs at 242 for 6. Haverhill opening batsmen S Youngs (95no) and N Winter (67) put Ipswich under pressure, which continued when A Dellar came to the crease. The finale saw D Wilkins striking out scoring the 10 runs wanted from the last over with a boundary and a straight six. The next match versus Worlingworth saw Youngs hit 87 and Winter 60 to put on an opening partnership of 147. This set the pattern for a another Haverhill win, said by the captain to be *"a superb win that the lads enjoyed, and that's important at the end of the day."* He added an invitation, *"Feel free to bring the family along to Manor Road for a pleasant afternoon, hopefully in the sun."*

The game versus Sudbury had Adam Dellar bowling figures of 6 for 50 runs with his off-spin. A victory put Haverhill on top of the league, moving them towards their objective; promotion two years in a row. Captain Youngs remarked, *"We wear the Haverhill Cricket Club logo with pride; we represent the town in Suffolk and Essex towns as best as we can. We want to improve people's perception of the town and a higher standard of cricket.*

Come on down to the Club, buy a soft drink, or a pint, and stay for a chat." A defeat to Tuddenham by one run was followed by a close win over Lakenheath. In the Lakenheath match, Haverhill got under the skin of the opposition by refusing to let their fielders move the sightscreens every time they were needed. The visiting batmen did not take kindly to this, and the game was played in a smouldering attitude all round. Yet another very close victory over Dunmow meant Haverhill were certainly working towards promotion the hard way.

The weather interrupted some matches but most of them managed to get a result. An exception was when Ipswich visited Manor Road, and Haverhill suffered a rare defeat by 11 runs. Worlington then won when Haverhill could not quite reach the opponent's total. More rain stopped the next encounter versus Sudbury after Haverhill finished their innings; Sudbury were not able to go in and the game was abandoned. In the top of the table clash with Lakenheath, N Winter posted his second century of the summer for a Haverhill victory by just 4 runs. A one run loss at Dunmow meant that the final match would decide the championship and promotion. This was a visit to Brockley with both opening batsmen absent. Nevertheless, the team pulled together, and with many air shots, reached 237 for 9. The bowling was first-rate as was the fielding. This was shown when a Brockley swipe took the ball high in the air. From near the boundary line came a shout from Dan Poole as he raced at breakneck speed to catch the ball firmly, with the batsman staring in amazement. Brockley were all out for 215 as Haverhill ended a very successful season. The Haverhill side for this important game was S Powell, R Sullivan, A Dellar, D Poole, P Jones, G Street, M Rinaldi, D Wilkins, R Davis, M Wilkins and J Woodley.

One interesting match took place again this year, the visit of the Lashings World XI cricket team; they had visited Haverhill for the first time in 2006. This season they included amongst their star line-up New Zealand's Chris Caines and Alvin Kallicharran from the West Indies. Unfortunately, the sun was not shining on the event this year and it was played out under dull and damp skies.

Two victories started the **2008** season well for the 1st XI. Right behind them were wins for the 2nd XI and the Sunday side, showing the club's strength in depth for the coming campaign. Haverhill travelled to Kelvedon on a very hot day,. intent on extending their unbeaten spell. Kelvedon were restricted to 210 for 9 with tidy bowling and some great catches, two from young Poole and Simon Youngs, who threw himself around, belying his years. Haverhill batted with some confidence as all the batsmen contributed to the cause, and they gained the win by 4 wickets. A washed out week-end was followed by a disastrous match against Brockley when the Haverhill Sunday XI were all out for a miserly 58, leaving their opponent's victors by 237 runs.

The Haverhill 1st XI's winning run then came to an end at Exning, who started their innings by losing a wicket in the opening over. Bowling figures of 4 for 37, Scott Webb helped restrict Exning to 217 from 41 overs, a total Haverhill were confident of overtaking. However, after a succession of failures from the top batting order, apart from Webb who hit 67, and little support from the tail, Haverhill were all out for a very disappointing 117. A further woeful display brought another loss to Brightlingsea by 118 runs. The club's honour, however, was kept up with wins for the 2nd XI and the Sunday XI, D Poole scoring a well-created 75 not out in the latter game.

A return to form by Haverhill came from the home fixture with Elmstead Grasshoppers. The weather conditions were trying and saw the visitors all out for 119. Haverhill's openers were low scorers before Scott Webb knocked up a quick 47, and the middle order stepped up to the plate. It was left for Dan Poole to finish the win with clouting 4 fours. Despite the victory, the team were beginning to show signs of inconsistency which was hoped to be redressed as soon as possible. Opening bat Winter and wicket-keeper D Wilkins were dropped to the 2nd XI to try and help them regain their form. When Haverhill went down again to Hadleigh by 9 runs, the captain stated the obvious, *"We did not make enough runs."*

The Sunday XI seemed to have caught the losing habit when they lost to Withersfield by five wickets. Haverhill putting up a small 107 which Withersfield passed with wickets to spare. Youth seemed to be the future for Haverhill, and teenagers Josh Meekings and Luke Youngs had already played for the 1st XI. When Sullivan was absent one week, Haverhill paraded their youngest captain in 18-year-old Adam Dellar. Haverhill 1st XI eventually won again against Woodbridge by 2 wickets, the match turned Haverhill's way by

19-year-old Sam Powell who hit a century (124), half the Haverhill total. The same week both the 2nd XI and the Sunday side won, but the Midweek XI was heavily beaten by Helions Bumpstead by 9 wickets.

Haverhill 1st XI extended their winning streak with a convincing win by 10 wickets over Kelvedon, N Winter (58) and S Webb (53) both not out saw the 1st XI to victory. The 2nd XI brought off its own first-rate win, bowling Felixstowe out for 44. P Turner took 3 wickets for 6 runs and Kettel 1 wicket costing just one run to give a low target for their batsmen. Unfortunately, two more reverses more or less ended the Haverhill dream of three promotions in a row. Rob Sullivan then gave up the captaincy owing to work commitments, and two more loses saw Haverhill drop perilously near the bottom of the league. When they did score freely, as they did against Hadleigh (243 for 6) Sam Powell putting up 100, it was not enough to gain the victory. However for the 2nd XI scored a fine win versus Eye by 40 runs, including a career best of 143 by Steve Taylor.

A final losing match against Woodbridge, which gained Haverhill three points, kept everyone waiting to see how the clubs around them performed in the league. As it was, these games went Haverhill's way and they kept their place in Division 2. The summer ended a season that promised so much but resulted in a lack of success.

The annual visit of the International Lashings XI to Haverhill attracted a good turn out, as well as the sunshine all day. It was competitive match as they brought a strong team. Gordon Greenidge, Richie Richardson, Brendan Taylor and A de Silva were amongst the runs as the stars compiled 288 for 5. D Poole had the privilege of bowling out West Indies star Richardson. Haverhill were not slow to put on the runs either as Dellar hit 69, D Poole 49 and N Winter 42, in their reply of 227 for 7.

In May **2009** the first side to start the season were the Haverhill II, who were away at Earl Stonham on a baking hot day. Haverhill were put into bat first, and with the sun on their backs, proceeded to put on the pressure when Chris Thompson and Rob Sullivan moved quickly to 60 for 0 in only 9 overs. Dan Poole then joined Sullivan, and with well-placed shots all round the wicket, it was soon 110 from 15 overs. Sullivan holed out at 80, these coming from 71 deliveries. Big hitter Russell pushed the score along, his 85 included seven massive sixes. Poole then reached his maiden century and finished the visitors' innings with a mammoth six into the field behind the ground. The first Earl Stonham wicket fell to a wonder catch by Joe Kettle. The home team batted steadily, but did not come anywhere near the Haverhill total of 345 for 2, and Haverhill took the win.

First to visit Manor Road this season were Witham who chose to bat first when they won the toss. They batted strongly and reached 232 for 9. A good fight back saw Haverhill take the game to begin the season with three wins in a row. This was unfortunately followed by a shocking performance at Easton when Haverhill lost by the large margin of 10 wickets; a very surprising result. However, it was soon back to winning form with a victory over Brightlingsea. They scored 259, and Haverhill started with 88 for 0 in the first 10 over's; this set the pattern as Webb reached his century and helped guide them to a good win. Setting a target of 221 by Haverhill, Hadleigh came up short as the 1st XI made it two wins on the trot and moved up the table to fifth.

The league leaders Maldon came to Haverhill full of confidence and took the points on offer in a hard fought contest. 149 for 9 was the Ipswich total when Haverhill went to visit, their bowlers performing well on a very hard wicket at first. However, Haverhill were soon in trouble in the dusty conditions, and runs were hard to come by; they could only manage to reply with 135, losing the encounter. Fielding probably one of the youngest sides, Haverhill went to Felixstowe, where the sea air suited them and they were winners by 60 runs. Confidence was high, and although they stuttered a bit, Haverhill were successful at home to Easton. Another victory at Brightlingsea kept the Haverhill 1st XI in the running for promotion.

Two more wins over Hadleigh and Mildenhall by the 1st XI were followed by a crunch game against Brockley, and Haverhill, with Chris Silverwood and Amit Gupta back in the team, gained the victory. Silverwood had signed for Haverhill at the beginning of the summer and played for the town when not needed by his county team Middlesex and did in fact play in half of the Haverhill games. This left the final match of the season versus East Bergholt that Haverhill had to win, as well as have other games go their way, in order to achieve promotion. Haverhill were hoping to write history and bring the highest level of cricket to the town. They did their part by winning by 6 wickets, captain Dellar closed the season by hitting the winning boundary. Unfortunately, this was not enough, as other results did not go Haverhill's way and they finished in third position.

Meanwhile in Division 7, the 2nd XI clinched promotion with a 5-wicket win at promotion rivals Eye. After a defeat against Sudbury, the 2nd XI won their last game to gain the league title. In his last game before retiring, captain J Poole said, *"It was a very tense game and at tea I thought we had blown it, but a strong batting, bowling and fielding display saw us home."* By winning their last two matches, the Sunday 2nd XI were also champions of Division 5 of their Sunday League.

When Haverhill ended the season, many wanted the feel good experience to go on into the winter months, so well had they been performing. Every team run by the club finished in the top three in their leagues. Haverhill II won the Two Counties Division Six, and Haverhill Sunday and the Sunday II won their respective divisions of the Hunts County Bats Suffolk Sunday League. The Midweek XI were runners-up in both the Midweek League and the Cup, while the Youth sides had unprecedented success as well. The Under 11 and 15 teams won their divisions, and the Under 13's ended second in the Border League. Chairman Steven Woodley remarked, *"We have three out of four week-end teams who have won their league, so I am very pleased at that, and it is unlucky that the firsts had not made it through. Cricket has got a big future in the town, and we have plans drawn up for the new pavilion ready for out 150 years celebrations in 2011."*

A plan to improve the pavilion and the surrounds was a £200,000 project, and would see the changing rooms and bar area increased and space for a larger kitchen space. This would see more prestigious matches being played at Haverhill. The England and Wales Cricket Board had told the club it was keen to develop the club into one of the premier sites in the county, after Haverhill was awarded Clubmark. This accolade had opened up funding from the ECB.

After getting over their near promotion the previous season Haverhill made up for this in 2010 by winning a place in the top division of the Cricket

League in Suffolk. Haverhill's first ever match in Division One game in the club's history was a journey on a sunny 23 April **2011** (St George's Day) to Woolpit. The home team took the bat first and began to build a big total. The score was well over 200 before the second wicket went down, and they ended with 356 for 3 from their fifty overs. Haverhill had a huge job to chase the runs and were soon 165 for 1. After Dellar was out for 87 and Brown for 54, it was too much to expect and they finished at 212 for 8, losing by 144 runs. Although the opponents were one of the stronger sides, it was a lesson for the 1st XI in what they could expect in the higher regions.

With the Royal Wedding of Prince William and Katherine Middleton out of the way, it was back to business with a tricky visit from Copdock. With some great fielding and bowling, Haverhill kept the runs down, and the visitors were all out for 158. Confident Haverhill started with two quick boundaries but a batting collapse then saw them being all out for 57, inside twenty overs. The captain said, *"As long as the boys learn from their mistakes and stick together we will be fine."* Entertaining top of the table Mildenhall, Haverhill were faced with Essex County bowler Mills. With rain the night before and more forecast, the captain's decided to reduce the match to 35 overs to try to get the game played. 161 for 4 was the Haverhill total after some careful innings. Unfortunately, the rain appeared again at tea, and there was no chance of resuming and the match was abandoned. The following match at Coggeshall provided the 1st XI with their first victory of the season by 4 wickets.

The first outing for the newly formed 3rd XI came against a young Linton Village College side. Called the Haverhill Wanderers, the new team were made up mainly of youth players with skipper Jon Watkins. .Linton were all out for 43 in a dozen overs with the Haverhill bowlers headed by Kieren Bailey (5 for 18) and Jack Mitchison (5 for 5). The Wanderers side quickly made up the winning innings in just seven overs. Other games in their small league included Babraham III, Madingley II and Linton III.

Mistley arrived at Manor Road with an unbeaten record but left with their tails between their legs as Chris Silverwood destroyed the visitors with the finest display of quick bowling seen for many a year. The ex-England International was in top form and Mistley were all out for 119. It was left for Adam Dellar to hit the winning Haverhill runs with a mighty six into the car park. There were several changes to the 1st XI versus Ipswich with a greatly reduced batting order. Standing one time at 52 for 8, Haverhill managed to reach 95. Ipswich lost several wickets in their reply but did enough to win the game. More Jekyll and Hyde performances left Haverhill third from bottom. The home fixture with Wivenhoe saw 16-year-old Anthony Phillips making his debut, and Bill Moran back in the fold after an absence of four years. A victory made it four wins after seven games.

Finally, a sunny week-end for Haverhill's trip to Mildenhall. The home team made 277 for 7 for Haverhill to aim for, however they only reached 182 before being all out. The return match versus Woolpit provided another race for a win, but the 1st XI could not overtake their opponent's score of 227. Haverhill started badly and although they rallied from 1 run for 3 wickets, they were six runs short at the end. Five catches were dropped by the fielders, which did not help the cause.

A game to be won was at home to Maldon, with both sides fighting against relegation. Haverhill were expected to win but slipped to a surprising defeat, a big blow as the 1st XI fought to stay in their division. The captain commented, "*It was frustrating as yet again our batting let us down, but yes, we were not helped by dubious decisions, but the application seems to be there just off the radar.*" A lucky share of the points came when they faced 2nd placed Wivenhoe. Haverhill were struggling at 138 for 6 when the heavens opened and the players rushed for shelter, not returning as the rain persisted. After a week of wet weather, only thirteen overs were possible versus Frinton before a halt was called. A comprehensive 20-point victory over Abberton saved Haverhill's place in Division One. "*They were a poor side, but we did what we had to do, and I'm delighted for the club. Things are moving forward at Manor Road and we can only go on from strength to strength.*"

Haverhill started the **2012** season with a friendly match at East Anglian Premier League side Sudbury. On a bright but chilly day, Haverhill came out on top against a team decidedly higher in the standings than Haverhill. It was a day for the young guns as the town side were victorious by one wicket. Missing for Haverhill were new signing Satyajit Sathbai, Chris Silverwood, Dave Brown, Tom Saville and James Smith. Coming in were 14-year-old

Calum Brunning, 16-year-old Ben Wilkins and two 17-year-olds, Anthony Phillips and Dan Pass. A completely new look Haverhill, but a team which did the club proud, with Sudbury 123 all out and Haverhill 124 for 9. Captain Simon Youngs was delighted by this victory, *"It was everything you want in a friendly and both teams had a good work out. Dan Poole had an excellent bowling spell and all the others backed him up, and the fielding was energetic and people were throwing themselves around, which was good. We are not getting carried away however, it was only a friendly."*

The opening league game was at Manor Road when last year's runners-up Mildenhall were the visitors. Haverhill paraded their new signing Satyajit Satbhai, who made his debut in place of Russell Davis who was working. Sunshine was in short supply but the rain was not; credit was owed to the groundsman that the match started on time. Father and son appeared in the Haverhill side as captain Simon Youngs was joined by his son Luke. Haverhill batted first and put up 140 for 8, but when the visitors were 31 for 2, the heavens opened. No more play was possible and the league points were shared.

It was not until the fourth week of the season that a match was completed for Haverhill at newcomers Elmstead Grasshoppers. Haverhill made a meagre 102 all out after being 46 for 4 at one time. The bowling of Haverhill's Gupta and Dan Poole soon unsettled their opponents, and the omens looked good at this small score. They destroyed the Elmstead batting and skittled the home team out for just 39. Gupta had figures of 5 for 16, and Poole 5 for 20.on a damp wicket. Some decent weather greeted the next home game versus Exning with Satbhai absent. He was playing for Cambridge University against Gloucestershire, so in came James Smith. Haverhill gained the 20 points with a victory by 36 runs. The match was noted for a hat-trick from Nigel Brunning, two caught and one clean bowled, as the spin bowlers were impressive. The Haverhill skipper commented, *"Our players are buzzing at the moment."*

Teenager Anthony Phillips shone in the win over Maldon, and Haverhill remained unbeaten, but only after a nail-biting finish with the difference between the sides only 3 runs. Haverhill were without Gupta who had returned to India for a while. Phillips had his best innings with the bat, and when he was handed the ball he promptly grabbed the wickets of the Maldon opening batsmen. Haverhill continued in their rich vein of success with a victory over Lakenheath after batting first, as they had done in all games so far. Unfortunately, the bubble burst the following week when they lost by 6 wickets to Frinton. They were all out for 117, which was soon passed by their opponents. Trying to speed up the scoring, Satbhai was out to a mighty hit, caught on the boundary line.

On Sundays there were two Haverhill sides, with Joe Woodley the captain of the Sunday I. After some poor results, a match at Mildenhall was an important one to avoid a drop in divisions. Unfortunately, they fell short, this after starting well and standing at 125 for 2 at one time. 208 was given to Mildenhall to aim for, but their opening batsman set about the Haverhill attack; this proved the difference as Mildenhall were the victors. The Sunday 1st XI also played in the Suffolk 20/20 Cup, going out in the quarterfinal round to Mildenhall. There was also a Sunday 2nd XI who were one of the unlucky Haverhill sides early in the summer when their first three matches were rained off. Haverhill Sunday II visited Nowton's picturesque ground on a warm day under captain Martyn Wilkins, and after a score of 201 for 3, the Haverhill side gave chase but ended up 19 runs in arrears. It was a decent performance with an under strength side against strong opposition, and it seems that some of the lessons were being learnt from earlier games.

On Saturdays there was also a Haverhill 2nd XI in Division 5 who put together an unbeaten run early in the season. Teenagers were given plenty of outings in this side. On one away trip, two players were caught in heavy traffic and the Haverhill side started without them, with just nine fielders until they arrived at a run; this match was then won. By the time they met rivals Mildenhall II at Manor Road, the league title was up for grabs. It was a low-scoring game and Mildenhall made 128 for 9. Although it seemed a low target, Haverhill steadily lost wickets before winning the match in the 35th over. The victory ensured promotion and the league title with two matches still to go.

Up against unbeaten Mistley at Manor Road, Haverhill 1st XI were missing captain Simon Youngs, leading wicket taker D Poole and star batsman Satbhai. The Mistley bowlers soon dismantled the brittle Haverhill batting line-up, and from 40 for 9 wickets they eventually reached 64. Haverhill started their bowling well and had their opponents at 22 for 2, but a strong stand then saw them fail to get the remaining batsmen out. The captains view was *"They were a class act and in a different league to us; losing the toss each week doesn't help either."* A journey to Wivenhoe saw Haverhill lose their third match in a row, but they got this out of their system when they turned on the style to thrash Elmstead by 85 runs. Openers Poole and Bill Moran swept to 60 for 0 in 10 overs and Haverhill posted a target of 264 for 7, which their opponents never looked like overtaking. *"This result more or less guarantees us Division One cricket next year, let's hope we can do the same next week."*

This was not the outcome as Haverhill went down again to Coggeshall by 104 runs. Players were missing owing to injuries, holidays and the Olympic Games. Three players made their first team debut, Jamie Boulton, Liam Botten and Ryan Fowler. It was weak batting which let the team down this time. Haverhill were then "outgunned but went down fighting" as the headlines said, when they lost again to Mistley, currently the top team in the league. Mistley made 377 for 5 in their fifty over's, and although Haverhill scored a respectable 253 for nine, they were well beaten. From their last league game Haverhill needed at least seven points to stop the drop to Division Two, and after a tight struggle these were obtained. Haverhill were now playing in one of the best league's in East Anglia and looking forward to the future in top class cricket, which is what the town cricketers deserves

****

DICK POOLE: I am the middle part of five generations of the Poole family to play cricket for Haverhill. My grandfather Stephen Poole was one of the first players for the cricket club, then my father Bert. After me were my son Julian and then my grandson Graham Poole. I went to watch my father play and was the 'tin-boy', which is putting up the scores on the scoreboard, and recall the very basic toilet arrangements and the trains rattling past on the railway embankment close to the ground. My first years of cricket were affected by the Second War, I had started to play for Haverhill in 1939 aged 16, then was called up for the RAF in 1942 and served until 1947. All the team played in their whites although some could hardly afford the expense; I was lucky as I inherited my father's gear. He was foreman at the old Echo Printing Works run by Mr Claydon. In the early days the nearest the cars could get to the ground was to park in Mount Road. There were some characters in the game then including the groundsman George Coote, he was the boss when it came to the playing area and his grass was precious. The horse that pulled the roller and cutting machines had pads on each foot to prevent imprints in the wicket. George worked on the cricket field in the summer and was employed in the Mat Factory during the winter. Another well-known gentleman was 'Budget' Willis who lived in Meeting Walk and was the team's umpire for many years; he only had one arm. I wonder how he signalled 'wide's' to the scorer. Then there was Harry 'Rastus' Farrant. In the wartime, there were several good cricketers stationed at RAF Stradishall and some used to play for Haverhill, one of the best being a Sharples who played in the prestigious Lancashire League. In the 1940's the transport for away matches was usually Burgoin's Coaches which picked everyone up on the Market Hill and stayed at the game to bring us all back to Haverhill. Very often, a stop was made halfway home for some fish and chips all round. As for the cricket meadow and the old pavilion, each Saturday the batting order was hung on a nail next to the steps. Working for the railway I was moved to Cambridge for a while and while there I played some games for the Cambridge Rail Cricket Club. At the age of forty, I gave up cricket and took up bowls, as several of the cricketers did. Even when in a pram Graham was taken to watch the cricket so it was natural he would carry on the Poole tradition and play for Haverhill. I myself was a batsman and only bowled when necessary, and I still go along to watch some games when I can.

MICK FARRANT: I played for Haverhill Cricket Club between 1957 and 1968, my father Harry Farrant, played in the 1930's when we lived in Meeting Walk, close to the cricket ground. I started by helping the scorer put up the runs on the scoreboard, and then became the scorer for the 2nd XI when I was 10. We travelled to away games in the back of Bill Scrivener's little van, which was always covered with horsehair. Coming home we often stopped at a pub for a drink, I had to stay outside with a lemonade. I remember being very proud one day when my father took 8 wickets for just 4 runs versus Courtaulds, and watched him come off the field as all the others applauded him. Being near to the ground, my father used to bring home a basket full of spirits from the pavilion, but had to leave the barrel of beer in place; this because break-ins to the old pavilion could be quite easy. I was captain of the Haverhill Y C when they won the West Suffolk Youth Competition and then started to play for the Haverhill Cricket Club youths in midweek. Clarence Hulyer was one of the biggest hitters of the ball seen at

Haverhill, and a friend of mine likened him to a village blacksmith as he walked out to bat. In one match he hit a whirlwind 31, including 3 sixes; two of these hit with a broken handle on his bat. Nevertheless, whatever Haverhill did, win or lose, there was a small group of spectators in a little shelter near the pavilion, always had a moan about something. We called them the critic's corner. In my early days there were no boundary ropes laid down, the boundary was marked as where the short grass met the bed of nettles one side, and the fence on some other sides of the ground. I recall an all-day match we played on Sunday at Hatfield House, starting at 11am. However, we had to all stop at mid-day to let the Rolls Royce of the owner pass by the cricket ground on his way home from church, then start again after he had gone by. We played a charity match one year against a TV Stars XI captained by Christopher Trace of Blue Peter fame, and Dinsdale Landen did the commentary. When David Pryke bowled one of his fast balls and clean bowled an actor who opened the innings, the All-Stars captain came on to the field and said to David, "They have come to see us, not you." Another story was when Tim Ralling was hit on his leg as wicket-keeper, he could hardly stand for the pain, and after persuading him to come off the field, the only way to get him off, as he was a bulky person, was to use the club's wheelbarrow to push him to the pavilion. Bill Easey brought a side from his home town of Leiston to play Haverhill one week-end, this included John Price, the Middlesex and England bowler. After two over's he had skittled out four Haverhill men for no runs, I stood waiting for him to bowl at me and had no time to lift my bat before it whistled past me. I was lucky to score a four as the next ball hit my bat as I was lifting to try to play a stroke, and it flew to the boundary; luck or what! Other top cricketers I remember coming to Haverhill were Ray East and Keith Boyce of Essex. Now I live in the Netherlands coaching youngsters, and bring some over each year to a tour of West Suffolk, including a match or two in Haverhill

****

2013 AND BEYOND

The 2013 season finds Haverhill Cricket Club in possibly the best shape it has ever been. Fielding three Saturday sides, two Sunday sides, four youth teams and a Midweek eleven, it is still struggling to find every member a regular game. Club stalwart Michael Rinaldi said, *"What a change in twenty years. We could really do with increasing the amount of teams, but struggle to find the facilities to play the additional matches. This is largely due to the* *youth policy we set in place a few years ago, which means we now have a constant conveyor belt of talented young cricketers coming through the ranks. There are currently in excess of sixty boys and girls under the age of fifteen who regularly attend our coaching nights on Fridays. Many of them who have come through are now playing 1st XI team cricket, and competing at the highest level. The club now trains twice a week throughout the year, and all this success means we have outgrown the latest pavilion. Ground designs are therefore in place to completely re-design the ground, with a new pavilion moving back to the site of the original one. We hope work will start on this soon. This club has provided some great memories and friendships for a lot of people for many years. Our job as a committee is to reallise we are merely guardians of the club for future generations, and do our utmost to make sure we leave office with the club in a stronger position than when we joined. With the current position of the club and the plans in place, I see no reason why the club cannot continue for another one hundred and fifty years.*

****

SOME OTHER BOOKS BY THE AUTHOR

Football

Spurs At War (1939-46)	1999
Tottenham Hotspur (1882-1952)	2000
Tottenham Hotspur since 1953	2003
Tottenham Hotspur 100 Greats	2006

Speedway

Mildenhall Fen Tigers (History) 1	2005
Mildenhall Fen Tigers (History) 2	2012

Local

Images Of Haverhill	2000
Haverhill Through Time	2009
Letters From The Front (WWI)	2010
Haverhill's Home Front (WWII)	1997
Haverhill Rovers (History)	2007
R.A.F. Castle Camps	2011
Empty Fields (farm labs strike)	1989
Glimpse of Haverhill Railways	1999
Portrait of Helions Bumpstead	1997

Theatre

The Festival Theatre (Cambridge)	1995